D0982685

WITHDRAWAL

Reducing the
Cost of Surveys

norc

**NATIONAL OPINION RESEARCH CENTER
MONOGRAPHS IN SOCIAL RESEARCH**

Reducing the Cost of Surveys

By

SEYMOUR SUDMAN

ALDINE PUBLISHING COMPANY
Chicago

The research reported herein was supported by
Research Grant No. 2-4402, National Science Foundation

First published 1967 by
ALDINE Publishing Company
320 West Adams Street
Chicago, Illinois 60606

Library of Congress Catalog Card Number 67-17611
Designed by Greer Allen
Printed in the United States of America

Preface

In its twenty-five-year history, the National Opinion Research Center has conducted studies of the most critical issues facing the American public—war, civil rights, education, religion, and medical care. Parallel to these interests, if less newsworthy, has been a continuing concern with survey methodology. As gatherers of social information, we recognize that improvements in data gathering procedures must accompany increases in our stores of social knowledge and in our theoretical understanding.

Past NORC methodological studies include *Interviewing in Social Research,* a study of interviewer effect by Herbert Hyman and the NORC staff published in 1954. In addition, the NORC interviewing manual, *Interviewing for NORC,* has long been a standard training manual for interviewers everywhere, as well as dozens of articles in professional journals dealing with methodological issues.

The present monograph follows in this methodological tradition. It describes NORC's recent efforts to understand the survey process better. The title does not completely describe the scope of its chapters. While the research deals with techniques for reducing survey costs, it also describes methods of getting more information for the same budget, thus increasing the yield per dollar spent. Underlying the entire project is the belief that a detailed understanding of how surveys are conducted and costs generated must ultimately lead to better cost control and reduced costs.

Three different research approaches are used in this monograph—theory, cost analysis, and experimentation. In combination they produce impressive findings. Thus, in the chapter on probability sampling with quotas, a theoretical explanation of a quota sample design is first offered, then detailed evidence in support of the theory is derived from analysis of several NORC studies, and finally further confirmation is given based on experimental results.

As the author's acknowledgments will indicate, this is a project in which many of us at NORC participated. Of course, it would not have been possible without the financial support of the National Science Foundation under Research Grant 2-4402. By recognizing the need for a detailed study of survey methods, the National Science Foundation made it possible to build experiments onto ongoing NORC studies and to uncover the valuable cost information hidden in basic interviewer documents.

Several chapters of this monograph appeared in somewhat different versions in various professional journals. We acknowledge with thanks permission to reprint granted by the *Journal of the American Statistical Association,* the *Journal of Marketing Research,* and the *Public Opinion Quarterly.*

Special mention should also be made of the information and advice received from the Bureau of the Census and the Survey Research Center at the University of Michigan. Several of the experiments discussed are attempts to adapt for the more typical survey organization the procedures used on a far larger scale by the Census Bureau.

Considering the millions spent annually on surveys for commercial reasons, the amount of methodological information published is sparse. This may indicate a lack of research activity, but it is far more likely that much research on methods is never published for fear of revealing trade secrets or because the authors are unduly modest about the value of their methods. Hopefully, one of the serendipitous effects of this monograph will be to stimulate new methodological research and the publishing of results.

PETER H. ROSSI
Director
National Opinion Research Center
March, 1967

Acknowledgments

This book is in the true sense of the word the combined effort of the entire NORC staff. Since the title page is not large enough to list everyone connected with this project, the senior author would like to gratefully acknowledge the help he received.

The project was conceived by Peter H. Rossi, then Director of NORC, and Jacob J. Feldman, then Director of Research at NORC and now at the Department of Biostatistics, Harvard School of Public Health. In addition to the valuable insights in the initial proposal they were both continuously helpful during the entire project.

Paul Sheatsley, Director of the NORC Survey Research Service, and Richard Jaffe, then Associate Director of NORC, read substantial parts of the manuscript and made cogent suggestions for revisions. They also facilitated many of the experiments described in the text. Herbert Goldstein and Henrietta Meredith offered important assistance in the collection of cost data.

The entire NORC Field Department cooperated in this research. Galen Gockel, then Field Director and now a study director at NORC, and Eve Weinberg, the current Field Director, both cooperated fully with the experiments involving field techniques and also read substantial parts of the manuscript. Fansayde Calloway, who was NORC's Office Manager and is now Associate Field Director, and Pearl Zinner, head of NORC's New York Field Office were also especially helpful.

Among NORC's study directors, Andrew Greeley, John Johnstone, Norman Bradburn, Alice Rossi, James Davis, and Leonard Pinto made valuable contributions, and all the participants at the NORC staff seminars helped clarify ambiguous ideas.

Difficult hand computations of costs were ably carried out by Harry Baitinger, Henry Kaplan, Caroline Underhill, and Loretta Mitchell. Caroline Underhill was also responsible for early work on the interviewer questionnaire which she handled with distinction.

The data processing aspects of this study were capably handled by Harold Levy, James Daniels, Patrick Page, and Frank Rothacker, who all gave valuable suggestions in this rapidly developing area. Abbie Littleton was in charge of coding the interviewer questionnaire.

Substantial thanks for improving the clarity of the prose are due to Bonnie McKeon, who edited the final manuscript, and to Ann Jacobs who edited earlier sections. The preparation of the manuscript was intelligently and expertly done by Toshiko Takahashi and Nella Seifert. The index was prepared by Mary A. Spaeth. Patrick Bova and his NORC library staff were continuously helpful in suggesting and tracking down references to other studies.

Outside of NORC, the author benefited greatly from the advice of other professional survey researchers. The staff at the Bureau of the Census were especially helpful—particularly Morris Hansen, Leon Pritzker, Dean Webber, and Jack Silver. Charles Cannell of the Survey Research Center, University of Michigan, was most helpful in his discussion of field problems as was Rueben Cohen of the Opinion Research Corporation. Allen Jung of Loyola University (Chicago), and Edward Schwartz of the School of Social Service Administration, University of Chicago, generously lent material from their files. Finally, Fredrick Mosteller, of Harvard University, and William Kruskal and Nathan Keyfitz, of the University of Chicago, made helpful suggestions on parts of the manuscript.

The final responsibility for remaining errors and ambiguities is mine. I would greatly appreciate it if the readers of this monograph would bring these to my attention, as well as any typographical errors.

S. S.

Contents

List
of
Tables

1
Introduction

The cost of conducting sample surveys has risen sharply in recent years, even though the number of surveys has increased even more rapidly. The National Science Foundation, recognizing the increased use of sample surveys, but also recognizing the increasing concern with rising costs, recently awarded the National Opinion Research Center a grant to study techniques for reducing the costs of survey research without materially affecting quality.

The results of the research on reducing survey costs are presented in this monograph. No single grand scheme for reducing costs is presented. Rather, each area of survey research methodology is examined separately. The reader will note that the research falls into five areas, dealing with sampling procedures, field techniques, interviewers, processing, and scheduling.

Some chapters deal with procedures for reducing costs. Others discuss methods for obtaining more information for the same money—another way of reducing the cost-value ratio. In addition to the methodological experiments, the book presents detailed cost analyses of many NORC studies.

It is always useful to specify the intended audience for a book. This work is directed to professional researchers who are familiar with basic survey techniques. It is not intended as a text in survey research methodology, and for this reason the balance of the sections by no means reflects the importance of the various parts of survey methodology. The sequence of the presentation is intended to reflect the chronological development of a survey, from its inception and the selection of procedures, through its implementation and to its completion and analysis.

Thus, Chapters 2 and 3 deal with sampling procedures. Chapter 2 shows that quota sampling—once the standard method of sampling but later discarded for strict area probability sampling—can be justified on theoretical and empirical grounds in certain situations. On the basis of detailed cost analyses, interviewing costs of a tightly controlled quota sample are shown to be only slightly less than the costs of a probability sample with call-backs, but the speed with which such a sample can be fielded will often make quota sampling useful. Chapter 3 describes the usefulness of obtaining advance information about the characteristics of respondents for use in future sampling. When a large population is being screened to obtain a sample of a relatively uncommon group, such as participants in an adult education program or victims of a crime, four-fifths of the sample may be ineligible. If a few key bits of information are obtained from these respondents, they may be interviewed on a later study. Thus, NORC's study of effects of parochial school education (Greeley and Rossi, 1966) utilized a sample of Catholics who had been located in the adult education survey. This chapter also discusses the problems due to families moving, and some techniques for locating such families.

Chapters 4 and 5 discuss field technique procedures, both in terms of increasing survey yield and of reducing interviewer travel costs. Chapter 4 describes a leave-and-pick-up procedure which, in combination with a personal interview, yields very high cooperation rates at costs substantially less than personal interviewing. Since differences between personal interviews and self-administered questionnaires are a possible source of difficulty with this method, these differences are also discussed. Chapter 5 discusses several different uses of the telephone to reduce interviewing costs. In many cases this cost reduction may also be connected with an increase in the quality of interviewing. There is a description of four successful NORC methodological experiments. In the first pair, the telephone was used to make appointments and to reduce wasted travel time. In the other two, interviews were conducted by phone with hard-to-reach respondents. In all experiments, there were substantial cost savings.

Chapters 6, 7, and 8—the longest section of the monograph—deal with the most important workers on a survey—the survey interviewers. In the past, short-lived efforts have been made to improve the efficiency of interviewers. The results of this section suggest that the prime methods for reducing interviewing costs are the better selection of interviewers and the establishment of cost standards rather than efforts to manipulate the work schedules.

Chapter 6, which contains a detailed cost and time analysis of interviewing based on a dozen different surveys, shows that only about one-third of an interviewer's time is spent on her main task—interviewing. In this chapter, unlike most of the others, results are available from other survey organizations and are compared to the NORC results. Since interviewers are paid in a unique way, comparisons are made between interviewers and social workers, salesmen, and public health nurses. Although salesmen generally work on commission and social workers on an annual salary, the surprising results presented in this chapter show that the time allocation of these three groups is remarkably similar. Only public health nurses spend substantially more of their time in their chief function, leading one to suspect that job tensions may be responsible for the remaining time being spent in non-tension producing functions such as travel and clerical activities. If this is so, then fiddling with the hours an interviewer works would be unlikely to increase the amount of time she spends interviewing.

Chapter 7 deals with a new procedure for paying interviewers, based on the establishment of standards for the various parts of the interviewing function. The effort here is not to reduce costs of all interviewers, but to identify those interviewers who are least efficient and some who may be cheating. The standards discussed are based on NORC cost analyses and are similar to standards developed by the Bureau of the Census for the Current Population Survey. A successful methodological experiment in which interviewers were paid by formula is also described.

Chapter 8 also utilizes the results of Chapter 7. Interviewers are characterized as being above or below standard costs for eleven NORC studies. They are also rated by the quality of their interviewing as determined by the number of errors discovered in a sample of their completed interviews. The rating method used is described in detail. Then cost and quality behavior are cross-classified with other characteristics of the interviewer obtained from an interviewer questionnaire. Finally, length of employment is cross-classified with the characteristics from the questionnaire. High education and intelligence, high need achievement, and enjoyment of outdoor activities characterize high quality, low cost interviewers. Enthusiasm for interviewing, on the other hand, appears to be related to high cost and low quality. Career orientation variables are related both to high quality and high cost. Family responsibility is related to low cost interviewers, but negatively related to longevity. None of the characteristics, however, are very useful for predicting longevity.

The next two chapters turn from interviewing to processing of results. Chapter 9 describes the use of computers in coding free response answers. The process uses a computer coding system called the General Inquirer, which has been used before in social research but never in this way. Based on the evidence of a single study, it is possible to develop a method that is as accurate as human coding and which, if used enough to offset the high set-up costs, is cheaper than manual methods. The major advantage of the technique, however, is the increased flexibility given the study director to analyze his results. Since the total response is keypunched and put on a computer tape reel, coding categories can be revised at any time, as new ideas occur or new results become available.

Chapter 10 presents the results of a methodological experiment on the use of optical scanners. A low cost IBM scanner primarily used for grading of examinations was found to be adaptable to survey research questionnaires. The speed and error rates of this procedure compare favorably to traditional keypunching methods. Optical scanners will probably be even more useful in survey research as the hardware improves and becomes more flexible.

Clearly the most important part of a survey is the analysis of results. This part of a survey is also the most difficult to analyze from a cost reduction viewpoint. The widely different personalities and work habits of study directors make generalizations in this area treacherous, and none are made here. Instead, the final chapter deals with the flow of a study. Observations made at NORC and other survey organizations suggest that one of the most expensive parts of any study are the times when the study director of that study is doing nothing because of unrealistic scheduling. While sometimes these delays are unavoidable, they are frequently due to impossible expectations about how quickly a study can be fielded and processed.

The reader now has a brief outline of the book. Hopefully, the monograph will inspire other survey organizations to attempt experiments similar to those described here or will stimulate new ideas. Since NORC is only a single survey organization and may differ in many unknown ways from other survey organizations, some of the successes reported here may not be reproducible. Nevertheless, we believe that continuing methodological research is vital, and we invite our readers to join with us in the search for and the publishing of better and cheaper ways of doing survey research.

2

Probability Sampling with Quotas

INTRODUCTION

Two decades ago, when the advocates of probability sampling met and defeated the defenders of quota sampling, the doctrine became established that there was an unbridgeable gulf between the two methods. While it was conceded that quota samples were cheaper, most sampling statisticians had no doubts that quota samples were far less accurate than probability samples and that, even worse, there was no way to measure the accuracy of a quota sample.[1]

[1]An illustration of the typical view held by sampling statisticians is given in Hansen, Hurwitz, and Madow (1953, Volume I, p. 71): "The so-called 'quota controlled' sampling method, which has been widely used, is essentially a sample of convenience but with certain controls imposed that are intended to avoid some of the more serious biases involved in taking those most conveniently available. . . . The restrictions imposed on the convenience of the interviewer by this method may possibly considerably reduce the biases. However, they may also be completely ineffective. What is worse, there is no way to determine the biases except by a sample properly drawn and executed."

In William Cochran (1953, p. 105), a similar, but slightly more favorable view is taken of quota sampling: "Another method that is used in this situation [stratified sampling where the strata cannot be identified in advance] is to decide in advance the n_h that are wanted from each stratum and to instruct the enumerator to continue sampling until the necessary 'quota' has been obtained in each stratum. If the enumerator initially chooses units at random, rejecting those that are not needed, this method is equivalent to stratified random sampling. . . . As this method is used in practice by a number of agencies, the enumerator does not select units at random. Instead, he takes advantage of any information which

This remains the general view today, although Stephan and McCarthy (1958, pp. 211–34) have given a justification of the measurement of sampling variability for quota samples. Meanwhile, there has been a major change in quota sampling methods, particularly since the failure of the polls in 1948 (Perry, 1960). The major change has been the establishment of tight geographical controls that the interviewer must follow. That is, in her search to fill her quotas, the interviewer follows a specified travel pattern, visiting predesignated households. While this quota procedure is now widely used and has produced meaningful data, no one has yet had the audacity to justify it on theoretical grounds.

It is the heretical intent of this chapter to attempt a rationalization of this procedure, which indicates that it is very close to traditional probability sampling. To differentiate it from older quota sampling methods that do not specify a travel pattern, the procedure will be referred to as "probability sampling with quotas." This procedure is not unbiased, but typically the bias is small. On the other hand, a careful cost analysis indicates that differences in direct interviewer costs between probability sampling with call-backs and probability sampling with quotas is also small. The major advantage of this new procedure may well be the

---

enables the quota to be filled quickly (such as that rich people seldom live in slums). The object is to gain the benefits of stratification without the high field costs that might be incurred in an attempt to select units at random. Varying amounts of latitude are permitted to the enumerators. . . . Sampling theory cannot be applied to quota methods which contain no element of probability sampling. Information about the precision of such methods is obtained only when a comparison is possible with a census or with another sample for which confidence limits can be computed."

According to W. Edwards Deming (1960, p. 31): "There is another kind of judgment sample called a quota sample. The instructions in a quota sample ask the interviewers to talk to a specified number of people of each sex and age, perhaps by section of the city, perhaps by economic level. The report of the results usually boasts of good agreement between the sample and the census in respect to the classes specified, but what does this mean? It means that the interviewers reported what they were supposed to report concerning these classes; it proves little or nothing with respect to the accuracy of the data that constitute the purpose of the study. . . . There is no way to compare the cost of a probability sample with the cost of a judgment sample, because the two types of sample are used for different purposes. Cost has no meaning without a measure of quality, and there is no way to appraise objectively the quality of a judgment sample as there is with a probability sample."

speed with which interviewing can be completed. Thus, when speed is critical to obtain immediate public reaction to a crisis such as the Kennedy assassination, probability sampling with quotas can be most useful. The National Opinion Research Center completed the field work on a national study of public reactions to the President's assassination in about ten days, using a probability sample with quotas. Quota studies with less urgency are finished in two or three weeks. On the other hand, regular probability samples usually take six weeks or longer.

The next section of this chapter describes the theoretical foundation of the argument. The following two sections present empirical data from various NORC studies that confirm the theory. The fifth section discusses procedures for computing sampling errors, and the sixth section discusses the costs of sampling with call-backs and quotas. The final section compares the results of three almost identical studies, two of which were done with call-backs and one with quotas.

ASSUMPTIONS UNDERLYING PROBABILITY SAMPLING WITH QUOTAS

In probability sampling with call-backs, the interviewer is given a specific household or individual to be interviewed. If the individual is not available on the first call, repeated call-backs are made until the interview is obtained or the respondent refuses to grant an interview.

In probability sampling with quotas, the basic assumption made is that it is possible to divide the respondents into strata in which the probability of being available for interviewing is known and is the same for all individuals within the stratum, although varying between strata. Any respondent's probability of being interviewed is the product of his initial selection probability times his probability of being available for interviewing. While these probabilities will not be identical for all respondents, they are known, and the sample is therefore a probability sample. There is an implicit assumption that an interviewer in a sample segment follows the same time pattern over repeated surveys and that the respondent has a pattern of availability depending on certain characteristics.

The quotas then used must clearly be associated with the probability of being available for interviewing. Essentially, the quotas should be based on the reciprocals of the probabilities of availability. If the probability of the individuals in Stratum A being available is twice as large as the probability of individuals in Stratum B, then the sampling rate for Stratum A should be one-half that for Stratum B.

In the usual situation, quotas are set for a given stratum based on the sampling rate and universe estimates of the size of the stratum. These quotas are normally determined for the smallest geographic area for which information is available. Thus, in metropolitan areas, census tract information is used, while in non-tracted areas the quotas are based on the characteristics of the locality or of the rural portion of the county. This method introduces the possibility of error because of inadequate universe estimates, but generally it is almost like the method that uses sampling rates directly.

This procedure is wasteful from a sampling viewpoint, since households with no one at home are skipped as well as households where the respondent is not available for interviewing at the time the interviewer calls, or households with respondents who do not fit the quota. The field cost savings, however, considerably exceed the increase in internal sampling costs.

Probability sampling with quotas has been used primarily for sampling of individual respondents. Where household behavior or opinions are wanted it would be possible to use the same procedure, but since size of household is highly correlated with availability it would be necessary to make it a major quota control. Since any knowledgeable adult is acceptable as the respondent in a household survey, probability sampling with call-backs of households is less costly than sampling of designated respondents in households. Generally, cost and time savings of probability samples with quotas of households will not be great enough to make this method very useful considering the possible biases.

The rationalization of probability sampling with quotas depends on a major assumption, while probability sampling with call-backs does not require this assumption. Fortunately, there is strong evidence to be presented in the next section that this assumption is almost true for the kinds of surveys generally conducted in the United States. To the extent that the assumption is not true, small biases are introduced, but the method still remains a probability sample.

Even in the usual probability sample with call-backs, biases exist due to non-cooperators. These same biases exist in probability sampling with quotas. We have not observed any major difference in the overall cooperation rates achieved by interviewers on probability samples with call-backs as compared to probability samples with quotas. These cooperation rates depend on both respondents and interviewers. Since respondents cannot be aware of the type of sampling, any difference would have to be due to the fact that the interviewer did not try as hard to convert a refusal into a cooperator. At least with NORC interviewers who do both types of interviews, there is no evidence that this is occurring.

It may be useful for the reader to compare the rationale for samples described above with the Politz-Simmons weighting method sometimes used to adjust for not-at-home bias (Politz and Simmons, 1949). In this procedure no call-backs are made and no quotas are used. Typically, the respondent is asked whether or not he was home on the preceding five nights, and his answers to this question determine the weight that he receives. Thus a respondent who had been at home all nights would get a weight of 1, while a respondent who had not been home on any of the preceding five nights would get a weight of 6, since only one-sixth of respondents of this type would be found at home on a random night.

The Politz-Simmons weighting has three disadvantages. First, the weighting depends on the respondent's memory of how he spent the last five nights, and, in general, respondents will tend to overstate their availability. Second, the use of weights increases the sampling variability substantially. Finally, the weighting method introduces the need for careful controls when the data are processed to insure that the weighting is done properly. It is my impression that not very many surveys currently use the Politz-Simmons weighting procedure because of these difficulties.

If one were willing to accept the answer to the at-home question as being reliable and did not worry about the cost of weighting, then it would be possible to develop a combined sampling method that used probability sampling with quotas to keep sampling variability low, and used the answer to the at-home question to eliminate remaining sample biases.

RESPONDENT CHARACTERISTICS RELATED TO AVAILABILITY FOR INTERVIEWING

How does one go about establishing strata within which individuals have the same probability of being available for interviewing, and how are these strata tested for homogeneity? Since direct data are unavailable, one must use past experience on probability samples. Many earlier studies have shown that women are generally more readily available for interviewing than are men. Primarily, this is due to the fact that more men than women are employed. When one imposes the additional control of employment status, one sees a substantial difference between employed and unemployed women, but the difference between men and women shrinks. In addition, age of men is of some importance. Thus, NORC developed a four-stratum system for its probability sample with quotas, comprising men under thirty, men thirty and over, unemployed women, and employed women.

Another major factor determining availability is the size of the community in which the respondent lives. The basic probability sample design, which is a multi-stage sample drawn with probabilities proportionate to size of the block or enumeration district, controls for this. No claim is made that the four strata are optimum. NORC plans additional research to find characteristics that may be more highly correlated with availability. One can certainly make the strata more homogeneous by splitting off additional strata from those that already exist, but this makes the search procedure more costly. Under some circumstances it becomes cheaper to make call-backs than to continue the search for a respondent with rare characteristics.

Tables 2.1 through 2.4 present in summary form the relationship between characteristics and availability for interviewing. While these results may also be valuable in planning new sample surveys, they are primarily presented to show that the NORC strata are reasonable, if not optimum. Table 2.1 presents the

Table 2.1 Average Calls Required To Complete an Interview on Various Probability with Call-back Samples

Sample	All Respondents	Males	Under 30	30+	Females	Employed	Unemployed
NORC:							
All places	2.7 (906)	3.0 (387)	3.2 (76)	2.9 (311)	2.5 (519)	3.0 (212)	2.2 (307)
10 largest SMA's*	3.2 (206)	3.2 (96)	3.4 (27)	3.2 (69)	3.3 (110)	3.9 (48)	2.8 (62)
Other SMA's	2.9 (357)	3.3 (155)	3.5 (30)	3.2 (125)	2.5 (202)	2.9 (91)	2.2 (111)
Non-metro counties	2.3 (343)	2.4 (136)	2.8 (19)	2.4 (117)	2.1 (207)	2.6 (73)	1.9 (134)
Survey Research Center:							
All places	2.2 (7,528)	2.3 (3,658)			2.1 (4,031)		
Large metro	2.5 (2,299)						
Other urban	2.1 (3,717)						
Rural	2.8 (1,512)						
Britain	2.3 (1,443)	2.4 (938)			2.0 (505)	2.3 (55)	2.0 (450)
Elmira	1.9 (1,029)	2.1 (452)			1.7 (577)		
Madison	2.0 (743)	2.2 (313)			1.8 (430)		

*SMA is a Standard Metropolitan Area.

average calls required to complete an interview by age, sex, and employment status for a typical NORC probability with call-back sample, and several other samples for which data are available.

The results obtained by NORC interviewers agree reasonably well with other published data on the number of calls required to complete an interview. Durbin and Stuart's data, when recomputed to put them into the format of Table 2.1, show the same relationship between availability of men, employed women, and unemployed women (1954, pp. 395–97). Mayer presents separate tables of availability by size of community and sex, and a cross-classification of these variables with first calls (1964, pp. 19–33). His results are also in agreement with the NORC and British results. Two local studies in Madison and Elmira are also in general agreement with the other studies (Lowe and McCormick, 1955; Williams, 1950).

For a better understanding of probability samples with quotas, however, it is also useful to consider the probability of completing an interview on the first call as well as the average number of calls required. There is a very substantial increase in the probability of finding a respondent after the first call. Thus, using average calls required over-estimates the probability of a respondent being available on a probability sample with quotas. Table 2.2 shows these first-call probabilities for the NORC study and the other surveys of Table 2.1. Naturally, these results are somewhat more variable since they utilize only a fraction of the data, but they show exactly the same relationships.

If household information is required, it is not necessary to specify which individual in the household should furnish it. Generally, any knowledgeable adult would be qualified. While this does not bias a probability sample, it could cause a substantial bias in a probability sample with quotas since, as indicated in Table 2.3 and as one would expect, larger families would be more likely to be found at home than would smaller ones. For this reason, any such sample of households would clearly need to control for household size.

Table 2.4 gives the probabilities of completing a call by number of calls for four NORC studies and compares these results to those at the Survey Research Center (Mayer, 1964, p. 24). Typi-

Table 2.2 Probability of Completing Interview on First Call by Age, Sex, and Employment Status with Call-back Samples

Sample	All Respondents	Males	Under 30	30+	Females	Employed	Unemployed
NORC:							
All places	.28 (906)	.23 (387)	.24 (76)	.22 (311)	.31 (519)	.19 (212)	.40 (307)
10 largest SMA's	.19 (206)	.18 (96)	.26 (27)	.14 (69)	.20 (110)	.10 (48)	.27 (62)
Other SMA's	.26 (357)	.21 (155)	.30 (30)	.18 (125)	.30 (202)	.16 (91)	.41 (111)
Non-metro counties	.35 (343)	.28 (136)	— (19)	.31 (117)	.40 (207)	.30 (73)	.45 (134)
Survey Research Center:							
All places	.32 (2,963)	.26 (1,340)			.36 (1,623)		
Large metro	.21 (1,724)	.15 (323)			.26 (401)		
Other urban	.32 (1,501)	.26 (659)			.36 (842)		
Rural	.42 (738)	.37 (358)			.47 (380)		
Britain	.44 (1,443)	.40 (938)			.51 (505)	.35 (55)	
Elmira	.38 (1,029)	.24 (452)	.18 (108)	.26 (344)	.49 (577)		.53 (450)
Madison	.40 (743)	.27 (313)	.21 (57)	.29 (256)	.49 (430)		

Table 2.3 Probability of Completing Interview with Any Household Member on First Call by Size of Household with Call-back Samples

Sample	All Respondents	Household Size					
		1	2	3	4	5	6 or More
NORC:							
All places	.56 (11,257)	.46 (1,465)	.52 (3,219)	.56 (2,074)	.58 (1,979)	.63 (1,242)	.67 (1,287)
10 largest SMA's	.44 (2,437)	.29 (351)	.36 (675)	.44 (478)	.50 (441)	.58 (260)	.59 (232)
Other SMA's	.56 (4,504)	.47 (548)	.51 (1,274)	.55 (835)	.58 (830)	.62 (484)	.67 (533)
Non-metro counties	.63 (4,316)	.55 (566)	.62 (1,270)	.64 (761)	.61 (699)	.66 (498)	.70 (522)
Elmira	— (1,029)	.36 (129)	.38 (662)	.37 (166)	.50 (50)	— (13)	— (9)

cally there is a substantial rise from the first to the second call and then a leveling-off on subsequent calls. This is true for the first two NORC studies and for the SRC data.

Tne third NORC study shown in Table 2.4 is an example of a survey where a screening call was made first and an interview then conducted with a special subsample of those screened. In that case, the interviewer has already obtained information from someone in the household, and her probability of completing a call is greatest on the first call. Looking at Table 2.8, one can see that the costs for this study are the lowest of the four studies presented. As an aside, another NORC experiment discovered that substantial reductions in travel costs were achieved when interviewers phoned for appointments before going to the segment.

The final NORC study was the short screening questionnaire which was the prelude to the survey described in the previous paragraph. Here, the interviewer was permitted to interview any adult in the household instead of a specified family member. Again the probability of completing an interview is greatest on the first call and drops slightly on the second and subsequent calls.

Table 2.4 Probability of Completing Call on Various Surveys by Number of Calls with Call-back Samples

Sample	N	1	2	3	4	5
National Opinion Research Center 1	2,211	.36	.66	.56	.54	.50
National Opinion Research Center 2	2,866	.42	.44	.52	.48	.48
National Opinion Research Center 3	5,083	.77	.53	.53	.39	.49
National Opinion Research Center 4*	12,441	.59	.50	.46	.47	.47
Largest SMA's	3,035	.48	.40	.37	.40	.41
Other SMA's	4,873	.58	.51	.48	.50	.49
Non-metro	4,533	.67	.58	.56	.57	.60
SRC—Total		.34	.39	.41	.39	.43
Large metro		.22	.30	.32	.36	.42
Other urban		.35	.41	.45	.42	.45
Rural		.43	.49	.50	.40	–

* Interview with any household member.

TESTING FOR HOMOGENEITY

Having selected these strata, or some other grouping, one must then test for homogeneity for probability samples with quotas. For this purpose it seems reasonable to use the geometric distribution as the theoretical distribution to which our empirical distributions are compared.

Assume that the interviewer for a probability sample with quotas is conducting a random search and that her probability of completing an interview at any random household is equal to the probability of completing an interview on the first call for a probability sample with call-backs in the same area. Let us pause for a moment to examine these two assumptions. While it is clear that the interviewer is not actually searching at random, the establishment of quotas makes it necessary for her to interview not only during the day, but also in the evening and on weekends so that her searching times approximate a random procedure. The second assumption is realistic since the same interviewers conduct both types of samples in their areas, and generally have the same time periods available for interviewing.

Using these assumptions, the number of calls required to complete an interview for probability samples with quota is a random variable which has the geometric distribution (a special case of the negative binomial or Pascal). The expected mean and variance of this distribution are known to be:

$$E(X) = 1/p; \text{ Variance } (X) = q/p^2$$
(See Feller, 1950, pp. 174, 217–18.)

The fit of this model to actual interviewing behavior can be seen in Tables 2.5 and 2.6. The first of these, Table 2.5, compares the means obtained on actual probability samples with quotas with the expected values obtained from the reciprocal of the probabilities of being home on the first call which were given in Table 2.2, and which are based on call-back samples. The actual means and expected means are generally in close agreement, which lends substantial credibility to the model.

It may be useful in considering these results to keep in mind how they were obtained. For NORC probability samples with quotas a detailed listing sheet is kept by all interviewers. This

Table 2.5 Actual and Expected DU[a] Approaches Required To Complete Interview for NORC Probability Sample with Quotas[b]

Sample	All Respondents	Males	Under 30	30+	Females	Employed	Unemployed
All places:							
Actual x̄	3.6	3.8	3.6	3.9	3.7	4.4	3.4
Expected x̄	3.6	4.3	4.2	4.5	3.2	5.3	2.5
N	(1,916)	(919)	(171)	(748)	(997)	(338)	(659)
10 Largest SMA's:							
Actual x̄	5.8	5.6	5.6	5.5	6.0	7.0	5.3
Expected x̄	5.3	5.6	3.8	7.1	5.0	10.0	3.7
N	(480)	(230)	(36)	(194)	(250)	(96)	(154)
Other SMA's:							
Actual x̄	3.4	3.8	3.9	3.8	3.4	3.6	3.3
Expected x̄	3.8	4.8	3.3	5.6	3.3	6.3	2.4
N	(763)	(359)	(73)	(286)	(404)	(152)	(252)
Non-metropolitan counties:							
Actual x̄	2.5	2.5	2.0	2.7	2.5	2.9	2.3
Expected x̄	2.9	3.6	—	3.2	2.5	3.3	2.2
N	(673)	(330)	(62)	(268)	(343)	(90)	(253)

[a] DU is the Dwelling Unit.
[b] Actual values derived from NORC probability samples with quotas. Expected values are reciprocals of values in Table 2.2 which are based on NORC call-back samples.

sheet shows every house visited, and the results obtained. While vacant dwelling units and commercial establishments are listed, they were not included in the counts, nor were households that had no respondent who fitted the quota. It should be noted that quota refusals are included, since generally these were not final refusals but rather respondents who were unavailable for interviewing at the time the interviewer called. The expected probabilities from the call-back samples are based on completed cases and do not account for hard-core refusals, or vacant or commercial units.

Table 2.6 compares the actual and expected variances for the probability sample with quotas. Since, unfortunately, the expected variances are sensitive to small changes in the mean, they are based on the combined means of both the samples in Table 2.5. For example, consider males under thirty in the ten largest SMA's. If the actual value of Table 2.5 is used, $p = 1/5.6 = .18$ and expected $\sigma^2 = (1-p)/p^2 = 22.2$. If the expected value is used based on call-backs, $p = .26$ and $\sigma^2 = 10.9$. Combining these estimates gives p a value of .213 and $\sigma^2 = 17.4$, which is the value shown in the table. The comparisons show close agreement for employed females and men over thirty everywhere, and generally good agreement for all groups in the non-metropolitan counties. Men under thirty and unemployed women have higher than expected variances in metropolitan areas.

While this is probably a weak test, the ratios in a few of the cells of Table 2.6 clearly suggest that there are biases still remaining in the groups with the higher than expected variances, but they do not insure the absence of biases in the other cells. That is, it is possible that some groups within a stratum have a substantially higher or lower probability of being found at home than the average for that stratum, and due to the large variance of the estimate of the variance of the mean, this cannot be detected.

It is possible to make some estimates of the maximum magnitude of the bias in the final results based on the data shown in Table 2.6. Suppose that each stratum is not homogeneous, but consists of two equal-sized substrata which are homogeneous within themselves. (It can be shown that the bias is maximized

Table 2.6 Actual and Expected Variance of DU Approaches Required To Complete Interview for NORC Probability Sample with Quotas*

Sample	All Respondents	Males	Under 30	30+	Females	Employed	Unemployed
All places:							
Actual σ^2	24.4	22.9	23.2	22.8	25.8	32.9	21.9
Estimated σ^2	10.6	12.4	11.3	13.4	8.5	18.7	5.8
Ratio	2.3	1.8	2.1	1.7	3.0	1.8	3.8
10 largest SMA's:							
Actual σ^2	57.4	45.4	50.3	43.9	71.2	76.9	62.8
Expected σ^2	25.3	25.8	17.4	33.4	24.8	63.8	15.8
Ratio	2.3	1.8	2.9	1.3	2.9	1.2	4.0
Other SMA's:							
Actual σ^2	16.3	20.4	23.3	19.7	12.5	14.5	11.4
Expected σ^2	9.4	14.2	9.4	17.4	7.9	19.6	5.3
Ratio	1.7	1.4	2.5	1.1	1.6	0.7	2.2
Non-metropolitian counties:							
Actual σ^2	5.6	6.2	2.0	7.2	5.0	7.0	4.2
Expected σ^2	4.6	6.3	2.0	5.8	3.8	6.5	2.8
Ratio	1.2	1.0	1.0	1.2	1.3	1.1	1.5

*Actual values derived from NORC probability samples with quotas. Expected values are $(1-p)/p^2$, where p is the reciprocal of the average of the actual and expected values given in Table 2.5, and is based on both quota and call-back samples.

with two equal-sized substrata rather than with a larger number of strata or unequal-sized strata.)

The estimated means of the substrata are shown in Table 2.7. These values are derived from the formula:

$$\sigma^2 (X_s) = \frac{1}{2} \left(\frac{q_1}{p_1{}^2} + \frac{q_2}{p_2{}^2} \right) + \frac{1}{4} \left(\frac{1}{p_1} - \frac{1}{p_2} \right)^2$$

Using the values for the observed variances from Table 2.6, the values for p_1 and p_2 can be easily derived. The bias in the estimate also depends on differential behavior between the two substrata. If the proportion of Substratum 1 with a given characteristic is R and the proportion of Substratum 2 with the characteristic is αR, then the bias in the stratum estimate is:

$$\frac{p_1 - p_2}{p_1 + p_2} \left(\frac{\alpha - 1}{\alpha + 1} \right)$$

While α will not generally be known, past experience would suggest that it would normally be about 1.5 or less, although it might be as high as 2 or 3. Table 2.7 also shows estimated biases for each stratum for α values of 1.3, 1.5, 2, and 3. It can be seen that the overall estimates of bias for an estimate range from 3 per cent to 12 per cent. These estimates do, of course, depend on the estimates of Table 2.6 as well as the estimates of α and so are subject to large error, particularly in the individual strata. Nevertheless, Table 2.7 indicates that, typically, differences between call-back and quota samples will not exceed 8 per cent and that most differences will be of the order of 3 to 5 per cent. Empirical verification of this is given in the final section of this chapter and in Table 2.10.

In summary, this section has presented empirical results that support the reasonableness of treating sampling with quotas as a form of probability sampling. The agreement in Table 2.5 between the number of dwelling unit approaches on a probability sample with quotas and the reciprocal of the probability of completing an interview on the first call for probability sampling with call-backs strongly supports the notion that these two kinds of sampling methods have much in common.

The results of Tables 2.6 and 2.7, however, indicate that some

Table 2.7 Estimated Biases in Quota Sample Results When Strata Consist of Two Substrata

Stratum	Probability of Completing Interview on First Call			Estimated Per Cent Bias in Results			
	Total	Substratum 1	Substratum 2	$\alpha = 1.3$	$\alpha = 1.5$	$\alpha = 2$	$\alpha = 3$
10 Largest SMA's:							
Men under 30	.22	.11	.33	9.4	10.0	16.7	25.0
Men over 30	.16	.12	.30	4.7	5.0	8.3	12.5
Women employed	.13	.09	.17	5.8	6.2	10.3	15.5
Women unemployed	.23	.10	.36	10.7	11.4	19.0	28.5
Other SMA's:							
Men under 30	.28	.16	.40	8.1	8.6	14.3	21.5
Men over 30	.22	.17	.27	4.3	4.6	7.7	11.5
Women employed	.22	.22	.22	0	0	0	0
Women unemployed	.36	.21	.51	4.9	5.2	8.7	13.0
Non-metropolitan counties:							
Men under 30	.50	.50	.50	0	0	0	0
Men over 30	.34	.27	.41	3.9	4.2	7.0	10.5
Women employed	.32	.30	.34	1.1	1.2	2.0	3.0
Women unemployed	.44	.33	.55	4.7	5.0	8.3	12.5
All strata	—	—	—	3.2	4.9	8.2	12.3

biases still exist in the probability sample with quotas, at least for the strata considered. That is, within some of the strata there are probably individuals belonging to substrata whose probabilities of being available for interviewing differ from the stratum mean. If there were no considerations of time or cost there would never be a reason not to use call-backs instead of quotas. When time and cost factors are considered to be more important than the biases (generally small) introduced by the use of sampling with quotas, this method becomes preferable.

SAMPLING VARIABILITY OF PROBABILITY SAMPLES WITH QUOTAS

There are no basic differences between methods for computing sampling errors for probability samples with quotas and the usual sample error computations. Of course, the naive use of simple random sampling error formulas for complex national samples is never appropriate for either quota or call-back samples.

Since stratification of samples of individuals generally does not significantly reduce sampling variability, the major difference between complex and simple samples is due to clustering. A probability sample with quotas is a cluster sample and will have about the same variability as a similar cluster sample with call-backs.

Direct methods of computing variances of complex samples are tedious, and almost all statisticians currently use short-cut procedures. These are very well described by Kish (1965) and Hansen, Hurwitz, and Madow (1953) and need not be repeated here. The suggested procedure of Stephan and McCarthy (1958, Chapter 10) is one of several possible appropriate methods. These procedures do not measure uncertainty about biases or response errors, and so are minimum estimates of error.

COSTS OF PROBABILITY SAMPLES WITH CALL-BACKS AND WITH QUOTAS

The chief argument made for the old quota samples was that they were cheap. The costs of probability sampling with quotas are still less than the costs of sampling with call-backs, but the differences are much narrower. This section compares the costs of various NORC probability call-back and quota samples, and indicates that a substantial portion of the cost differential between them is due not to field activities but rather to other aspects of the study unrelated to sampling.

Let us first compare the total costs of six NORC probability call-back and four quota studies. It can be seen from Table 2.8 that call-back sample costs per case are typically three times as high as the costs per case of quota samples; the probability with call-back samples have a median cost of about $52.00 per case as compared to a median of about $19.00 for probability samples with quotas.

A brief examination of the table, however, reveals that a substantial part of this difference is due to differences in planning, processing, and analysis between the two surveys. Almost always, the planning and analysis of call-back samples is costlier, and takes a larger part of the total cost of the study. It seems clear that it is not the sample design that determines the cost of a study, but rather the cost that determines the sample design.

To be more explicit, where survey results will receive very sophisticated analysis or when critical decisions will be based on them, it will be worthwhile to pay a substantial cost to achieve high standards of sampling, processing, and control. Thus, the Census Bureau rightly has very high standards on their current population surveys. On the other hand, many exploratory studies do not require such high standards since the analysis may be more limited and the questionnaire may itself be a major source of error. Here quota sampling would be justified.

On the other hand, the relationship goes both ways. One reason why analysis costs are higher on call-back samples is that the analysts spend more time waiting for results to become available. Very often the field data collection period is extended for several weeks, which delays the processing for an additional time period. While this waiting time may sometimes be useful in developing codes and modes of analysis, it is frequently wasted.

If one looks only at total field costs, which include both direct and supervisory costs, the ratio of the costs of probability samples with call-backs to probability samples with quotas drops from three:one to two:one. The median field cost per case for call-back

Table 2.8 Field and Other Costs for NORC Surveys (in Dollars)

Costs	Probability with Call-backs						Probability with Quotas			
	Study 1	Study 2	Study 3	Study 4	Study 5	Study 6	Study 1	Study 2	Study 3	Study 4
Direct field costs	$ 31,800	$ 21,000	$ 19,500	$ 5,000	$22,000	$16,900	$ 8,900	$ 9,900	$ 8,500	$ 9,000
Field supervision	8,100	29,500	4,900	2,500	9,500	6,000	1,900	1,700	1,200	1,900
Other survey costs	173,100	106,200	93,400	31,400	38,500	26,500	16,000	18,600	14,100	14,800
Total costs	$213,000	$156,700	$117,800	$38,900	$70,000	$49,400	$26,800	$30,200	$23,800	$25,700
Total cases	(2,380)	(2,810)	(2,200)	(760)	(2,500)	(1,500)	(1,200)	(1,500)	(1,300)	(1,500)
Cost per case	$ 89.50	$ 55.80	$ 53.50	$ 51.20	$ 28.00	$ 32.90	$ 22.30	$ 20.20	$ 18.30	$ 17.10
Direct field cost per case	$ 13.40	7.50	8.90	6.60	8.80	11.30	7.40	6.60	6.50	6.00
Total field cost per case	$ 18.70	$ 18.00	$ 11.10	$ 9.90	$ 12.60	$ 15.30	$ 9.00	$ 7.70	$ 7.50	$ 7.30

samples on the six studies is $14.00 as compared to $7.50 per case for the quota samples.

This comparison can be carried still one step further. The major difference between the two types of samples is the cost of supervision. When one examines only the direct cost of interviewing, the difference shrinks to about $2.50 between the median direct field cost per case of $9.00 for call-back samples and $6.50 for quota samples.

This difference represents the one extra hour per case that the average interviewer on a call-back sample must spend to find her respondent, as well as some additional travel expenses. It is clear that this difference is less important than the difference in the cost of supervision. Thus, it would seem possible to reduce the cost of a call-back sample almost to the level of a quota sample if one could reduce supervisory costs.

Again it should be noted that not all of the difference in supervisory cost is due to the sampling method. Some of this difference can be attributed to the greater quality control checks generally used in the more expensive samples. The additional effort generally made in training interviewers on call-back samples requires more supervisory time. There are, however, some characteristics of a call-back sample that do generate greater supervisory costs. Typically, the interviewer is told to make three call-backs and then to check with the supervisor for further instructions if she has not completed an interview. The decision process whereby this occurs is quite costly in supervisory time, as are the letters and long-distance calls which accompany the revised instructions. If methods can be found for standardizing the follow-up procedures and eliminating most of the ad hoc decisions now made, a substantial part of field supervisory costs could be eliminated.

Another aspect of call-back sampling which leads to higher supervisory costs is the time period required to complete the interviewing. Since some respondents will be temporarily unavailable at the interviewer's initial call, she will need to return at a later time. If the respondent is on vacation or in the hospital, it may take several weeks before the interviewing is completed. Proper allowances should be made for this when scheduling, and the flow of completed questionnaires should be watched carefully. Nevertheless, some added cost due to the stretching-out of the time period cannot be avoided with call-back samples.

In summary, Table 2.8 shows that the direct interviewer cost difference between call-back samples and quota samples is about $2.50, or one hour of interviewer time per case. Much larger differences are due to added supervisory costs, some of which might be eliminated by the standardization of call-back procedures. The greater length of time required to complete a sample with call-backs is another factor in increasing supervisory and other overhead costs, and there is no way to avoid this increase.

MARGINAL COST OF CALL-BACKS

The small difference between direct field costs of call-back sampling and quota sampling is due both to the fact that quota sampling as described in this chapter is more costly than uncontrolled sampling, and that the marginal cost of call-backs is not as large as is generally believed. This is not a new finding (Birnbaum and Sirken, 1950, pp. 189–90) but it seems worthwhile to present additional evidence to support this result.

The data in Table 2.9 show that the marginal travel cost of additional calls remains fairly constant, although sampling variability causes differences as the number of cases becomes small. That is, it is generally less expensive to continue call-backs than to draw an additional sample. Table 2.10 shows the same relationship when the costs are separated by size of place.

One would think that travel costs per case would have to rise on repeated call-backs since relatively fixed costs are divided among fewer cases, but this is compensated by the increased probability of finding a respondent at home and the interviewer's greater familiarity with the area she is sampling.

The allocation of travel costs requires some arbitrariness. While the NORC procedure adopted is certainly a valid one, there are other allocation methods which might be equally valid and which would probably also lead to similar results. Travel costs are divided into two parts—travel time within a segment and travel time to and between segments.

Table 2.9 Average Travel Cost and Marginal Cost To Complete Interview by Number of Calls for Four NORC Call-back Samples

Calls Required To Complete Interview	Study 1			Study 2			Study 3			Study 4		
	N	Average Total Cost	Marginal Cost	N	Average Total Cost	Marginal Cost	N	Average Total Cost	Marginal Cost	N	Average Total Cost	Marginal Cost
One	792	$3.23		1,202	$2.89		7,285	$0.89		3,894	$1.13	
Two	791	4.14	$0.91	738	3.50	$0.61	2,562	1.34	$0.45	631	2.55	$1.42
Three	349	5.30	1.16	480	3.72	0.22	1,187	1.98	0.54	293	3.68	1.13
Four	152	6.98	1.68	215	4.43	0.71	661	2.50	0.52	103	4.33	0.65
Five	64	8.46	1.48	112	5.24	0.81	351	3.13	0.63	79	4.59	0.26
Six	34	8.67	1.21	42	7.06	1.82	176	4.22	1.09	35	6.12	1.53
Seven or more	29	9.22	0.55	77	8.13	1.07	219	5.97	0.67	48	9.26	1.12
Total N	(2,211)			(2,866)			(12,441)			(5,083)		

Table 2.10 Average Travel Costs and Marginal Costs To Complete Interview by Size of PSU* for Four NORC Call-back Samples

Calls Required To Complete Interview	10 Largest Metro			Other Metro			Non-metro		
	N	Average Travel Cost	Marginal Cost	N	Average Travel Cost	Marginal Cost	N	Average Travel Cost	Marginal Cost
Study 1:									
One	1,442	$1.09	$ –	2,811	$0.89	–	3,032	$0.80	–
Two	643	1.78	0.69	1,045	1.30	$0.41	874	1.06	$0.26
Three	351	2.46	0.68	485	1.79	0.49	351	1.66	0.40

	10 Largest Metro			Prince Georges			Warren		
Four	237	3.10	0.76	268	2.45	0.66	156	2.06	0.40
Five	149	3.67	0.57	130	2.90	0.45	72	2.44	0.38
Six	86	4.60	0.93	68	3.25	0.35	–	–	–
Seven	59	5.33	0.93	27	4.16	0.91	–	–	–
Eight or more (av. = 10)	68	8.04	0.90	39	7.10	0.98	–	–	–
Study 2:									
One	724	1.55	–	1,402	1.12	–	1,768	0.97	–
Two	158	3.60	2.05	263	2.46	1.34	210	1.86	0.89
Three	88	4.95	1.35	127	3.72	1.26	78	2.18	0.38
Four	32	6.19	1.24	49	4.26	0.54	22	3.27	1.09
Five	20	6.95	0.76	34	5.47	1.21	25	4.05	0.78

	Metro			Non-metro			Detroit		
Study 3:									
One	150	3.14	–	697	2.97	–	147	2.42	–
Two	132	3.50	0.36	294	3.41	0.44	121	3.62	1.20
Three	135	3.58	0.08	148	3.84	0.43	76	4.44	0.82
Four	59	3.86	0.28	55	4.86	1.02	37	4.70	0.26
Five	38	4.60	0.74	22	4.98	0.12	23	6.44	1.74
Study 4:									
One	345	3.80	–	370	2.88	–	208	2.79	–
Two	425	5.04	1.24	336	3.20	0.32	191	3.56	0.77
Three	229	5.69	0.65	117	4.25	1.05	121	3.73	0.17
Four	120	6.03	0.34	34	4.62	0.37	64	4.98	1.25
							29	5.34	0.36

*PSU is the Primary Sampling Unit.

Travel to Segment

Travel to segment is derived from the travel column on the time report. It includes time to the segment from the interviewer's home and return. It also includes any travel time from one segment to another. It is generally not too difficult to separate this time from the time spent by the interviewer within the segment.

Travel costs to a segment are allocated equally, but only to the completed interviews made on that trip. That is, not-at-home calls were not charged any travel time to a segment unless there were no completed interviews on that trip. The rationale behind this allocation is that if the interviewer has been in the segment anyway (either with or without an appointment) and has completed one or more interviews, then any additional calls she makes in the segment are gravy, as far as travel time to the segment.

Travel in Segment

Travel in segment is defined as all time in a segment not spent on the actual interview. Travel in segment includes all waiting time, and time in a respondent's home spent in conversation not part of the interview, as well as time spent locating the proper house in the segment and knocking on doors. Also included here is the time the interviewer spends on the telephone making appointments for interviews. This type of travel time is not always directly noted by interviewers filling out the present time sheet. It is sometimes included under travel time, sometimes under interviewing time and sometimes under other time. In coding the time reports, cross-checks are made with questionnaires. If the interviewer combines waiting time or other time within the segment with the interview, the length of the interview as obtained from the questionnaire is subtracted from the total time shown and the balance is called "travel in segment." Even where the interviewer has separated her time, cross-checks still are made to the questionnaire to insure that dates and times agree. If not, the normal procedure is to adjust the time report to the questionnaire since times in the questionnaire were presumably filled out immediately while the time report is generally filled out later.

Travel costs within the segment were allocated equally to all the calls made in the segment on that trip. That is, all calls, whether or not they resulted in a completed interview were charged with the same fraction of the travel costs within the segment.

COMPARISON OF SURVEY RESULTS ON PROBABILITY CALL-BACK VS. QUOTA SAMPLES

This final section compares the results of three NORC studies, conducted for Professor Jiri Nehnevajsa of the University of Pittsburgh, all of which dealt with attitudes of the American public on questions dealing with world tensions (Nehnevajsa, 1964). On each of these surveys, five questions were asked in exactly the same way, and the responses to these questions are presented in Table 2.11. In addition, a large number of demographic characteristics, which were obtained on all three surveys, are compared.

As is to be expected from the previous discussion, the differences between the three surveys are small, and can mostly be accounted for by sampling variability, the different times at which the three studies were conducted, and small differences in the ages of eligible respondents. The first sample with call-backs was conducted in June, 1963, the second in June, 1964, while the sample with quotas was conducted in December, 1963, midway between the other two. On the first call-back study, respondents over sixty-five years old were excluded, while on the last two studies all adult respondents were eligible.

These results do not prove the lack of biases in the probability sample with quotas, but they support the view that for most items these biases cannot be large. The reader may also wish to compare these results to those of Moser and Stuart (1953) who found only small differences on most items between probability samples with call-backs and uncontrolled quota samples. For uncontrolled quota samples, the best explanation of close agreement with census data and probability samples is that the interviewing biases are not highly related to responses. For the probability samples with quotas described here, some of the agreement with the call-back samples may also be attributed to the low correlation be-

Table 2.11 Comparison of Survey Results for NORC U. S. National Samples: Probability with Call-back and Quota (Per Cent)

Opinions on World Affairs	Call-back		Quota
1. *The amount of world tensions just about now:*			
0 No tensions at all	0.3%	0.8%	0.3%
1	0.1	0.5	0.4
2	0.8	0.9	1.2
3	2.4	2.7	3.4
4	4.9	6.7	4.1
5	16.3	16.6	20.0
6	14.0	13.2	11.6
7	21.2	16.5	14.9
8	19.1	17.8	17.6
9	8.8	8.5	6.3
10 Extremely high tensions	12.1	15.8	20.2
Total	100.0%	100.0%	100.0%
N	(1,416)	(1,452)	(1,393)
$\bar{x}$	6.95	6.92	7.03
$s_{\bar{x}}$	0.08	0.08	0.09
2. *World tensions just about two years from now:*			
0 No tensions at all	0.5%	0.7%	0.5%
1	0.6	0.7	0.8
2	1.7	3.1	3.2
3	4.1	4.6	6.5
4	6.7	7.2	7.8
5	12.5	13.6	17.1
6	11.0	9.3	12.3
7	14.8	14.8	13.8
8	19.8	17.8	15.7
9	13.2	11.5	8.3
10 Extremely high tensions	15.1	16.7	14.0
Total	100.0%	100.0%	100.0%
N	(1,416)	(1,452)	(1,393)
$\bar{x}$	7.03	6.90	6.54
$s_{\bar{x}}$	.09	.09	.09
3. *World tensions five years from now:*			
0 No tensions at all	1.0%	1.7%	1.6%
1	1.1	1.5	2.2
2	4.4	4.1	5.7
3	7.2	7.6	8.0
4	7.9	10.0	9.5
5	15.1	17.8	23.1
6	11.3	11.1	9.5
7	11.9	11.4	9.9
8	14.7	12.9	12.2
9	10.8	8.4	6.7
10 Extremely high tensions	14.6	13.5	11.6
Total	100.0%	100.0%	100.0%
N	(1,416)	(1,452)	(1,393)
$\bar{x}$	6.51	6.22	5.91
$s_{\bar{x}}$	.10	.10	.11

(Table 2.11   continued)

Table 2.11 *Continued*

Opinions on World Affairs	Call-back		Quota
4. *World tensions two years ago:*			
0 No tensions at all	0.6%	1.1%	0.4%
1	0.6	1.7	0.8
2	3.1	3.5	2.7
3	6.0	5.7	4.1
4	8.5	8.3	5.6
5	14.4	12.9	11.8
6	14.0	11.8	7.9
7	14.1	13.5	14.6
8	19.3	17.8	19.2
9	11.2	11.2	14.2
10 Extremely high tensions	8.2	12.5	18.7
N	(1,416)	(1,452)	(1,393)
$\bar{x}$	6.51	6.57	7.18
$s_{\bar{x}}$	.09	.09	.09
5. *Average world tensions:*			
Two years ago	6.51%	6.57%	7.18%
Now	6.95	6.92	7.03
Two years from now	7.03	6.90	6.54
Five years from now	6.51	6.22	5.91
N	(1,416)	(1,452)	(1,393)
6. *When will the cold war end?*			
Within two years	4.6%	7.0%	3.4%
Within five years	22.4	21.9	20.4
Within ten years	22.8	23.6	23.2
Ten to twenty years	16.5	14.8	18.6
Twenty-one to fifty years	5.0	6.1	5.9
Over fifty years	5.5	5.7	7.0
Never	13.5	14.0	15.4
Don't know	9.7	6.9	6.1
Total	100.0%	100.0%	100.0%
N	(1,416)	(1,452)	(1,393)
Median years	10.1	9.5	11.6

Demographic Characteristics	Call-back		Quota	
7. *Sex:*				
Male	45.6	44.8	48.1	48.3
Female	54.4	55.2	51.9	51.7
N	(1,434)	(1,464)	(1,557)	(1,482)
8. *Race:*				
White	87.9	85.6	86.8	89.8
Other	12.1	14.4	13.2	10.2
N	(1,434)	(1,464)	(1,557)	(1,482)
9. *Service (or spouse's service in armed forces):*				
Yes	55.9	48.3	50.1	–
No	44.1	51.7	49.9	–
N	(1,434)	(1,464)	(1,557)	–
10. *Service in combat if served in armed forces:*				
Yes	37.1	38.3	39.0	–
No	62.9	61.7	61.0	–
N	(726)	(645)	(715)	–

(*Table 2.11* continued)

Table 2.11 *Continued*

Demographic Characteristics	Call-back		Quota	
11. *Political affiliation:*				
Democrat	52.9	54.7	58.5	53.6
Republican	31.6	28.0	28.0	27.7
Other	4.9	0.9	5.6	2.3
None or independent	10.6	16.4	7.9	16.4
N	(1,434)	(1,464)	(1,557)	(1,482)
12. *Religion:*				
Protestant	68.6%	69.2%	67.6%	66.2%
Catholic	24.4	23.3	23.4	25.7
Jewish	2.7	3.4	2.3	3.2
Other	2.0	1.5	2.8	2.5
None	2.3	2.6	3.9	2.4
N	(1,434)	(1,464)	(1,557)	(1,482)
13. *How strongly do you feel about your religious beliefs?*				
Very strongly	37.9%	43.6%	38.4%	–
Strongly	27.6	22.8	28.4	–
Moderately	29.1	28.3	27.1	–
Not so strongly	3.9	3.3	3.5	–
Not strongly at all	1.5	2.0	2.6	–
N	(1,434)	(1,464)	(1,557)	–
14. *Marital status:*				
Single	8.7%	7.4%	9.4%	–
Married	79.1	75.9	77.4	–
Divorced	3.6	3.8	3.0	–
Widowed	5.9	10.4	7.6	–
Separated	2.7	2.5	2.6	–
N	(1,434)	(1,464)	(1,557)	–
15. *Social class perception:*				
Upper	2.2%	3.8%	1.9%	–
Middle	44.4	42.5	44.5	–
Working	47.3	46.7	49.0	–
Lower	3.9	2.8	2.6	–
There are no classes	0.8	2.0	–	–
Don't know	1.4	2.2	2.0	–
N	(1,434)	(1,464)	(1,557)	–
16. *Own or rent:*				
Own	63.6	64.5	61.2	–
Rent	36.4	35.5	38.8	–
N	(1,434)	(1,464)	(1,557)	–
17. *Household size:*				
1	8.1%	12.0%	6.8%	–
2	24.9	29.2	24.5	–
3	18.1	15.5	20.6	–
4	21.5	16.7	19.4	–
5	13.7	13.1	12.8	–
6	6.8	7.8	8.0	–
7	3.4	2.8	4.0	–
8	1.9	1.7	1.9	–
9 or more	1.6	1.2	2.0	–
N	(1,434)	(1,464)	(1,557)	–
x	3.62	3.42	3.70	–

(Table 2.11   continued)

Table 2.11   *Continued*

Demographic Characteristics	Call-back		Quota	
18. *Education of respondent:*				
0–8 years	21.7%	26.5%	26.0%	25.4%
9–11 years	22.8	20.3	22.9	22.5
12 years	30.2	29.6	28.2	28.7
13–15 years	13.3	13.2	13.7	13.6
16 years	7.5	6.0	6.0	5.8
17 years or more	4.5	4.4	3.2	4.0
N	(1,434)	(1,464)	(1,557)	(1,482)
Median years	12	12	12	12
19. *Education of spouse of respondent:*				
0–8 years	20.1%	25.7%	26.5%	–
9–11 years	23.5	20.1	21.3	–
12 years	32.8	32.2	31.7	–
13–15 years	11.7	11.8	9.8	–
16 years	8.3	6.9	6.5	–
17 years or more	3.6	3.3	4.2	–
N	(1,434)	(1,464)	(1,557)	–
Median years	12	12	12	–
20. *Main wage earner:*				
Respondent	53.5%	–	51.9%	–
Spouse	38.7	–	37.8	–
Others	7.8	–	10.3	–
N	(1,434)	–	(1,557)	–
21. *Income:*				
Under $3,000	17.0%	21.1%	18.6%	23.1%
$3,000–4,999	20.0	19.4	22.4	22.1
$5,000–7,499	29.2	26.3	29.1	26.6
$7,500–9,999	16.4	15.9	15.4	15.4
$10,000–14,999	11.9	11.9	10.8	8.9
$15,000–24,999	4.4	4.1	2.6 ⎫	3.9
$25,000 and over	1.1	1.3	1.2 ⎭	
N	(1,434)	(1,464)	(1,557)	(1,482)
Median	$6,100	$5,900	$5,800	$5,500
22. *Occupation of main earner:*				
Professional	13.3%	12.6%	13.6%	
Farmers, farm managers, and farm laborers	7.2	8.7	8.6	
Managers, officials, proprietors	12.4	13.4	12.8	
Clerical workers	7.4	7.5	6.5	
Sales workers	5.4	4.7	4.6	
Craftsmen, foremen	19.7	18.5	16.9	
Operatives	16.5	15.4	19.4	
Service workers	7.7	9.4	9.4	
Laborers	10.4	9.8	8.2	
N	(1,434)	(1,464)	(1,557)	

(Table 2.11   continued)

Table 2.11 *Continued*

Demographic Characteristics	Call-back		Quota
23. *Children under 13:*			
0	51.7%	58.8%	53.5%
1	18.5	13.8	17.6
2	15.0	13.1	13.2
3	7.5	8.2	7.7
4	4.7	4.1	5.0
5 or more	2.6	2.0	3.0
N	(1,434)		(1,557)
$\bar{x}$	1.05	.93	1.04
Children 13–21:			
0	66.9	69.3	73.1
1	18.8	15.3	13.9
2	10.3	9.6	9.0
3	2.6	4.2	2.7
4	1.0	1.1	0.7
5 or more	0.4	0.5	0.6
N	(1,434)		(1,557)
$\bar{x}$	.54	.54	.46
Children over 21:			
0	75.4	67.1	69.9
1	11.2	12.5	10.8
2	6.8	9.4	8.2
3	3.4	5.1	4.5
4	1.4	2.3	2.3
5 or more	1.8	3.6	4.3
N	(1,434)		(1,557)
$\bar{x}$	.51	.76	.76

tween sample bias and response, but, most important, the sample biases themselves are small.

The questions dealing with world tensions show mixed results when comparisons are made between the three surveys. On the first question dealing with "world tensions at this time" there are no differences between the three samples. On the second question dealing with "anticipated world tensions two years from now" the sample with quotas is significantly more optimistic than the call-back samples, and this greater optimism is also seen in the question dealing with "world tensions five years from now." Conversely, respondents on the probability sample with quotas perceived "tensions two years ago" as being higher than did respondents on the call-back samples. Looking at item 5, which summarizes the first four questions, one can conclude that quota respondents believe that world tensions are being, and will be, steadily reduced. The call-back respondents show no clear pattern, but there is no reason that they should. The final item on tensions asks, "When will the cold war end?" Here the call-back samples are more optimistic than the quota sample. It is possible that the assassination of President Kennedy a month earlier may have affected the answers of the probability sample with quotas, but if one disregards this, the possible biases due to differential availability range from 0 to 10 per cent on the four items, averaging about 6 per cent, which agrees with the data in Table 2.7.

Obviously, it would be desirable to have additional substantive questions for comparison, but unfortunately minor or major wording changes in the remaining items, as well as the inclusion of different items, make such comparisons impossible. There remain, then, the demographic items, which have the virtue of being asked in the same way on all three studies.

Of the seventeen demographic comparisons, there are no differences except for sex and household size. Naturally since there is a quota on sex, the probability sample with quotas matches census data. The call-back samples were both deficient in males because of non-cooperation. That is, since the cooperation rate among men is lower than among women in the ordinary call-back sample, the sample with quotas is superior on this characteristic.

The comparisons of household size suggest that the quota sample is deficient in one- and two-member households. These results suggest that some of the remaining availability bias in the quota sample could be eliminated by imposing a household size control in addition to the controls now in effect. NORC plans to experiment with this control in future surveys.

3

Advance Listing of Special Populations

INTRODUCTION

Although national probability samples of all adults or all households in the United States or some other country are still best known and are used frequently, there has been an enormous growth in the sampling of special populations as users of survey results become increasingly sophisticated. These samples are not to be confused with haphazard convenience samples that purport to represent the entire population, but that usually reflect only the behavior and characteristics of a freshman psychology class. Rather, these are carefully designed probability samples of special populations chosen because the populations themselves are of special interest. From among hundreds of such studies, five recent NORC studies are cited as examples of the wide variety of special populations:

1. A 1964 study attempted to measure the social effects of the Catholic educational system (Greeley and Rossi, 1966). The population for study consisted of all United States Catholics, twenty-three to fifty-seven years of age. The age limits were set so that at the lower end most respondents would be through with college, at least at the undergraduate level. The upper age limit was set to eliminate older Catholics whose education had not been in American parochial schools or who had been trained in American parochial schools far different in character from those of today. The curious reader may well wonder why that particular upper age level was selected. It represents a compromise between the desire to keep the upper age limit as low as possible for the reasons just mentioned and the sampling problems of finding sufficient respondents if the age limits were too narrow.

2. A study now in progress of the effects of crimes on households and individuals requires a national sample of crime victims. It should be

noted that the use of police records for sampling is inadequate since many crimes never are officially recorded by the police.

3. A 1962 study of the characteristics of adults participating in adult education programs required a population of recent participants which was defined as persons over twenty-one (or over eighteen and married) who had received instruction in subjects other than Bible studies or traditional religious training during the previous year.

4. A 1964 study of the attitudes and behavior of men related to their employment required a universe of all males aged sixteen or older working twenty-five hours a week or more, who were currently employed in civilian occupations.

5. Several recent NORC studies have utilized the population of all graduating college seniors in a given year, or of graduate students in various fields of study.

This chapter discusses some efficient techniques for sampling some of these populations, using advance listing. The basic procedure is described in the next section. Problems relating to classification and to household moves are discussed with some suggested solutions. Finally, the appendices to this chapter contain some examples of forms used for prelisting.

METHODS FOR SELECTING SPECIAL POPULATIONS

Lists

There are three basic procedures for locating special populations. The easiest procedure is the use of lists that are available or can be obtained relatively easily. Thus, a sample of public health professionals can be efficiently drawn, using combined lists (excluding duplicates) of the major public health professional organizations. A sample of college seniors is somewhat more difficult. It is first necessary to draw a sample of colleges from the excellent lists that are available.

Then, as a second stage, the list of graduating seniors is obtained at each selected school. These lists are prepared at all schools, but mail, phone, or personal visits may be required to obtain them for sampling purposes, assuming that the aims and sponsors of the study meet with the schools' approval.

There are many lists available, and list sampling should always be considered carefully before going to a more expensive procedure. In many cases, the lists are so fragmentary that they cannot be considered as representative of the entire population. Thus, subscription lists of Catholic newspapers and magazines are insufficient to obtain a good national sample of Catholics, although for some purposes the readers of such publications are an important special population.

Screening

If lists are unavailable, the general population must be screened to determine those individuals with the desired characteristics. It is assumed that the organization doing the screening already has a national sample frame and is interviewing a large number of households within this frame. In general, the costs of sampling and of hiring and training interviewers are so high that all organizations conducting national samples use the same sampling frame repeatedly, although, of course, not the same respondents.

It is not generally recognized that screening costs are only a little lower than actual interviewing costs. In a strict probability sample with call-backs, the total cost of screening interviews may nearly equal that of regular interviews, although the screening may take only five or ten minutes once a household respondent is located. These costs depend on many factors, including the length of the screening interview, the length of the full-scale interview, the rarity of the special population, and the amount of clustering in the screening. Since study, clerical, and travel costs are also present in screening interviews (see Chapter 6), and call-backs are required for these interviews also, the major difference is the length of the interview.

While there are some efficiencies in conducting a full-scale interview immediately upon completion of a screening interview, this will only be possible in a minority of the cases. Although screening costs cannot be avoided, it is sometimes possible to amortize them over several studies, thus reducing the cost to each individual study.

Advance Listing

Basically, advance listing merely means the use of screening information obtained on one study to eliminate the need for new screening on a future study. Two types of advance listing are possible. In the first, and more usual case, the advance listing collects basic demographic information about all individuals who fall into the sample. As an example, the screening interview for the study of adults participating in adult education programs obtained the following information for each member of the selected 12,000 sample households: age, sex, marital status, occupation, education, race, religion, household income, type of structure, and household telephone.

The complete form used is found in Johnstone and Rivera (1965) and, of course, also included several questions on adult education activities. The Appendix contains the two sheets of the questionnaire that asked for the demographic information (pp. 198–99).

Demographic information can be used for a wide variety of future studies. The information from the screening on the adult education study was used a year and a half later to draw a national sample of Catholics. Its use was considered for the study of employed males, but the sample size of that study was so large that it required a new screening. The adult education screening was also used to draw a national sample of respondents sixty-five years old and older, but this was not an advance listing, since this survey was designed to be in the field simultaneously with the major adult education questionnaire.

In most cases, much of the demographic information would need to be obtained on the screening questionnaire for analysis of the results of the initial survey, so that there is no additional cost attributable to these demographic questions. Even if there are no analytic reasons for including them, the marginal time and costs are so low that this should be a standard procedure for survey organizations with national samples.

The second type of advance listing involves special, non-demographic questions. However, such special questions should be asked on screening questionnaires only when the survey organization already knows about its future needs for a sample of a special population. NORC's study of crime victims requires a new sample screening since we could not anticipate several years ago that we would be studying such a special population. However, on the screening questionnaire for this study, we are asking for information on book reading in addition to the usual demographic information, because a study of book readers is being planned for next year. The screening questions for this new sample are included in the Appendix (pp. 200-203).

CLASSIFICATION CHANGES

With any special population the problem of misclassifications exists. Misclassification can occur because of response error, interviewer mistake, or incorrect processing of the results. The most efficient way to store screening information for future use is on computer tape, but this does not eliminate the possibility of some error along the way. This section does not discuss the problems of error present in any study but only those errors due to change in the respondent's classification through time. For example, employment status may change from one year to the next as women get married and have children, men retire, and students enter the labor force. An improper classification into the special population is not too serious. It merely means a wasted visit to the respondent, since the interviewer would ordinarily discover at the start of the new interview that the respondent no longer fits the requirements. The greater problem is with persons excluded from the special populations who now belong in it. If this group is large or important enough, it will make advance listing impractical.

For many studies, however, the likelihood of change in classification is small or can be anticipated. Changes in date of birth, sex, race, and type of structure can occur only because of misclassification. Changes in religion and education (if education has been completed) are highly unlikely, and changes in household income and occupation, although more common, would not usually be large enough to change a respondent's classification into the special population.

Occupation and marital status are much more likely to change for younger respondents, and it may be efficient to reinterview this group to see if they now belong in the special population,

rather than screening an entirely new sample. Much of this rein-
terviewing may be conducted by telephone so that travel will not
be required.

MOVERS

A major problem with using lists one or two years old is that
respondents move. If the earlier listing is to be useful, these respondents must be followed and located. Although the initial sample was of dwelling units, the new sample is a sample of individuals
with a specified characteristic that would remain with them unless one were interested in the characteristics of the dwelling unit
or neighborhood in which they lived.

Fortunately, most movers remain in the same general area, and
only a few move to a location where it is uneconomical to send
an interviewer. Even in these cases, long distance telephoning may
be possible. The major problem is to trace the respondent to his
new address. NORC has tried several different procedures, all of
which have some usefulness. They are listed here in order of increasing cost:

Mail tracing.—As a service to mailers, the Post Office will
attempt to provide, when requested, the new address of a person
at a specified address who has moved.[1] This is done only for persons who have left permanent forwarding addresses. Where no
forwarding address is available, the name is crossed from the list.
The charge for this service is five cents per name. Obviously, this
service is a bargain for samplers, since a sample of two thousand
cases would cost only one hundred dollars. The lists must be submitted at local post offices, and local interviewers or supervisors
can handle this, or the lists can be mailed to the local post offices.
The critical link in the process is the local mailman whose records
may or may not be in good condition and who may object to the
extra work load of correcting a list. Time is also an important
factor since forwarding addresses are not retained in files beyond
two years, and the likelihood that the record is misfiled or lost
increases sharply after the first few months. Still, a check of the
sample in the first year should generally get about two-thirds of

[1]See Section 123.5 of the *Postal Manual,* United States Post Office Department,
or contact your local postmaster for information.

the new addresses and indicate the remaining movers who need to be traced.

Telephone tracing.—If the telephone number is obtained on the screening interview then an appointment can be made to interview a respondent for a study of a special population. The advantages of this procedure are discussed in Chapter 5. In addition, if the call indicates that the respondent has moved, it will generally be possible to obtain the new phone number if the move has been in the same locality. Again, even when it is not possible to find the new telephone number or address, this method also identifies the families who have moved and need to be traced.

Use of other informant.—A useful procedure is to ask at the end of a questionnaire for the name and address of someone who would know where the respondent has moved and could give a forwarding address. This would generally be a relative or a close friend.

Neighbors or new tenants.—As a final technique, a canvass of the neighbors near to the last known address of the respondent may be rewarding but will probably be far more expensive than the other procedures.

Even with the use of multiple tracing procedures, 5 per cent of the original sample will not be found, or will have moved to an area which cannot economically be reached. There will be some additional unavailabilities due to deaths or misclassifications. These losses increase as the listing becomes older and are related to the mobility of the population. They also depend on how much one is willing to spend to find the hardest 5 per cent on the original list.

SUMMARY

Special populations are frequently of great importance for survey users, but they may be very expensive to locate unless lists are available. Advance listing of these populations on earlier surveys of special populations is a method for reducing these listing costs. The marginal costs of advance listing are so small that it will always pay to pick up a wide range of demographic information in advance. Behavioral information should be obtained only if the need for it is already known.

Some attention must be paid to the possibility of changes in classification, but usually this will not be a major problem, and it may be more efficient to reinterview the subsample of the population most likely to change classification, rather than to screen an entirely new sample.

Movers are a major problem, especially as the list ages. Several techniques are useful for tracing movers, including mail, telephone, and personal efforts. While the costs of these procedures become important as the most difficult cases are followed, the total cost of the entire advance listing procedure is far lower than a new screening. The sample biases introduced by the respondents who cannot be located, or who have moved to areas where they cannot be economically reached by interviewers, are likely to be small relative to the cost savings.

4

The Use of Self-administered Questionnaires

INTRODUCTION

As the costs of personal interviewing rise, it becomes more important to obtain the maximum information from each interview. The prime method of doing this is to lengthen the interview so that more information is obtained from the respondent.

Gradually survey organizations have lost their fears of the long interview, and interviews lasting an hour are standard at the National Opinion Research Center and other survey organizations, with two- and three-hour interviews no longer uncommon. Since actual interviewing time is only one-third of total interviewer time, lengthening the interview increases costs much more slowly than it increases information (see Chapter 6). In addition, if one considers cross-relationships, increasing the length of an interview very greatly increases the possible cross-classifications. Thus, if the interview is twice as long, there are approximately eight times as many possible three-way tables and sixteen times as many four-way tables as originally, if the sample sizes remain sufficient.

There are limits on the length of the interview. Both interviewer and respondent fatigue begin to take their toll as the interview gets past two hours. Cooperation, as well as quality, are affected. Travel costs are also increased since the interviewer can complete only a single interview per trip and must make more trips.

In addition to information about a specific respondent, it is often valuable to obtain information from more than one member of a household. Even where intra-family comparisons are not the

This chapter was co-authored by Andrew M. Greeley and Leonard Pinto.

major focus of interest, this method provides an economical way of increasing the sample size of subgroups. Thus, interviewing both husband and wife in a household may not appreciably reduce the variability for the total sample, but can substantially reduce the variability for women in a particular age group, or men in a given occupation, to cite just two examples.

Where one wishes to observe differences or similarities between husband and wife, or between parents and children, one must either obtain this information from the separate individuals or rely on one member of the family to report on the attitudes of the others. While the latter method may sometimes produce reasonably good results (Rossi and Katz, 1960), it is generally better to get the data directly from individuals.

Personal interviews are the most common, but not the only way of obtaining information from additional household members. An alternative is to interview one member of the household and to leave self-administered forms for other household members from whom data are desired. This has the advantage of not requiring the interviewer to return to the household for another interview if additional household members are not available, or if the first interview takes too much time. Thus, both travel and interviewing time are saved. It has the advantage over other leave-and-pick-up methods (or mail questionnaires) that the personal interview has established a feeling of rapport between the interviewer and the household so that cooperation is likely to be better.

This chapter describes an NORC study where such leave-pick-up techniques were attempted, and gives the cooperation rates for alternative methods attempted, as well as a comparison of the responses for the self-administered questionnaires and the personal interviews.

ALTERNATIVE LEAVE-PICK-UP METHODS

During the spring and summer of 1964, NORC conducted a national survey of Catholics and a control group of Protestants to determine the effects of Catholic schools on the knowledge, attitudes, and behavior of those who attended them as compared to Catholics who attended public schools (Greeley and Rossi, 1966). Initially, it was decided to interview about 3,500 respondents. As part of the continuing research program on reducing the cost of surveys, it was decided to attempt to obtain another 1,000 respondents using self-administered questionnaires. Half of these added respondents were to be other adult members in households where a personal interview had been conducted, and half were to be teen-agers in these households.

Three methods using different intensities of effort were compared to see how costs and response rates varied. The methods from the least to the most intensive are described below:

Method A
The interviewer left the self-administered questionnaire at the respondent's home, and the questionnaire was mailed back to NORC's Chicago office by the respondent.

Method B
The interviewer left the self-administered questionnaire at the respondent's home, and the questionnaire was mailed back to the interviewer's home. If the interviewer did not receive the questionnaire after several days she phoned the respondent.

For both Methods A and B, the final step of the process was a personal call to the home of those respondents who had not returned questionnaires. This personal call was only made, however, when the interviewer still had other personal interviews to do in the area. If she had completed her assignment of personal interviews and so had no other reason to travel into the area, no further efforts were made to obtain the self-administered forms.

Method C
The interviewer left the self-administered form at the respondent's home and returned to pick it up. Call-backs were made until either the completed form was obtained or the respondent refused to cooperate.

COOPERATION RATES OBTAINED
Tables 4.1 and 4.2 show the results for adult and teen-age respondents by each of the three methods. It can be observed that for the adults the most intensive Method C produced a coopera-

Table 4.1 Cooperation Rates for Self-administered Questionnaires as Compared to Personal Interviews with Catholic Adult Respondents

Cooperation Rates	Personal Interviews		Method A (Mail to NORC)		Method B (Mail to Interviewer)		Method C (Interviewer Pick-up	
	N	Per Cent	N	Per Cent	N	Per Cent	N	Per Cent
Original sample	2,753	100	344	100	330	100	348	100
Completed by initial method	1,872	68	159	46	168	51	223	64
Completed on call-backs	212	8	62	18	43	13	31	9
Total completed	2,084	76	221	64	211	64	254	73
Initial refusals or not reassigned	50	2	35	10	28	8	9	3
Final refusals	498	18	63	19	78	24	69	20
Total refusals	548	20	98	29	106	32	78	23
Not at home or other loss	121	4	25	7	13	4	16	4

Table 4.2 Cooperation Rates for Self-administered Questionnaires with Catholic Teen-age Respondents

Cooperation Rates	Method A (Mail to NORC)		Method B (Mail to Interviewer)		Method C (Interviewer Pick-up)	
	N	Per Cent	N	Per Cent	N	Per Cent
Original sample	298	100	297	100	313	100
Completed by initial method	159	53	179	60	249	80
Completed by call-backs	87	29	62	21	29	9
Total completed	246	82	241	81	278	89
Initial refusals or not reassigned	17	6	22	8	8	2
Final refusals	21	7	25	8	21	7
Total refusals	38	13	47	16	29	9
Not at home or other loss	14	5	9	3	6	2

tion rate just about equal to that obtained on the personal interviews, while the cooperation rate for both Method A and Method B was about 10 percentage points less. For the teen-agers, Method C again produced the highest cooperation rate, but the cooperation rate for each of the methods was above 80 per cent. It is clear that high cooperation rates can be obtained using self-administered questionnaires, and that teen-agers in particular will respond very well to this method.

While Methods A and B produce ultimately the same cooperation rates, Method B, as expected, produces more initial returns. There is also an indication from these results that the cooperation achieved by Methods A and B could reach that achieved by Method C if the interviewer always made a personal call to respondents who had not returned questionnaires, even if she had no other personal interviews in the area. Naturally, this would be a more expensive method than either Method A or Method B. The comparative costs of the three methods and of various other alternatives are discussed in the next section of this chapter.

Some comments should be made about the absolute values of the cooperation rates. Normally, on a national study, cooperation rates of over 80 per cent are obtained by NORC on surveys of the length and complexity of the one used here. The cooperation rate achieved on the personal interviews in this study was about 5 percentage points lower than normal, although every effort was made to achieve maximum cooperation. Two major demographic factors are responsible for the below-average cooperation:

1. Location of respondents: The Catholic and Protestant respondents in this study were concentrated in the largest metropolitan areas of this country, where the impersonality of the surroundings has always made it most difficult to obtain cooperation on surveys.

2. Age of respondents: Older people with more spare time who are generally more willing to respond were excluded from the current survey. Thus, while this was a national sample of the universe it was intended to represent, this universe is substantially more difficult to survey than a sample of all adults or households. The cooperation rates achieved on the self-administered forms should be compared to the cooperation rates achieved by intensive at-

tempts to complete personal interviews on this survey, and not to some other norm. In general, one would suspect that on an easier national study the cooperation rate on the self-administered forms would rise as much as 5 or 10 percentage points.

One issue, however, tends to confuse these comparisons. It should be noted that NORC's interviewing staff is largely non-Catholic and that some of the refusal rate on the personal interviews may have been due to the fact that interviewers anticipated problems because of the nature of the questionnaire. That this was a problem found only in the interviewer's mind is demonstrated by the fact that only three respondents refused to complete the survey after they started answering questions. In cases where the interviewer is not comfortable with the personal interview form, a self-administered version may achieve a cooperation rate closer to that obtained by personal interview than would normally be the case.

One final point before closing this discussion. The experiment described here involved the personal placing of a self-administered form with a respondent after the interviewer completed a personal interview in the household. The interviewer who has done her job well has established substantial rapport with the household by the time she has finished her personal interview, and finds it much easier to obtain cooperation on the self-administered form than an interviewer who spends only a few minutes in the household before dropping off a questionnaire. It is not surprising, therefore, to note that the cooperation obtained in this study is higher than that usually obtained on a leave-pick-up questionnaire, and, of course, much higher than could be achieved by mail alone.

COSTS OF EXPERIMENTAL METHODS

Table 4.3 shows the total costs and the costs per assigned and completed case for each of the three experimental methods. These costs are not very far apart, with only an 11 per cent difference between the cost per case of the most expensive Method A and the least expensive Method B. All three methods cost about $7.00, which is only one-half as much per completed case as the cost of a probability sample of equal difficulty.

As between methods, the more intensive Methods B and C,

Table 4.3 Costs per Assigned and Completed Cases

Summary	Total		Method A (Mail to NORC)		Method B (Mail to Interviewer)		Method C (Interviewer Pick-up)	
	Costs	N	Costs	N	Costs	N	Costs	N
Direct interviewing costs	$30,396.52		$10,550.45		$9,721.48		$10,124.59	
Personal—Catholic and Protestant		3,406		1,135		1,198		1,073
Self-administered—Catholic and Protestant		2,178		726		708		744
Total cases assigned		5,584		1,861		1,906		1,817
Personal		2,620		873		921		826
Self-administered		1,661		537		517		607
Total cases completed		4,281		1,410		1,438		1,433
Cost/total cases assigned	$ 5.44		$ 5.67		$ 5.10		$ 5.57	
Cost/total cases completed	7.10		7.48		6.76		7.07	
Cost/personal cases assigned	8.92		9.30		8.11		9.44	
Cost/personal cases completed	11.60		12.09		10.56		12.26	

which had the interviewer phone or make personal calls on the respondent, turned out to be less costly on a completed case basis, since cooperation was higher and fewer call-backs were required eventually. The results of this experiment suggest that Method C is the most useful procedure when considering both cost and co-operation. Method C, which used call-backs until the completed form was obtained or the respondent refused, achieved a substantially higher cooperation rate than either of the other two methods, while its costs per completed case were only about 5 per cent higher than the cheapest Method B.

The data suggest that call-backs are not only cheaper when made early in conjunction with other trips to the segment, but that they are also more effective if made before the contact established by the interviewer with the household is forgotten. This, in turn, suggests one modification in the procedure which will be incorporated in a later experiment. If the interviewer does not find it convenient to return for the questionnaire in the day or two following the personal interview, or if she finds no one at home, she will be instructed to call and encourage the respondent to complete the questionnaire and to make an appointment for picking it up.

The experiment has shown that it is possible to achieve high cooperation on self-administered questionnaires left with respondents in a household where a personal interview has been made. Costs per completed case are reduced by about one-half as compared to the usual sample if the self-administered forms are considered as valuable as the personal interviews. Of course, the method discussed here is not the only one possible. Lengthening the interview, or conducting two personal interviews on the household (either on the same or on different topics), will also reduce the cost.

Maximum cooperation on self-administered questionnaires is achieved by personal placement and follow-ups, after initial rapport has been established. The added cost of these follow-ups is more than compensated by the increased response.

RESPONSE DIFFERENCES BETWEEN PERSONAL INTERVIEWS AND SELF-ADMINISTERED QUESTIONNAIRES

Many previous studies have shown that respondents will answer some questions differently in a personal interview as compared to what they will write on a self-administered questionnaire (Hyman, 1954, pp. 139–45). It is frequently stated that the respondent will give the interviewer the answer he thinks the interviewer wishes to hear, or that boosts his ego. This is not always the case, however. If the respondent feels very strongly about an issue, or if he doesn't know what the most socially acceptable answer is, his answers on a personal interview may be identical to those on a self-administered form.

Before combining results from personal interviews and self-administered forms, it is necessary to compare them to see if they differ. This is done in Table 4.4 for forty-four statements. On thirty-one of these forty-four statements the differences are less than 5 per cent. For the remaining thirteen statements, differences range from 5 to 16 per cent. On ten of these thirteen statements, as one would expect, the responses to the personal interview appear to be those which a Catholic respondent would consider more socially acceptable when made to a non-Catholic interviewer. For instance, 72 per cent of the Catholics who were personally interviewed, but only 62 per cent of the respondents on the self-administered form, said that God doesn't really care how He is worshipped so long as He is worshipped. Sixty-five per cent of personally interviewed Catholics said that a good man can earn heaven by his own efforts alone, while only 58 per cent said this on the self-administered form. The other three statements, for no obvious reasons, are in the reverse order—that is, the more socially acceptable answer is given more frequently on the self-administered form.

Surprisingly, the largest difference is on the statement, "It would be wrong to take considerable time off while working for a large company, even though the company would not be hurt by it

Table 4.4 Agreement to Statements in Catholic and Protestant Personal Interviews and Catholic Self-administered Questionnaires

Statement	Percentage Agreeing		
	Catholic Personal	Catholic Self-administered	Protestant Personal
Personal answers more socially acceptable (differences larger than 4 per cent):			
Taken altogether, how would you say things are these days—would you say that you are very happy or not too happy? (Those answering very happy.)	36	23	40
Even though a person has a hard time making ends meet, he should still try to give some of his money to help the poor	81	74	76
God doesn't really care how He is worshipped so long as He is worshipped	72	62	69
Negroes shouldn't push themselves where they are not wanted	60	68	62
Have you spent any time by yourself in the past few months helping someone who needs help?	64	52	57
A good man can earn heaven by his own efforts alone	65	58	53
The United States should do more to help the poorer nations by building hospitals, schools, and homes in these places	70	63	65
I would strongly disapprove if a Negro family moved next door to me	37	43	40
A student should be free to make up his own mind on what he learns in school	59	54	60
Two people who are in love do not do anything wrong when they marry, even though one of them has been divorced	52	47	87
Personal answers less socially acceptable (differences larger than 4 per cent):			
It would be wrong to take considerable time off while working for a large company, even though the company would not be hurt by it at all	50	66	55
It is all right to refuse to talk to some member of the family after a disagreement, especially if the argument was the fault of the other	27	20	25
Rules should never be relaxed because children will take advantage of it	65	60	61
Not significant (differences smaller than 4 per cent):			
There is no definite proof that God exists	21	22	31
God will punish the evil for all eternity	73	74	55
Science proves that Christ's resurrection was impossible	12	11	13
Jesus directly handed over the leadership of His Church to Peter and the Popes	87	89	26
Books written by communists should not be permitted in public libraries	57	57	45
Complete abstention from liquor is the best thing	36	35	47
People who don't believe in God have as much right to freedom of speech as anyone else	86	87	85

(Table 4.4   continued)

Table 4.4   Continued

	Percentage Agreeing		
Statement	Catholic Personal	Catholic Self-administered	Protestant Personal
Not significant (differences smaller than 4 per cent):			
Jewish businessmen are about as honest as other businessmen	80	80	80
Jews have too much power in the United States	19	21	19
Negroes would be satisfied if it were not for a few people who stir up trouble	52	51	51
White people have a right to live in an all-white neighborhood if they want to, and Negroes should respect that right	73	75	75
There is an obligation to work for the end of racial segregation	79	81	78
It is as important for a child to think for himself as to be obedient to his parents	85	84	88
When parents are wrong, they should always be willing to admit it to their children	83	83	87
Usually parents are just too busy to explain the reasons behind the orders they give their children	65	66	70
The federal government should give religious schools money to help pay teachers' salaries and build new buildings	73	73	35
The federal government should provide aid for the local public schools	79	78	74
The government is responsible for checking wide-spread unemployment	62	62	61
Working men have the right and duty to join unions	78	77	71
Each country should be willing to give up some of its power so that the United Nations could do a better job	68	68	68
I would try to stop the planned parenthood association from having a meeting in my community	26	23	11
In the long run, war with the communists is almost certain	50	46	51
Laws should change with the times	88	89	90
It is not really wrong for an engaged couple to have some sexual relations before they are married	12	12	18
A married couple who feel they have as many children as they really want are not doing anything wrong when they use artificial means to prevent conception	45	43	91
A family should have as many children as possible and God will provide for them	41	37	12
Even though you find some people unpleasant, it is wrong to try to avoid them	58	56	59
A salesman has the right to exaggerate how good his product is when a customer is too suspicious	24	22	22
It is all right to ask an insurance company for more money than you deserve after an auto accident if you think they might cut your claim	34	33	25
If the government wastes tax money, people don't have to be too exact on their income tax returns	13	10	10
Have you spent any time with others in the past few months helping someone who needed help?	56	59	60

at all." Sixty-six per cent of respondents on the self-administered form but only 50 per cent of the personally interviewed respondents gave the socially acceptable answer and agreed with this statement.

More understandable is the fact that 36 per cent of personally interviewed respondents, but only 23 per cent of respondents on the self-administered form, said they were very happy when the question was asked, "Taken altogether, how would you say things are these days—would you say that you are very happy, pretty happy, or not too happy?" Compare these results to Hochstim (1962) who, when he asked respondents how they would generally rate their health—excellent, good, fair, or poor—found that 44 per cent of personally interviewed respondents, but only 30 per cent of respondents to a mail questionnaire rated their health as excellent.

All in all, these comparisons do not show large differences between the two methods except on a handful of items, suggesting that it will generally be possible to combine the answers from personal and self-administered forms. Where there are large differences, the self-administered forms seem to give a better measure of the true feelings of respondents than do the personal interviews, and in analyzing such data the personal interviews should be treated cautiously.

5

Some New Uses of Telephone Methods in Survey Research

The use of telephone interviewing in market and survey research has become a common practice in recent years. The method has always had much to recommend it. By eliminating travel, costs are substantially reduced and it becomes possible to make almost unlimited call-backs if respondents are not home or unavailable.[1] In many cases, this reduction in cost is accompanied by an increase in quality, since the interviewer is more at ease working from the comfort of her home, while the respondent is more candid than he would be in a face-to-face interview (Hochstim, 1962).

This chapter describes some additional uses of telephones that have proved successful in four recent NORC studies. Two experiments were conducted in which the interviewing was done by face-to-face methods, but where appointments were made with respondents using the telephone. This eliminated wasted travel time to a segment where no respondents were available for interviewing. The other two experiments involved the use of telephones to locate and interview samples of respondents who are particularly hard to reach. The first of these samples consisted of physicians who were reached by long-distance telephone, while the other sample consisted of households in which at least one member was blind.

[1]Sindlinger and Company have an ingenious variation to the procedure of making repeated call-backs. Initially, the interviewer makes up to six telephone calls to reach a sample number. If the respondent is still not available he is included in a later sample until finally he is reached. Each sample consists of new numbers and former not-at-homes or not availables.

USE OF TELEPHONE CALLS TO MAKE ADVANCE APPOINTMENTS

National Sample of Adolescents

In the spring of 1962, NORC conducted a large study of adult education in the United States. As a follow-up to this study, a special study was made of adolescent, adult, and formal education. The results of this study have been reported by John Johnstone and Ramon Rivera (1965).

Since phone numbers had been obtained previously, it was possible to split the adolescents into two groups—those who were approached directly and those with whom an appointment was made by telephone. There was no difference in the cooperation rates between the two groups, which in both cases was 81 per cent. There were very few actual refusals, but a large number of adolescents were not living at home and were not available for interviewing. They were away at college, in the armed services, or had taken a job elsewhere during the summer when the interviews were conducted.

There was a reduction of about one-fourth in the average number of calls required to complete an interview where a telephone appointment had been made first. An average of 1.7 calls/completed case were necessary with the phone appointment, while 2.3 calls/completed case were necessary where no appointment had been made in advance. Table 5.1 shows the detailed number of calls for the two groups. This reduction is due to the much greater probability of completing an interview on the first call if a telephone appointment is made.

The sample sizes for the two groups are not exactly the same, although the initial samples were identical. This is due to the fact that about 10 per cent of the group which was selected to receive the initial phone call did not have phone numbers available.

It should be noted that there was very little clustering in the sample of teen-agers, which made it unlikely that more than one respondent could be contacted on any visit to a segment. Thus, any trip made when the respondent was not available for interviewing was usually wasted. On the other hand, where there is more clustering, it may be possible to interview an alternate respondent if the initial one is not available.

Happiness Studies in Prince Georges County, Maryland

Another opportunity to test telephone appointments was presented when early in 1963 Norman Bradburn and David Caplovitz of NORC conducted a large study of mental health related behavior which became known as the Happiness Study (Bradburn and Caplovitz, 1965). As part of this study, a special sample was drawn in Prince Georges County, Maryland, using as its major source the street address listing of the area telephones supplied by The Chesapeake and Potomac Telephone Company. Since phone numbers were available for most selected households, interviewers were instructed to make a phone appointment with at least one household in a segment before travelling to the area. Once in the area, they could make additional calls on other selected households. The purpose of these instructions was to eliminate those trips to the segment which resulted in no completed interviews.

Table 5.1 Number of Calls Required To Complete Interview of Teen-agers by Type of Initial Contact (NORC Study of Adult Education, 1962), Per Cent

Number of Calls Required To Complete Interview	Telephoned for Appointment	Direct Initial Contact
One	61.6	40.5
Two	24.4	29.3
Three	6.9	15.2
Four	2.5	5.8
Five	2.8	3.6
Six	0.6	1.7
Seven	0.6	1.7
Eight	0.3	0.8
Nine	–	0.6
Ten	0.3	0.8
Total	100.0	100.0
N	(320)	(361)
Average number of calls	1.69	2.28

There has been some feeling among field supervisors that it is easier for a respondent to refuse to be interviewed if the request for an appointment is made by phone. For this study, interviewers were told to ignore phone refusals. That is, if the respondent refused to make an appointment when the interviewer phoned, the interviewer made a personal call (or repeated calls) until an interview or a firm refusal was obtained.

While a controlled experiment in Prince Georges County would have been desirable, it was not attempted, since nearly all the interviewers used in this study had no previous experience. Thus, the experiences in Prince Georges County must be compared to those in the other cities where normal methods were used. These comparisons are given in Table 5.2 which shows the cooperation rates and number of calls in each of the sample locations.

The major problem in interpreting Table 5.2 is to decide which place or places to compare with Prince Georges County. The sample of the top ten standard metropolitan areas is perhaps the best group for comparison, but it includes New York, Chicago, and Los Angeles, where interviewing is especially difficult. The sample of Warren, a suburb of Detroit, consists entirely of single-family dwelling units, while many Prince Georges County households live in large apartments. The lower-class Negro neighborhood in

Table 5.2 Cooperation Rates and Number of Calls Required by Type of Initial Contact (NORC Happiness Study, 1963)

Cooperation and Calls Required	Initial Contact in Segment by Phone: Prince Georges County	Personal Contact			
		Top 10 Metro Areas	Chicago, Ill.	Detroit, Mich.	Warren, Mich.
Total number of cases	1,150	226	283	504	384
Completed number of cases	909	165	221	451	328
Cooperation rate	79.0%	73.0%	78.1%	89.5%	85.4%
Number of calls/ case	2.15	3.33	3.38	3.63	2.65
Ratio: $\frac{\text{PG County}}{\text{Other areas}}$	1.00	.65	.64	.59	.81

Detroit and the white ethnic neighborhood in Chicago are also not comparable. The best that can be done is to note that the cooperation rate in Prince Georges was about average for the other areas, and that the number of calls per case was reduced 20 to 40 per cent, depending on the area used for comparison.

Having established the usefulness of telephone methods, a controlled experiment was conducted in Prince Georges County on the third wave of the Happiness Study. Interviewers were randomly divided into two groups. The experimental group was instructed to call for an appointment before making a personal visit. It should be remembered that all respondents had already cooperated once and were being revisited to observe changes in happiness states. The control group were given no special instructions on how the initial contact should be made, but some of them also used phone contacts, since phone numbers were available from the first wave and most of the control group interviewers had earlier used phone contacts.

Table 5.3 compares the cooperation rates of the two groups as well as the number of calls, number of trips, and total travel time required. There were no differences in the cooperation rate, but there was a reduction of 10 to 15 per cent in the calls and travel time required by the group instructed to make phone appointments. This difference probably would have been larger if some of the interviewers in the control group had not also used telephone contacts.

Table 5.3 Cooperation Rates, Number of Calls, Number of Trips, and Total Travel Time by Type of Initial Contact (NORC Happiness Study—Wave III: Prince Georges County)

Cooperation, Calls, Trips, and Travel Time	(1) Instructed to Telephone for Appointment	(2) No Special Instructions	Ratio $\frac{(1)}{(2)}$
Total number of cases	690	576	
Completed number of cases	541	452	
Cooperation rate	78.4%	78.5%	
Calls/case	2.17	2.60	.83
Trips/case	.90	.95	.95
Travel time/case (in minutes)	109	124	.88

USE OF TELEPHONE CALLS FOR THE SCREENING
OF RARE POPULATIONS

The proportion of blind persons in the population is variously estimated as between fourteen and twenty per thousand population, depending on the severity of the visual impairment. It is clear that a very large number of households must be screened to obtain sufficient cases for any detailed analysis of the blind. A screening based entirely on personal interviews would be very expensive, even if only a few minutes were spent in each household.

During the winter of 1963, the American Foundation for the Blind in collaboration with Western Reserve University undertook a pilot study of visual impairment in Cleveland. The actual sampling and field work for this study were conducted by NORC (Josephson and Sussman, 1964). It was decided to use telephone screening methods wherever possible and to supplement these telephone interviews with a smaller sample of personal interviews in households which had no listed telephone. Based on past experience, we felt that cooperation rates using phone methods would be the same as those using face-to-face interviews and that costs would be very much lower. The pilot test was designed to verify this hypothesis, and it did, as can be seen in Table 5.4. In addition, the pilot test was designed to compare the accuracy of reporting of visual impairment by phone as compared to other procedures.

The sampling frame for this study consisted of the 1961 edition of the Cleveland Street Address Directory. This directory was two years old at the time of the study, but the timing of the pilot test made its use necessary. (The new directory was published shortly after the study was completed.) Because of the age of the directory and the control requirement that families which had moved be excluded, there were substantial losses from the initial sample due to vacancies and moves. These losses were greater among the households without listed telephones, which merely means that the poorest households without telephones were more likely to move than were average households.

Similarly, the cooperation rate was lower among households without phones, mainly because of the greater difficulty in locating them. In any event, Table 5.4 indicates that the cooperation rate among the households screened by phone was 83 per cent, which is as good, or slightly better, than the cooperation rate usually achieved in Cleveland by face-to-face methods.

Since the costs of phone screening in Cleveland were only one-third as much as the costs of face-to-face screening, the optimum allocation of sampling resources would suggest that the sampling rate for unlisted phones should be about 60 per cent $(1/\sqrt{3})$ that of phone households (Hansen, Hurwitz, and Madow, 1953, pp. 220–23). Naturally, households without listed phones cannot be ignored, since they differ substantially from households with phones.

The pilot test also demonstrated that accurate reporting of visual impairment could be obtained over the phone. While it was encouraging to note that the rate per thousand population of those reported as having serious trouble seeing even when wearing glasses was almost identical in the telephone screening and in the National Health Survey (19.3 and 19.8, respectively), this could not be regarded as conclusive since the samples are by no means identical. Instead, direct validation of phone results was conducted.

To check for under-reporting of visual impairment, 174 households were re-interviewed, providing data on about 550 household members. Only one new case of visual impairment was reported in

Table 5.4   Cooperation Rates and Costs in Cleveland Pilot Study of Visual Impairment

Cooperation and Costs	Phone		Face-to-Face	
	N	Per Cent	N	Per Cent
Total original sample	2,778		309	
Vacant or designated house-hold moved	333		71	
Net sample	2,445	100%	238	100%
Completed	2,018	83	183	77
Refusal or break-off	254	10	22	9
Not home	115	5	26	11
Miscellaneous unavail-ability (ill, language problems, etc.)	59	2	7	3
Cost/completed screening	$1.50		$4.50	

these face-to-face interviews, and even here the impairment was not severe, with the individual being reported as able to read a newspaper with glasses. Even with this small sample, it seems clear that there could have been no substantial under-reporting due to the use of phone screening, as compared to face-to-face interviews.

Over-reporting of impairment was similarly checked by the use of eye charts with 122 respondents who had been reported as having visual impairment. It should be noted that over-reporting is not a critical problem, since with a rare population one would usually obtain more complete information in a follow-up interview after the screening.

Generally, the pilot test proved highly successful and plans are now being made for larger studies of the blind, utilizing the techniques developed in Cleveland.

USE OF LONG-DISTANCE TELEPHONE INTERVIEWING WITH PHYSICIANS

Surveys of physician attitudes on various health issues are often difficult and costly because doctors are so busy that they are seldom available for interviewing. Doctors are an especially difficult group to contact, but other occupations, primarily managerial, professional, and sales also present the same problem on a lesser scale. Telephone interviews are frequently more convenient for the respondent and the interviewer.

A demonstration of the usefulness of telephone methods was provided recently in a study of New York State physicians conducted by NORC for the Columbia University School of Public Health and Administrative Medicine. Telephone interviews averaging an hour and a half in length were completed with 80 per cent of the selected sample. While most of the interviews were done over the telephone, a small subsample of cases were conducted in person to allow for comparison between the two methods. The comparison of physician responses has been made by Colombotos (1965). He finds that generally the response differences between the phone and face-to-face method are negligible. Where there are any differences, the phone method appears to obtain responses which are less distorted in the direction of social acceptability than are responses obtained in face-to-face interviews. This confirms earlier results which suggest that the less personal the method, the less the bias toward socially acceptable answers. (See Chapter 4.)

The cost comparisons shown in Table 5.5 indicate that telephone interviewing reduced interviewer costs about 22 per cent in New York City and about 26 per cent in Orange County. It should be noted, however, that toll charges in other upstate New York counties were substantially larger than toll charges in Orange County, particularly if the calls originated from New York City. It is clear that careful consideration must be given to telephone rate structures before deciding to use long-distance telephones.

The major advantage of long-distance phones, however, is the ability to do a study quickly without hiring and training a new staff of interviewers. In this Upper New York study, the doctors were widely scattered. To have conducted all interviews face to face would have required the hiring and training of new inter-

Table 5.5 Costs per Completed Case for Phone and Personal Interviewing

	New York Physicians		
Costs	(1) Phone	(2) Personal	Ratio $\frac{(1)}{(2)}$
New York City:			
Total cost/case	$ 8.45	$10.88	.78
Total cases	(34)	(37)	
Orange County, New York:			
Interviewing costs/case	$ 6.65	$16.12	
Toll costs/case	5.21	–	
Total costs/case	11.86	16.12	.74
Total cases	(24)	(40)	
Other New York counties:			
Interviewing costs/case	$ 6.24		
Toll costs/case	8.93		
From New York City toll costs/case	12.47		
From other places toll costs/case	7.55		
Total costs/case	15.17		
Total cases	(645)		

viewers, since some of the doctors who fell into the sample lived several hundred miles from the nearest interviewer. Hiring and training a new staff adds substantially to the interviewing costs, as well as the time required to complete the study. This additional time to hire and train, and conduct the interviews face to face would not be reflected in the direct interviewing costs, but would show up in costs of analysis and overhead charges, and thus in the total study costs.

SUMMARY

The experiments described in this chapter give additional examples of the value of telephone methods in the interviewing process. The use of telephones to make appointments before interviewing reduced the number of calls required by about 25 per cent. Telephone screening for visual impairment cost only one-third as much as personal screening. Finally, telephone interviewing of doctors reduced costs about 25 per cent as compared to personal interviewing in New York, and made it possible to sample a scattered population in upper New York State without hiring and training new interviewers. In none of these experiments was there any indication that the telephone results were less satisfactory than those obtained from personal interviews.

The telephone is not always appropriate for survey interviewing. Where the study design requires the respondent to be presented with cards to read or other visual stimuli, personal interviewing remains necessary—at least until visual phones become standard in American homes. Meanwhile, telephones remain an extremely versatile tool for reducing the cost of surveys without affecting quality.

6

Time Allocation of Survey Interviewers and Other Field Occupations

INTRODUCTION

The survey research interviewer and the job that she does should be of particular interest to social scientists. The interviewer is the chief collector of the raw data used in social analysis. Her work influences both the quality and cost of social research. Hyman and others (1954) of the NORC staff have discussed in detail the effects of interviewers on the interviewing situation. Cost data, however, have not been generally available, but have become even more necessary as survey costs have risen precipitously over the past two decades, largely because of increases in interviewing costs. In order to reduce costs, it is necessary to recognize how they originate, and this is the first aim of this chapter.

Moreover, the occupational role of the interviewer is of intrinsic interest. Interviewers spend most of their time in the field under very little supervision. In this respect, they are similar to salesmen, social workers, and public health nurses. The pay method for interviewers differs from that of the other occupations, since interviewers are paid on an hourly basis, while the others work for either a fixed salary or commission. This might be expected to influence the interviewer's shaping of her job. A comparison of interviewing with other field occupations is given in the second part of this chapter.

The two parts of this chapter are closely connected, since better understanding of the interviewing role leads to hypotheses about methods for controlling or reducing interviewing costs. These will be discussed in the next chapter.

METHODS OF DATA COLLECTION

Each of the tables to be presented in this chapter will be described in detail, so that the differences in the methods used will be clear. In general, the results are based on analysis of time sheets submitted either for the special study or routinely. These figures are certainly subject to memory or clerical errors by the person submitting them, and even the likelihood of deliberate distortion should not be overlooked. Nevertheless, they appear to be of sufficient accuracy for the types of analysis attempted here.

Somewhat more troublesome is the fact that time records are not always kept the same way, so that some of the differences observed may be artifactual. For example, to anticipate the detailed discussion below, it is often difficult to separate the actual interview from time spent in the home in introduction and in general conversation.

The nature of the task, and of the organization conducting the field work also have an influence on the time allocations. This will be discussed when the tables are analyzed, but a discussion of individual interviewer differences is left to Chapter 8. Finally, however, it should be noted that even with all the possible reasons for non-comparability, there do appear to be great similarities between survey organizations and between interviewing and other field occupations, and it is these similarities, rather than the differences, which are the most significant findings presented.

NATIONAL OPINION RESEARCH CENTER INTERVIEWER
TIME ALLOCATION

Table 6.1 presents the actual time and percentage of interviewer time spent on various tasks for six NORC studies conducted during the period 1958–1964, and for an earlier 1947 study. Since the methods used for obtaining these results were generally similar for all studies, they need only be fully described once. The differences that are observed are due not to different methods of data gathering, but to the peculiarities of the particular studies.

The two main sources of information on time spent by NORC

Table 6.1 Percentages of Interviewer Time Spent on Various Tasks and Actual Times for Seven NORC Studies

Task	Percentage of Time Spent							Actual Times/Interview in Minutes (Study and Clerical Time Is Total/Study)						
	Probability Samples			Block-quota			1947 Quota							
	Study 1	Study 2	Study 3	Study 4	Study 5	Study 6	Study 7	Study 1	Study 2	Study 3	Study 4	Study 5	Study 6	Study 7
Study	17	8	4	13	12	9	} 47	704	424	172	199	178	85	—
Clerical	8	7	1	2	10	4		307	366	73	26	150	39	—
Editing	11	11	11	13	9	12		39	11	24	23	14	15	—
Travel to segment	21	22	29	17	17	18		74	21	67	29	27	23	—
Travel in segment	11	19	17	15	14	16	32	40	19	39	27	22	20	35
Interviewing	32	33	38	40	38	41	21	114	32	86	70	60	52	23
Total	100	100	100	100	100	100	100							
Total interviews	2,115	15,690	2,563	1,470	1,449	1,688	1,223							
Total interviewers	186	295	119	161	160	231	88							

interviewers are the questionnaire itself and the Interviewer's Time Report. At the beginning and end of each questionnaire the interviewer records the time so that length of interview is known. While interviewers are instructed to enter the times concurrently with the interview, there is some indication that there are two possible sources of error in these figures; some interviewers record the times that they enter and leave the house, while some interviewers forget to enter the times during the interview and fill them in by recall when they edit their questionnaires. In both of these cases, the tendency is for the interviewer to overstate the length of the interview by including non-interviewing time in the household such as waiting and post-interview conversation. In addition, this method does not account for any interruptions in the middle of an interview. For interviews which average about an hour or longer, these errors do not appreciably change the percentages shown in Table 6.1, but for short interviews (such as the Census Enumeration) these errors could be large.

The other source of information on interviewer time allocation, the Interviewer's Time Report, is the form routinely used by interviewers to report their time so they can get paid. A copy of this form is included in the Appendix (p. 229). The Time Report is divided into three sections: travel, interviewing and other time. Other time includes study, clerical, and editing time.

Study time is defined as the time spent by the interviewer in reading the instructions and specifications for a study and in doing any practice interviews required. It does not include any time spent in personal training by a field supervisor or in group sessions. When these personal training sessions are held, the interviewers involved are generally paid a fixed amount.

Clerical time is time spent filling out forms, including the time report, and in sending and receiving mail in connection with a study. It includes trips to and from the post office to pick up packages or mail completed questionnaires. It may also include the mailing of special letters explaining the purposes of a survey to respondents, if this is done.

Editing time is the time spent by the interviewer after the interview to insure that her writing is legible, that no questions have been erroneously omitted, and that any ambiguous answers are clarified. There is great variability between interviewers on this category, since some interviewers use shorthand during the interview and transcribe later. There is some difficulty in separating out editing time from travel time within a segment. Many interviewers do their editing while waiting for the next respondent to become available, and thus their time sheets show a combined category of editing and waiting. In these cases, the time spent editing a questionnaire is estimated from those questionnaires of the interviewer which were edited when no waiting time was involved.

Travel to segment is derived from the travel column on the time report. It includes time to the segment from the interviewer's home and return. It also includes any travel time from one segment to another. It is generally not too difficult to separate this time from the time spent by the interviewer within the segment.

Travel in segment is defined as all time in a segment not spent on the actual interview. Travel in segment includes all waiting time, and time in a respondent's home spent in conversation not part of the interview, as well as time spent locating the proper house in the segment and knocking on doors. Also included here is the time the interviewer spends on the telephone making appointments for interviews. This type of travel time is not always directly noted by interviewers filling out the present time sheet. It is sometimes included under travel time, sometimes under interviewing time, and sometimes under other time. In coding the time reports, cross-checks are made with questionnaires. If the interviewer combines waiting time or other time within the segment with the interview, the length of the interview as obtained from the questionnaire is subtracted from the total time shown and the balance is called "travel in segment." Even where the interviewer has separated her time, cross-checks still are made to the questionnaire to insure that dates and times agree. If not, the normal procedure is to adjust the time report to the questionnaire since times in the questionnaire were presumably filled out immediately, while the time report is generally filled out later.

SPECIAL INTERVIEWER RECORDS

Segment Call Record

Because of difficulties encountered with the time report a new method of accounting for interviewer time was used on the last probability sample study (Study 3) described in Table 6.1. For this study, a very much simplified time sheet was used in combination with a segment call record sheet. The two forms are included in the Appendix (pp. 230–31). The segment call record, which is kept by the interviewer while she is in the segment, records the times for each of the following steps in the interviewing process: travel to and from segment, travel within segment, waiting for respondent, seeking or talking with respondent, and actual interviewing.

Naturally, a cost analysis of interviewer time using this form is far easier and more exact than one which uses recall on time records. On the other hand, some interviewers found the record keeping of this form to be burdensome. Currently, the segment call record is being used for those studies where detailed cost analyses are required, but is not used routinely.

Interviewer Log

The results of the 1947 quota sample shown as Study 7 in Table 6.1 were based on an interviewer log developed especially for that study. Data are not available separately on the amounts of study, clerical, editing, and travel time to segments. The analysis of the field operations on this study were done by Stephan and McCarthy (1958).

INTERVIEWER TIME ALLOCATION AT THE CENSUS BUREAU AND SURVEY RESEARCH CENTER

1960 Census

Table 6.2 gives the percentage of enumerator time spent on various tasks, both for the 1960 census and the Current Population Survey. The figures have been re-worked from the census documents to make them as comparable as possible to the data in Table 6.1 Naturally, different methods make full comparability impossible. Thus, the training for the 1960 census was done on a personal basis, so there is no study item included. The Current Population Survey also has no provision for study since this is not measured on CPS time sheets. CPS interviewers are paid a fixed amount for studying any special instructions sent them.

The 1960 census results are found in Enumeration Time and Cost Study (U. S. Censuses of Population and Housing, 1960, 1963). During Stage I of the enumeration, information was obtained on five characteristics for each member of the household and for ten characteristics of the housing unit. If the household had filled in an Advance Census Report form, the enumerator transcribed the information from the form to the enumeration book; if not, he obtained the responses by questioning the household member.

At one-fourth of the housing units, enumerators left additional forms to be filled out and mailed. During the Stage II enumeration, the enumerator received all the individual questionnaires that were mailed in, and made additional visits or phone calls to obtain missing information.

Information on enumerator activities was obtained by having a records clerk accompany randomly selected enumerators and record what they did and how long it took. The Census Bureau

Table 6.2 Percentages of Enumerator Time Spent on Various Tasks, 1960 Census[a] and Current Population Surveys[b]

Task	1960 Census		CPS
	Stage I	Stage II	
Clerical (transcription)	21	38	20
Editing (field review)	6	7	–
Travel to segment	6	–	35
Travel in segment	30	12	14
Interviewing	30	23	31
Miscellaneous	7	20	–
Total	100	100	100

[a] United States Censuses of Population and Housing 1960 (1963, pp. 27, 32, 36).
[b] Bureau of the Census, Miscellaneous Data Memorandum No. 3 (1958).

made no attempt to estimate what the effect of the records clerk was on the enumerator. Clearly, it led to more accurate recording of time than would a time sheet, but it could also have influenced the enumerator's work habits.

Transcription to the various FOSDIC schedules was not measured in the field, but was estimated by the Census Bureau from established standards. In general, this work was done after the canvass was completed. Editing time (field review) was defined to include the quality control inspection of the enumerator's work by a crew leader or field reviewer, the time it took the interviewer to travel to the field review, the time the interviewer waited for the reviewer and the time spent on payroll computation.

Travel time to the segment was an insignificant part of the enumerator's task and is not even shown for Stage II. For Stage I it averaged seventeen minutes one way or thirty-four minutes round trip per average assignment of thirty-two. Thus the average travel time to segment per household was about one minute.

Current Population Survey

Interviewer allocation of time on the Current Population Survey is found in Miscellaneous Statistical Data Memorandum No. 3 of the Bureau of the Census.[1] In general, the definitions used there are comparable to those of NORC. The data for the CPS are obtained from interviewer time records, which were kept to obtain this detailed information. The standard CPS time sheet asks only for starting and finishing times each day.

Survey Research Center

The data in Table 6.3 are from a paper by Goodman and Cannell of the Survey Research Center, University of Michigan (n.d.). The data were compiled from detailed time and expense reports submitted regularly by interviewers. As at NORC, these were the same records that were used to compute the pay an interviewer received. Both surveys were national probability samples, with the interview lasting forty-five minutes to an hour. On the first study the interviewer took notes and transcribed these

---

[1] I am grateful to Dean Webber, the author of this memo, for making it available to me.

notes afterwards. On the other survey, answers were written on the questionnaire during the interview.

COMPARISON OF THE VARIOUS NORC STUDIES

This section will discuss the reasons for the differences in interviewer allocation of time on the various NORC studies. No attempt is made here to examine differences between interviewers on the same study. This analysis is left for Chapter 8.

Table 6.1 suggests that while actual interviewer times vary considerably from survey to survey, percentages are more stable. Study and editing time would normally be expected to increase with the complexity of a study, as would the length of interview. Travel time remains fixed with respect to length of interview, but is larger for probability samples. Some more specific comments on reasons for variability for each task may indicate how the nature of the assignment determines interviewer time allocation.

Study Time

Study time for a survey depends mostly on the complexity and length of the specifications. There is a correlation of .94 between length of specifications and actual study time required for the six studies. Roughly, each page of specifications requires on the average about five minutes of study time with an additional fixed time of an hour regardless of size. While these figures are crude, since they are based on only six studies, they do give some basis for suggesting to the interviewers how much time should be allocated to studying.

Table 6.3 Percentages of Interviewer Time Spent on Various Tasks on Two Survey Research Center Studies

Task	Survey A	Survey B
Study, clerical and miscellaneous	21	24
Editing	26	–
Travel to and in segment	30	44
Interviewing	23	32
Total	100	100

Source: Roe Goodman and Charles F. Cannell (n.d.).

The size of specifications for the six studies were:

Study No.	Pages of Specifications	Total Study Time (Minutes)
1	118	704
2	97	424
3	42	172
4	14	199
5	14	178
6	7	85

Clerical Time

Interviewer time spent on clerical tasks can be almost completely determined by the field department. The variability in the clerical times seen in Table 6.1 is due to the different tasks required of interviewers. For example, on the first study in Table 6.1, interviewers were required to use stamps to mail packages of completed interviews back to the office instead of using business reply envelopes which have since become standard. This meant frequent trips to the post office to have the packages weighed and to buy stamps as well as additional entries on the time sheet. On the second and seventh studies clerical time included the filling out of special records showing how interviewers spent their time.

Generally, it is more efficient to have clerical jobs done in a central office. This suggests that whenever possible, questionnaire kits and other interviewer material should be assembled before mailing, rather than by the interviewer, and that interviewer trips to the post office be avoided by putting stamps on mailing envelopes in advance or by paying postage when questionnaires are returned.

If one were only concerned with reducing clerical time, the use of detailed logs of interviewer time should be avoided. These records are very valuable, however, in the kinds of studies discussed in this chapter.

Editing Time

Editing time is directly related to the length and difficulty of the questionnaire. There is no direct measure of this, but the length of time required to conduct the interview is a good indication of this. Editing time is correlated .96 with interviewing time, and generally requires about one-third as much time as does the interview for the six NORC studies in Table 6.1

Travel to and in Segment

Travel to and in segment depends on the number of trips required, which is partly a function of the cluster size and call-back instructions. Naturally, the location of the interviewing staff in relation to the segments is also important, but this is usually unchanged from survey to survey. Since travel costs form a large part of the total costs of an interview, they will be discussed in detail in the next chapter, which will examine the effects of location and size of primary sampling unit as well as call-back instructions and cluster sizes.

The comparisons between probability samples and quota samples in Table 6.1 indicate some differences, but the magnitude of these differences is smaller than might be expected. For travel in segment, there is hardly any difference between the probability and quota samples. For travel to segment, quota samples require somewhat less time, since call-backs are not required and the number of trips is reduced. The quota samples in Studies 4 through 6 are those which specify the starting address for an interviewer and the path she must follow but do not require her to return to a dwelling unit if no one is available. In addition, these studies all specified the proportion of employed and unemployed women to be interviewed, as well as the proportion of men over and under thirty years of age.

In contrast, the 1947 quota sample imposed no geographic limitations, but required the interviewer to obtain a specified number of respondents in each of several rent levels. The high proportion of travel time on that study was probably due to the fact that the rent quotas used at the time were out of date, requiring a long search by the interviewer to find respondents in the lowest rent levels. In addition, the search procedure of interviewers at the time was inefficient, since many tried to fill their lower rent levels by searching in higher rent neighborhoods.

Interviewing

The length of time spent interviewing depends on the length

and complexity of the questionnaire. So far as is known, there is no good way to estimate how long it will take to administer a questionnaire without actually pretesting it. Table 6.1 shows, however, that the percentage of time spent interviewing is fairly stable for the first six NORC surveys, varying only from 32 to 41 per cent. Only for the 1947 quota study does the percentage of interviewing time drop to 21 per cent. There are two reasons for this: (1) the large percentage of time spent traveling, which was discussed above, and (2) even more important, the fact that this 1947 interview took only about fifteen minutes in contrast to the other studies where the interview was three or four times longer. It is clear that short interviews of a half-hour or less result in less time spent interviewing, but there is no increase in this percentage as interviews get longer than about forty-five minutes. The very long interviews make it hard for the interviewer to complete more than a single interview per trip, and this balances the increase of the ratio of interviewing time to travel time per trip.

COMPARISON OF NORC, CENSUS, AND CPS

The chief difference between the NORC studies and the CPS and census enumeration is the length of interview. The average NORC studies in Table 6.1 are about an hour long, while the census enumeration was less than ten minutes, and the CPS interviews run about fifteen minutes. This explains why NORC interviewers spend slightly more of their time on actual interviews. Thus, for the 1960 census, the actual time spent interviewing was only 5.4 minutes in Stage I and 2.8 minutes in Stage II. With such short interviews, the amounts of time spent in the house before and after the interview were large relative to the actual interview. If one included all time in the house as interviewing time, then the Stage I percentage of interviewing time would be 45 per cent instead of the 30 per cent shown in Table 6.2, and the Stage II percentage would be 28 per cent instead of 23 per cent. Perhaps these percentages as well as those in Table 6.2 should be considered when making comparisons to NORC and Survey Research Center results.

Of greater significance than the differences are the similarities. Note the percentage of time spent interviewing on the CPS, which follows a strict probability sample design as compared to the three NORC studies using probability samples. The CPS figure of 31 per cent of time spent interviewing is quite close to the three NORC percentages of 32 per cent, 33 per cent, and 38 per cent. This close agreement between different survey organizations on percentage of time spent interviewing is also confirmed by the data of the Survey Research Center in Table 6.3.

It can be seen that for Survey B, which is the more usual type of survey, the Survey Research Center percentage of interviewing time, 32 per cent, is in good agreement with the CPS figure of 31 per cent and the NORC percentages of 32 per cent, 33 per cent, and 38 per cent. For Survey A, if interviewing and editing are combined, they account for 49 per cent of the time of Survey Research Center interviewers. Similarly on the three NORC probability sample studies, interviewing and editing combined account for 43 per cent, 44 per cent, and 49 per cent of the total time.

To summarize these results: Although there are substantial differences between the requirements for different studies, and although different survey organizations have different requirements and measure interviewer time allocation in different ways, there is a surprising uniformity in the percentage of time which interviewers spend on their chief task—interviewing. For probability samples, it is a safe generalization that interviewers spend about one-third of their time interviewing and two-thirds of their time on less critical tasks.

How this compares to other occupations is the subject of the next section of this chapter. It will be seen that these results for interviewers are remarkably similar to those of other field occupations.

OTHER FIELD OCCUPATIONS: SOURCES OF DATA

Salesmen

Tables 6.4 and 6.5 show how salesmen, social workers, probation officers and public health nurses allocate their time to various tasks. Table 6.4 summarizes five different reports on salesmen. The data on wholesale drug salesmen is from Davis (1948). The time study was conducted by having an observer spend a complete day with a salesman from the time he left his house or hotel in the morning until he returned at night. Since Davis felt that the work of the salesman would be conditioned by the knowledge that he was being timed, the salesman was not told of the time-study. Rather the salesman was told that notes were being taken on the methods he used for selling, and how effective they were. A total of thirty-eight country salesmen and thirty-two city salesmen were observed.

Selling time, which corresponds to interviewing time, included promotional selling, dealer assistance, want-book selling, sales promotion and collection and adjustment. Travel in is the time in the store spent waiting at the start of an interview or if interrupted, general conversation and idle time. Travel to includes travel and meals. Clerical time is the time spent in writing up orders and phoning orders into the wholesale house.

The second study that deals with oil company salesmen is from a study by the Atlantic Refining Company reported in *Salesweek* (1960). Details of how this study, and the other salesmen studies in Table 6.4, were conducted are not available. Ordinarily, one would not be willing to give much credence to these studies, except that they all seem to say about the same thing. The study of carpet salesmen is cited by Brown (1961), while the study of miscellaneous salesmen is also in the *Salesweek* article mentioned above. It is based on a study of 255 salesmen in nineteen different fields. The data on steel salesmen are from the personal files of Allen Jung of Loyola University (Chicago), who obtained them while working in the steel industry.[2]

Social Workers

Table 6.5 shows the time allocation of social workers and public health nurses. Three different studies of social work occupations show great stability in the percentage of time spent interviewing.[3] The first study deals with probation officers in Contra Costa County, California (Contra Costa Probation Department, 1959). Individual deputies kept daily logs for a seven-week period, and

[2] Personal communication from Allen Jung.

[3] I am indebted to Edward Schwartz of the School of Social Service Administration, University of Chicago, for bringing this data to my attention and making it available to me.

the tasks were coded using the following classifications: interviewing included personal and phone contacts with the probationer; study included conferences with supervisors and with other deputies, psychologists, etc.; clerical included all office paper work; travel appears to be what would be called travel to segment

Table 6.4 Percentages of Salesman Time Spent on Various Tasks

	Wholesale Drug[a]		Oil[b]	Steel[c]	Carpet[d]	Miscellaneous[e]
	City	Country				
Study (preparation)	–	–	–	–	–	19
Clerical	4	2	–	6	–	–
Travel to	33	32	37	} 72	–	–
Travel in	26	25	16		–	45
Selling	37	41	45	22	40	36
Miscellaneous	–	–	2	–	60	–
Total	100	100	100	100	100	100

[a]Davis (1948, p. 59).
[b]*Salesweek* (December 12, 1960, p. 13).
[c]Personal communication from Allen Jung.
[d]Brown et al. (1961).
[e]*Salesweek* (December 12, 1960, pp. 12–13).

Table 6.5 Percentages of Time Spent on Various Tasks by Social Workers and Public Health Nurses

Task	Social Workers			Public Health Nurses	
	Probation Officers[a]	Foster Home Placement[b]	Independent Adoption[c]	National[d]	Georgia[e]
Study (conference)	9	13	24	2	–
Clerical (record keeping)	22	24	20	23	13
Travel	15	16	21	20	32
Interviewing (in-home care)	39	38	35	54	55
Miscellaneous	15	9	–	1	–
Total	100	100	100	100	100

[a]Contra Costa County Probation Department (1959).
[b]Jewish Child Care Association of New York (1952).
[c]Department of Social Welfare, State of California (1956).
[d]Department of Public Health Nursing, National League for Nursing (1956).
[e]Akin (1962, pp. 544–46).

by interviewers; and miscellaneous most closely corresponds to travel in segment for interviewers. The probation officers are the only male group of social workers in Table 6.5, but they are no different than the other two groups.

The second study concerns thirty-seven caseworkers of the Jewish Child Care Association of New York (1952). They kept tally sheets for twelve working days recording meetings and conferences, telephoning, paper work, dictation, and travel. The actual interviews and record reading in preparation for them were not recorded separately, but were obtained by subtraction. Thus, there is no way to separate out interviewing time from what we would call study time. In Table 6.6, conference time is treated as study time. Dictation and clerical work are both included under clerical, although dictation from notes, which accounts for 13.5 per cent of the total time worked, could correspond to editing shorthand questionnaires for interviewers. The 9 per cent of the time spent on the telephone was classified as miscellaneous, although it might also be compared to the interviewer's travel time in segment, since it involved making appointments for visits.

The final study by the Bureau of Management Analysis of the State of California Department of Social Welfare concerns independent adoptions caseworkers (Department of Social Welfare, State of California, 1956). It is based on returns of a questionnaire to seven agencies asking them to estimate time spent on various tasks. Since adoption is a complicated process, each of

Table 6.6 Comparison of Percentages of Time Spent Interviewing, Traveling, and in Other Tasks by Survey Interviewers and Other Field Occupations

Occupation	Interviewing	Traveling	Other	Total
Interviewers:				
NORC				
Probability samples	34	40	26	100
Block-quota samples	40	32	28	100
Census	26	24	50	100
Current Population Survey	31	49	20	100
Survey Research Center	28	37	35	100
Salesmen	37	52	11	100
Social workers	39	17	44	100
Public health nurses	55	26	19	100

the items in Table 6.5 is the sum of many individual steps. The study and editing tasks are combined because the record of one step becomes the material to be studied for the next; dictation, however, is classified as a clerical task.

Study time includes prepetition activity, preliminary steps, review of case material after interviews, and conferences with supervisors, attorneys and other professionals. Clerical includes all dictation and preparation of files. Interviewing includes interviews with the adopting parents, the natural parents, the child, and with other family members if needed. Travel time includes actual time spent traveling and time spent telephoning to arrange for appointments.

Public Health Nurses

Two studies are available on how public health nurses spend their time. The first study is by far the more comprehensive one (Department of Public Health Nursing, National League for Nursing, 1956). It is a nationwide study of eleven public health nursing agencies conducted by the Department of Public Health Nursing of the National League for Nursing. Each agency did two analyses five years apart, using special forms kept by the nurses. Although no averaging is done in the report, the figures in Table 6.5 are the simple averages of the twenty-two numbers. Total home visiting time is divided into three parts: actual time in the home, travel time, and preparation or post-activity. Staff education is classified as study time, while community activities are put into miscellaneous.

The second study is from *Nursing Outlook* and presents information on a study of Georgia Public Health Nurses (Akin, 1962). One hundred and eight nurses in five local health departments kept daily time records for one week. For the visiting nurses, time was divided into actual time in the home, travel time, and preparation and post-activity.

TIME ALLOCATION

Salesmen

Table 6.4 shows that about 37 per cent of a salesman's time is spent in actual selling, with only small variation around this average. Only the steel salesmen are substantially below average, and while it is not clear why this is the case, it may be due to the fact that their customers are more widely separated.

What is surprising is that salesmen do not appear to be much different from survey interviewers in the way in which they allocate their time. This would suggest that method of payment (commission *vs.* hourly rate) probably does not have a very large effect on the percentage of time either interviewers or salesmen spend on their main task. The difference of five percentage points between the time spent selling and the time spent interviewing is probably a maximum estimate of the effects of changing the compensation system for survey interviewers.

Social Workers

The time spent in interviewing on all three social work occupations averages 37 per cent and varies only from 35 to 39 per cent. It is also striking to note that this is exactly the same average percentage of time spent selling by salesmen, and is very close to the percentage of time spent interviewing by survey interviewers. Before speculating as to why these percentages are so close, data will be presented for public health nurses who show a sharply different pattern.

Public Health Nurses

Public health nurses spend a substantially greater part of their time on in-home care (which corresponds to interviewing or selling) than do any of the other occupations studied.

It can be seen that nurses spend better than half their time (54–55 per cent) in their chief function as compared to the other occupations which average about one-third time. Table 6.6 provides a concise summary of the results of the earlier tables. Certainly one is led to speculate as to reasons why interviewing, selling, and social work show such strong similarities, and why nursing differs. These speculations are presented in the final section.

SIMILARITIES IN VARIOUS FIELD OCCUPATIONS

In considering why interviewing, selling, and social work show such similar patterns, certain reasons can probably be rejected. It might be argued that the agreement is coincidental, but this seems extremely unlikely, given the fact that twenty different studies are compared. While the argument that this is a chance occurrence can never be fully discarded, there does appear to be a reason that has a more rational appeal.

Since there is some ambiguity in the data for all these studies, it might be thought that this agreement is artifactual—that the summarization of the data was done in such a way as to bring them into line with a preconceived hypothesis. This does not seem to be the case. The greatest ambiguity in the data are in categories other than interviewing. While there is often a question as to whether something should be classified as study, clerical, or miscellaneous it is generally easy to separate the actual interviewing or selling from travel or waiting time in the reports analyzed, although this does not insure the initial accuracy of these reports. In addition, the results shown above differed substantially from the initial hypotheses. Prior to data collection, it was felt that there would be real differences between interviewers, social workers, and salesmen. Using a monetary reward framework, it was felt that salesmen would spend the most time in actual selling, since their commissions depended on the number of contacts they made, while interviewers would spend the least time in actual interviewing, since the longer it took them in non-interviewing activities such as travel and study, the more they received. Clearly, this indicates that method of payment is not the reason for the similarities.

Nor does it seem likely that the characteristics of the persons in these occupations are enough alike to cause these similarities. Sex is not important since interviewers are mostly women, salesmen are men, and social workers are both (at least, in this analysis). Education is not an important variable since social workers generally have some graduate work, interviewers some college, and salesmen are generally high school graduates (Davis, 1948, pp. 41–53). Neither age nor family status are identical—interviewers tend to be middle-aged women with children in or through with school, while social workers tend to be younger.

The reason for the similarities seems to lie in the job situation itself. The three occupations—interviewing, selling, and social work—are all highly stressful in their most crucial component—the personal contact with the respondent. The interview has generally been arranged at the request of the interviewer rather than the respondent, and there is always the possibility of a slammed door or a curt refusal. Even when the interview has started, the interviewer is always conscious of the effort to keep it flowing smoothly to a successful conclusion. The process can be so wearing emotionally that the interviewer needs time to recuperate, and so other activities are included as part of the job, be they traveling, waiting, studying or clerical tasks.

It may be argued that social workers are not in the same fix as are interviewers and salespeople, but for the three examples given in this chapter there do appear to be real reasons for tension between the social worker and the respondent, and the social workers have come to expect this tension. The data on the visiting nurses seem to confirm this conclusion by contrast. The visiting nurse is almost always invited into the home to give medical care, and does not expect to overcome any resistance in getting into a home or during the treatment. Since there is less stress on her, she is able to spend a larger part of her time in the home.

If this is a valid conclusion, it has this consequence: It suggests that manipulation of compensation or of details of the job would have very little effect on the percentage of time which the interviewer spent on the interview. The only way to increase time spent interviewing would be to reduce tension, but this may not be possible. It may be that certain individuals are less sensitive to this tension, and are thus able to spend greater parts of their time on the actual interview. These people may not make the best interviewers, however, since this lack of sensitivity could result in more interviews of lower quality.

This analysis is not intended to suggest that each day will be allocated the same way by workers in field occupations. Some days may be spent entirely in interviewing, while on other days no interviews may be conducted. It is suggestive, however, that a majority of NORC interviewers never spend more than four hours per day interviewing, either on probability or quota sample studies.

FURTHER RESEARCH SUGGESTED

The generalizations presented above suggest several areas of additional study. It is not clear what part of the tensions are due to the efforts required to keep the interview going, and what part to the initiation of the interview with a possibly unwilling respondent. It should be possible to obtain records or devise experiments where appointments have been made for the interviewer. If interviewer time allocation did not then change, one would conclude that the tensions were primarily due to interpersonal contact. On the other hand, there are cases that require an initial contact with a respondent, but no additional interactions. Such tasks as store auditing and leave-and-pick-up questionnaires are examples. Again one would look for changes in interviewer time allocation as indicating effects of interpersonal contacts.

It would be extremely useful to obtain data on other occupations where a great deal of interpersonal contact is required, but where the meetings are not initiated by the interviewer. Thus, employment interviewers, sales clerks, and school teachers come to mind as groups worth investigating. The time allocation of people in occupations with little interpersonal contacts, such as scientists and engineers, would also be illuminating.

7

The Control of
Interviewing Costs

INTRODUCTION

There has been a continuing sharp dialogue between survey organizations and survey interviewers about the cost of interviewing. Most survey organizations bemoan the steady increase in the cost of field work, while interviewers complain that the increase has not been rapid enough. What is clear is that interviewing costs have, in general, not been subject to meaningful controls, so that there is no sensible way to analyze the cost argument. The purpose of this chapter is to suggest methods for controlling field expenditures. These controls do not insure the reduction of field costs, although they increase the probability of such cost reductions. The purpose of controls is to insure that interviewers are paid in a way that seems rational both to them and to the survey organization.

The current pay method, in almost universal use, is to pay the interviewer at an hourly rate for all the hours she spends, including portal-to-portal pay. Since the interviewer is not under supervision, this is indeed a unique method of payment. Other field workers such as mailmen, social workers, or public health nurses work on a salary, or, if salesmen, on a combination of salary and commissions. Hourly workers are generally under tight supervision and control through supervisors and time clocks.

The origin of the current pay procedure goes back to the early days of survey research when geographically uncontrolled quota sampling was the sampling method used. Survey organizations that wanted their interviewers to cover wide areas of the city rather than to do all their interviews in a small area near their homes found that paying interviewers by the hour and paying travel expenses encouraged them to travel more. Of course, the uncontrolled nature of the sampling made any method that paid on a per case basis unsatisfactory to the interviewer.

There was the additional problem of interviewer cheating. It was feared that payment on a per case basis would encourage interviewers to invent results or at the least would lead to sloppy work.

The gradual shift to area probability sampling caused no major changes in the pay method since it had become so well established, and since interviewers claimed that there was still much uncertainty in finding a respondent home for any given call. During this period, the control of interviewer time sheets generally consisted of checking the interviewer's arithmetic. Some of the more rigorous field organizations had a home office supervisor check the time sheets for unusual entries, but as work load increased this was one of the first checks that was dropped.

Although the pay method described above has been in almost universal use for more than thirty years, some major problems are connected with it:

1. The current procedure tends to reward the least experienced and least efficient interviewers who spend the greatest amount of time searching for respondents.

2. The interviewer is faced with the constant temptation to pad her time sheet since neither she nor anyone else knows how long it should take her to complete an assignment.

3. Internally, there is no good way to estimate the field costs of new studies in advance, and it is frequently noted that field estimates are too low as compared to actual costs.

4. Checking of time sheet records is in itself a long costly operation that generally accomplishes very little.

To summarize, the lack of controls of interviewer costs leads to reduced efficiency both among interviewers and in the internal supervision of interviewers. It makes it difficult to plan new surveys and run a tight survey ship.

ESTABLISHMENT OF CONTROLS BY THE BUREAU OF THE CENSUS

The Bureau of the Census has been a pioneer in the development of controls for field work, just as it has pioneered in many other survey research areas. In 1956 the Bureau recognized the need for such controls and the possibility of building them for repetitive studies such as the Current Population Surveys. Later this program was expanded, with only minor changes, to the National Health Survey and the surveys of retail establishments for the Census Current Business Reports. Primarily responsible for this work have been Jack Silver and Dean Webber of the Field Methods Research Branch.[1]

Since the census procedures have not been previously published, it seems worthwhile to discuss them in detail, using the Current Population Survey as a specific example. The basic procedure used is the analysis of the various parts of the enumerator's job and the establishment of standards for each of these parts based on past experience. The standards depend on the size of the PSU in which the enumerator works and the distance from her home to the sample segments.

Consider, first, time spent enumerating. The standard may be expressed as:

$$T_a = Ht_1 + Tt_2 + Bt_3 + Lt_4 + (H + T)t_5,$$

where T_a is the standard time allowed for enumerating,

H = the number of households completed by personal interview,

[1] The following memoranda, all within the Bureau of the Census, Department of Commerce, describe the production standards programs for enumerators: Proposed Model for Controlling the Cost of Enumeration in Field Surveys (July 27, 1956); General Administrative Memorandum No. 48, A Revised Procedure for Computing Production Standards for Field Offices and Individual Enumerators (October 8, 1956); Proposed Model for Controlling the Cost of CCBR Enumeration (December 11, 1957); Proposed Models for Controlling the Cost of NHS Enumeration (April 15, 1958); General Administrative Memorandum No. 70, Procedure for Computing Performance Ratios for National Health Survey Interviewers (May 28, 1958); General Administrative Memorandum No. 71, A Revised Procedure for Computing CCBR Performance Ratios for Field Offices and Individual Enumerators (June 3, 1958); Proposed Model for Controlling the Cost of QHS Enumeration (June 11, 1963); and Production Standards Memorandum No. 8, Procedure for Computing Production Ratios for QHS Interviewers (June 18, 1963).

T = the number of households completed by telephone interview,

B = the number of dwelling units for which no interview is required,

L = the number of segments prelisted or brought up to date, and where $t_1|$ = in-segment time per completed personal interview other than travel time,

t_2 = time per completed telephone interview,

t_3 = time per dwelling unit where no interview is required,

t_4 = time per segment prelisted or brought up to date, and

t_5 = handling time per completed interview—time spent at home on clerical tasks related to the schedules.

The values for the standards by PSU size are shown in Table 7.1. These were the original 1956 values based on detailed time records and may have since been revised by later field experience.

Next, to this time must be added travel time to, between, and within the segment. Travel time standards depend on number of trips required per segment, speed, and distance from the interviewer's home to the segment. The formula is expressed as:

$$T_b = \left(\lambda_1 \, S \, - \, \frac{H}{\lambda_2}\right) d_1 r_1 \, + \, 2 \, \frac{H}{\lambda_2} \, d_2 r_2 \, + \, \lambda_1 \, S \, d_3 r_3,$$

where T_b = total travel time,

λ_1 = number of segment visits per segment,

λ_2 = average number of households completed per round trip,

H = number of households completed by personal interview,

d_1 = average distance between segments,

d_2 = average distance from enumerator's home to a segment,

d_3 = average distance travelled within segments,

r_1 = average time per mile between segments,

r_2 = average time per mile to and from home,

r_3 = average time per mile within segments, and

S = number of segments visited personally.

The various values for the parameters are also shown in Table 7.1. Taken in order, the three terms of the formula are (1) time spent travelling from one enumeration segment to another, including call-backs and excluding travel to and from home; (2) time spent travelling to and from home; and (3) time spent in a car travelling within enumeration segments. (All travel from door to door on foot is included in t_1.)

From these rather formidable-appearing formulas it is possible to develop easy computational procedures that depend only on the size of the PSU and the distance that the interviewer lives from the segment.

To see how the formula would work in practice, consider an enumerator who was assigned sixty households in four segments and, in addition, was assigned one segment for prelisting. From his map it is found that the average distance (d_2) between his home and any segment is fifteen miles, and that the average dis-

Table 7.1 Basic Unit Allowances for CPS Enumeration by PSU Group[a]

Line No.	Workload Unit	Type of Allowance	Allowance by PSU Group			
			1	2	3	4
Households completed by:						
1	Personal interview	minutes	14.8	12.6	12.2	10.1
2	Telephone interview	minutes	9.1	9.4	8.9	9.9
3	Type B non-interview	minutes	5	5	4	4
Allowance for auto travel:						
4	Between enumeration segments, per mile	minutes	3.5	3.1	2.4	2.2
5	Between segment and home, per mile	minutes	2.9	2.1	2.0	1.8
6	Within enumeration segments, per segment	minutes	1.0	2.7	7.8	18.0
7	Segments listed or brought up to date	minutes	17	22	27	43
8	Homework time per completed interview	minutes	6.7	7.2	7.7	5.6
9	Call-back rate (visits per enumeration segment)	visits	1.56	1.56	1.56	1.56
10	Round trips from home[b]	trips	$H/8$	$H/10$	$H/9$	$H/11$

[a]CPS in the Census Population Survey; PSU is the Primary Sampling Unit.
[b]Total households completed by personal interview (H) divided by average number completed per round trip.
Source: General Administrative Memorandum No. 48, Bureau of the Census (October 8, 1956).

tance between segments (d_1) is ten miles. If the enumerator closed out his CPS assignment with fifty-five completed personal interviews, two telephone completions and one Type B non-interview, his allowance could be computed directly from the foregoing formula by making substitutions as follows:

Travel: $(1.56 \times 2.2 \times 4 \times 10.1) - \left(\dfrac{55}{11} \times 2.2 \times 10.1\right) + \left(\dfrac{2 \times 55}{11}\right) \times 1.8$
$\times 15 + (1.56 \times 18 \times 4) = 137 - 110 + 270 + 112 = 409$ minutes,

enumeration: $(10.1 \times 55) + (9.9 \times 2) + (4 \times 1) + 5.6\,(55 + 2) + (43 \times 1)$
$= 556 + 20 + 4 + 319 + 43 = 942$ minutes,

so that the total allowance would be: $409 + 942 = 1{,}351$ minutes.

There is, of course, the danger that the introduction of production standards could cause a drop in quality of interviewing or an increase in the non-interview rate. As in their other programs having production standards, the Census Bureau evaluates interviewers on the basis of their quality of interviewing as well as on their meeting of production standards. The introduction of standards reduced total interviewing costs of the Current Population Survey about 10 per cent with no decline in the quality of interviewing. The major change in the behavior of enumerators was the use of more efficient travel patterns.

Currently, enumerators whose costs are 80 per cent or less of standard receive a bonus for their efficiency, while enumerators who are substantially above standard are subject to firing. In practice, very few enumerators have been fired, but some have resigned because they found themselves unable to meet standards. The Census Bureau believes that the introduction of standards weeds out the least efficient interviewers and, even more important, provides a guide for improving overall efficiency.

ESTABLISHMENT OF FORMULA PAY METHOD AT NORC

The same general method for establishing standards has been used at NORC with modifications for the variation in the length of time required to complete the interviewing on different surveys.

Travel time to the segment and in the segment remain constant for an interviewer from survey to survey. The time required for interviewing, editing, clerical operations, and study time is determined from the pretest results. In some ways, the formula is simpler than the Census Bureau formula since it ignores interviewer travel between segments and treats all travel time within segments as constant.

For regular probability samples with call-backs, the formula for all time except travel time is:

$$T_a = S + C + nI,$$

where T_a = total time except travel,

S = fixed study time, which depends on length of interview and is determined by the pretest results,

C = fixed clerical time, which is determined on the basis of the clerical tasks associated with a particular study,

I = average length of time per interview based on pretest, and

n = number of completed cases.

Travel time standards are:

$$T_b = rHN + .75N,$$

where T_b = travel time to and within segment,

H = one-way travel time to the segment from the interviewer's home. (This information was obtained on a special questionnaire for all interviewers, along with actual distances for payment of mileage allowances. A copy of the questionnaire is included in the Appendix (p. 232).

N = total assigned cases, and

r = number of one-way trips to the segment from the interviewer's home.

The values of r obtained from several NORC studies are:

r = 1.5 in non-rural PSU's,

r = 1.3 in rural PSU's.

Thus, the first term of T_b is the allocation for travel time to segment. The second is the term for travel time in segment. Again, based on NORC experience, an average of three-quarters of an hour per case has been allocated for locating respondents. For probability samples with quotas where no call-backs are required, the non-travel costs are computed just as before. The travel time standard is now:

$$T_q = 6Hs + s,$$

where T_q = travel time for probability samples with quotas. H is, as before, the one-way travel time to the segment from the interviewer's home, and s is the number of segments in which interviewing is done.

Since a typical segment in a quota sample has seven or eight cases, it can be seen that the per case standards for this type of sample are about half of the corresponding standards for a sample with call-backs.

USE OF FORMULA PAY METHOD

The formula pay method has had three distinctly different applications at NORC. The first application has been in the field department where it has been used to decide whom to assign to a given study. All else being equal, it seems reasonable to assign the interviewer nearest the segment, since she should be able to complete the assignment in the least time at the lowest cost. Prior to the collection of information from interviewers on time required to travel to a segment, the home office supervisors making the assignment did not generally use this as one of the selection criteria, since the information was not readily available.

A second use for the formula pay method has been in the classification of interviewers as above or below average in their costs. This classification becomes the basis for a study of the relation between interviewer costs and characteristics which is described in Chapter 8.

Finally, and most importantly, the formula pay method has been used on an experimental basis as a method of payment of interviewers. The major advantage of using such a payment method is that it eliminates the need for checking interviewer time sheets for most interviewers. The standards have been set so that, on the average, interviewers earn just what they did before with, however, the more efficient interviewers earning more than they did before, while the less efficient interviewers earn less.

For the experiment, interviewers were told about the formula pay method and given the choice of participating or using the regular time sheet. The letter sent to interviewers describing the experiment is included in the Appendix (pp. 233-34). Of the one hundred interviewers who were given the choice, eighty-four agreed to try and were paid by the formula pay method, while sixteen were paid using the regular pay procedure. For control purposes, only half the interviewers were included in the experiment. The remaining hundred interviewers were not told about the new pay method, but were paid in the usual way.

Table 7.2 gives the direct field costs for interviewers paid by the formula pay method as compared to the regular time sheet method. It can be seen that the differences between interviewers paid by the formula pay method and the control group are not significant, but that those interviewers who chose not to try the new pay method are significantly higher. Some of this may be due to the particularly difficult segments in which they were to conduct their interviews, while the rest is due to their inefficient travel patterns. Following the principle of management by exception, the formula pay method makes it possible to check thoroughly those

Table 7.2 Average Cost per NORC Interview by Method of Payment and Size of Place

Size of Place	Total	Formula Pay Method	Regular Refused To Try F.P.M.	Regular Control Group
All places	$6.76	$6.60	$8.68	$6.56
N—number of interviewers	(200)	(84)	(16)	(100)
10 Largest SMSA's	7.72	6.99	9.36	7.63
N	(48)	(17)	(8)	(23)
Other SMSA's	6.41	6.48	8.04	6.10
N	(84)	(33)	(6)	(45)
Non-metro counties	6.73	6.46	6.49	7.12
N	(29)	(17)	(1)	(11)
Rural counties	6.36	6.61	9.45	6.02
N	(39)	(17)	(1)	(21)

interviewers who present special problems while most interviewers are paid with no further fuss.

The results of Table 7.2 are in very close agreement with costs of other NORC quota samples (see Chapter 2). The conclusion is that the standards that have been developed do give an accurate picture of the interviewing task.

Interviewer reaction to the experiment has been highly favorable. A brief questionnaire was sent to the interviewers who participated in the experiment asking for their reactions. Most interviewers expressed satisfaction with the method, willingness to try it again, and relief at not being required to fill out time sheets. Table 7.3 summarizes the results of the questionnaire. Given the usual reluctance of most of us toward changes in routine, these results are most encouraging.

SUMMARY

The formula pay method as used at NORC gives every indication of providing needed control of interviewing costs:

Table 7.3 Interviewer Reactions to New Formula Pay Method (Number of Interviewers)

1. Would you be interested in participating again in a pay method experiment such as the Formula Pay Method?	
Yes	77
No	2
2. What was your personal reaction to the Formula Pay Method? Did it work well for you or not?	
It worked well for me	73
Did not work well	6
3. If you had a choice on future block sample (quota) studies, would you prefer to be paid by the Formula Pay Method, by time sheet, or doesn't it matter to you?	
Formula Pay Method	52
Time sheet	3
Doesn't matter	10
Not sure yet	14
4. Which of the following statements comes closest to how you feel about filling out time and expense sheets?	
I like to do it	3
I don't like to do it, but I don't mind	35
It's one part of the job I don't care for, but I do it because I have to	29
It's the worst part of the job and I was glad not to have to do it	12

1. It eliminates the long, costly job of routinely checking interviewer time sheets and makes it possible to concentrate on unusual situations.

2. It enables the interviewer to know in advance how much she will make on a given study, and at the same time makes it possible for the field department to estimate in advance the total direct field costs of new studies.

3. It rewards efficient interviewers and tends to discourage the less efficient interviewers. In the long run, it should lead to a field staff composed of the most efficient interviewers.

8

Cost and Quality of Interviewers

INTRODUCTION

The selection of the proper person for a specific job is a critical part of any administrator's function. This is also true for field supervisors who must select interviewers. The initial hiring and training costs are high, and the supervisor is always trying to select applicants who will do high quality interviewing at reasonable costs and who will not need to be replaced in a short time. The results of the last two chapters suggest that the proper selection of interviewers is more likely to reduce survey costs than are procedures that attempt to manipulate the interviewers' time schedules.

This chapter presents some results that should eventually enable the field supervisor to improve her selection procedures. It is certainly not the intent of this research that the selection of interviewers ever become an objective process based on a pencil-and-paper test. The chief ability required by an interviewer is her ability to interact with other people. The sensitive field supervisor can best judge this characteristic during the personal interview and training period. As in other areas of survey research, however, a folklore has arisen about the qualities needed by a good interviewer. Some of the results of this chapter confirm this folklore, but there are several results that contradict the common beliefs. Our results are preliminary and need much more testing before they can be considered reliable. Still, they may be useful to field supervisors, particularly if used to modify earlier beliefs that automatically reject applicants with certain characteristics.

An example may be useful. Some supervisors avoid hiring

interviewers with too much education or intelligence because they believe that these interviewers will have difficulty establishing rapport with lower-class respondents. Our results indicate, however, that the most highly intelligent and educated interviewers are most likely to be high quality, low cost interviewers. This does not mean that no person with less than a college degree should ever be hired. In some areas, the only available interviewers may have only a high school education, and some of these applicants will do quite well. What it does mean is that applicants with graduate training should not be automatically rejected.

Three different (but not completely independent) measures of interviewer performance are discussed in this chapter—quality, cost, and length of service. A full description of how these measures were obtained is given below. In addition, we present the results of a detailed questionnaire which was returned by four hundred female NORC interviewers. The questionnaire, which is given in the Appendix, is mainly concerned with non-demographic personality characteristics and attitudes related to interviewing performance. In the following sections, we group these characteristics into these categories:

Education and intelligence
Need achievement
Career orientation
Attitudes toward interviewing and interviewing activities
Previous experience and knowledge of other interviewers
Family responsibilities
Efficiency and self-sufficiency
Activities enjoyed
Political party preferences
Machiavellian attitudes
Self-perception of quality-cost behavior
Some variables that don't work

To reduce the possibility that we are merely observing chance relations, individual items are generally combined into indexes. These indexes are formed in two ways. Some, such as the Machiavellian scale, were built directly into the questionnaire. In the more usual case, such as the Activities Enjoyed Index, the question asked about sixteen activities, of which half were correlated with each other using as a lower bound a product-moment correlation of .15. These items were then combined to form the index. Note that, in general, the relation between any index and the dependent variables—cost, quality, and length of service—will be smaller but more stable than the relation between the dependent variables and the single items most highly related to them.

Finally, we combine indexes using regression methods to summarize our findings and to estimate how well the combined variables explain performance. The sample, based on successful NORC interviewers, cannot be generalized to the universe of all interviewing applicants and thus used as an instant selection device. We are not certain that NORC interviewers are typical of those at other survey organizations, although some earlier work of Sheatsley (1950), as well as the results of Chapter 6, suggest that this may be the case. The only way to determine this is to use the same procedures and questionnaires elsewhere. We are encouraging other survey organizations to use revised versions of this questionnaire and to publish their results. In addition, for some items—particularly those dealing with attitudes toward interviewing—we do not know whether the attitudes expressed are due to the socialization that has resulted from interviewing or were held at the time the applicant first became an interviewer. In the future, we intend to use a revised version of the questionnaire for all new applicants.

The next section presents a summary of the major findings of this chapter. This is followed by a brief discussion of earlier published results. The balance of the chapter then discusses the measures of performance and their relation to the characteristics of the interviewers.

SUMMARY OF FINDINGS

Four measures of interviewer value are discussed in this chapter —quality, cost, quality-cost, and years employed by NORC.

Quality

The following variables appear to be useful in predicting high quality interviewers:

Education and intelligence variables, including high school grade average, perceived intelligence, estimated intelligence, subjects liked in school, and total years of school completed;

Need achievement, as determined in a projective scale that asks about characteristics most and least important for children to have;

Career orientation, including items on child-rearing, and marital and household attitudes;

Attitudes toward interviewing and interviewing activities, including items on the status of interviewing that are negatively correlated with quality and the enjoyment of interviewing tasks that are positively correlated;

Activities enjoyed, including mainly outdoor sports activities and verbal activities, such as gossiping and making a speech;

Political party preference, although probably related to geographic and socioeconomic variables; and

Self-perception of quality.

Cost

The following variables are related to high cost interviewers:

Education and intelligence variables, discussed above (negatively correlated);

Previous experience and knowledge of other interviewers, if the experience has been other than at NORC and the interviewers work for other organizations;

Family responsibility, as measured by the number of children and adults the interviewer is responsible for (negatively correlated);

Activities enjoyed (negatively correlated);

Career orientation;

Attitudes toward interviewing and interviewing activities;

Political party preference; and

Self-perception of cost behavior.

Quality-Cost

Some of the variables are related positively to both high quality and high cost and thus are not useful as predictors of high quality in relation to cost. The following remaining variables are related to high quality and low cost:

Education and intelligence;

Need achievement;

Activities enjoyed;
Attitudes toward interviewing (negatively correlated);
Child-rearing attitudes;
Household attitudes (negatively correlated);
(The combined index of these two measures shows no relation since it is related to both cost and quality.)
Knowledge of other interviewers (negatively correlated);
Family responsibility;
Efficiency;
Political party preference; and
Machiavellianism.

Years Employed by NORC

While none of the variables are strongly related to years employed, the following have some relation. In some cases, years employed may predict attitudes, rather than attitudes predicting longevity.

Education and intelligence;
Household attitudes;
Attitudes toward interviewing;
Family responsibility (negatively correlated);
Efficiency; and
Political party preference.

Some readers may wonder why we do not spend more time discussing multiple regression results and giving estimates of beta coefficients, correlations and sampling errors. While it is possible to compute these formally, the limitations of the sample and the search procedure for explanatory variables would keep these results from being exactly true for other populations. Nevertheless, we believe that the factors we discuss are related to interviewing quality and cost, and that it should be possible to develop such regression estimates with future samples.

For those readers who are willing to extrapolate these results to a wider universe of interviewers, a brief word on sampling errors may be useful. The interviewers are usually divided into three groups of about one hundred each. Using simple formulas, the standard error for any percentage figure shown is about 5 per cent and the standard error of any difference is about 7 per cent. The tables in this chapter omit differences which are less than 10 per cent.

The multivariate regressions suggest that the variables we considered are generally independent of each other so they are discussed separately. When combined, however, they still account for only a minor part of the variability between interviewers. It is possible that variables not considered in this chapter may also be important. We have ignored sex and marital status, since almost all NORC interviewers are married women. Age and income are not related to quality and cost of interviewing, but size of city is certainly a cost factor and has been made a part of the formula for standard costs.

NORC believes that the results to date are promising enough to test on new applicants, although in the next stage the results of the questionnaire will play no part in the hiring decision. The results of the questionnaire will be used to predict the cost and quality behavior of applicants who are hired, and to detect differences between those hired and those not hired by field supervisors. In the final stage, a questionnaire will be used as part of the hiring decision, although the major part of this decision will remain the responsibility of the field supervisor.

In general, the better interviewers have characteristics which would make them desirable employees for many different jobs. Fortunately, their interests and commitments have made them select interviewing. We who use their services should recognize their value and rareness and treat them with the care they deserve.

PREVIOUS STUDIES

The work closest in spirit to this chapter was done at NORC by Paul Sheatsley (1950). Sheatsley studied 1,161 NORC interviewers and related demographic characteristics found on the application forms to performance as measured by number of assignments handled and quality of performance. He found that middle-aged married women with some previous college education and some previous interviewing experience made the best interviewers. He noted, however, that demographic variables alone could not explain interviewer performance and pointed out in his perceptive conclusion that attitudes may be most critical:

A more likely prospect of success appears to lie in the gradual development of new and more appropriate tests which would measure each of the several aspects of interviewer performance, and which would, in the course of time, be validated against actual performance records. With the cooperation of researchers all over the country, it should not be too difficult to analyze the interviewer's job, break it down into the several types of required skills, and devise our own suitable tests to measure these skills. Such tests must not content themselves, however, with the mere measurement of skill. An interviewer may have all the skill in the world and yet be guilty of poor performance; a much less skillful interviewer may turn in superior work. In order to predict total performance, we must be able to measure not only skills, but such other factors as the interviewer's job motivations, his ambitions, his attitude toward research, etc. No industry has yet found perfect predictors of job performance, but it is strange that the research profession, which employs questionnaires and interviewing procedures as its stock in trade, should lag behind so many other fields in its development of more precise instruments to predict employee behavior.

This is the direction taken by this chapter.

More recently Hauck and Steinkamp (1964) used an application blank, references, and the Edwards Personal Preference Schedule with a group of sixteen interviewers and related this to pick-up rate which was their quality measure. Pick-up rate was obtained by multiplying the proportion of respondents who cooperated by the proportion of validated savings accounts the interviewer was able to discover. They discovered that three factors explained 71 per cent of the variance among the interviewers: (1) self-confidence of the applicant as rated by references; (2) dominance as measured by the EPPS; and (3) hours available for interviewing.

Again these results indicate the importance of personality factors, but as Hauck and Steinkamp point out, the results are limited by the small sample size and the special nature of the study.

Most other studies of interviewers have attempted to relate interviewer characteristics to variability on various questions.

This approaches a quality measure when characteristics are related to the proportion of "no answers" or "don't knows" on a question or series of questions. Thus, Hanson and Marks (1958) found in a study of census enumerators that the Enumerator Selection Aid Test with questions on reading comprehension, map reading, and ability to follow census-type instructions was useful in differentiating better from poorer interviewers based on "don't knows" and "no answers." There is also a discussion of the effects of interviewer characteristics on the variability of responses. This area has been most fully discussed by Hyman and his NORC colleagues (1954) and is not pursued in this chapter.

EVALUATING INTERVIEWER COSTS

As has been discussed in Chapter 7, high and low cost interviewers can only be identified in comparison to standards which have been established. The methods of Chapter 7 were used to develop cost standards for eleven studies. Comparisons were made between standard and actual costs for each interviewer. While the computations for a single interviewer on a single study are simple, the procedure is tedious when required for many interviewers on many studies and is best carried out on tabulating equipment.

The ratio of actual to standard costs was obtained for all studies in which the interviewer participated. The median ratio was used as an average measure of interviewer costs so that unusually high costs on a single study did not unduly affect the rating. Interviewers were classified as high cost, standard cost, or low cost with some interviewers omitted if no cost data on them were available.

MEASURING INTERVIEWER QUALITY

The quality measure used in this chapter derives from the continuing NORC rating of its interviewing staff. Most studies are rated and the interviewer's average quality score is computed for the studies she participated in. The interviewers have been grouped into three categories which are labeled high, average, and low quality. Those interviewers who are too new to have been rated are omitted from the analysis.

In some of the tables, the average group has been split in half and put into the high and low quality groups so only two groups are compared. The reasons for this are related to data processing requirements and to the fact that these tables were run at different times with different programs. As one would expect, the results for quality split two ways are virtually identical to those when quality is split three ways. Both quality and cost ratings are subject to measurement error particularly for the newer interviewers who worked on only a few studies. These measurement errors tend to reduce the relation between quality, cost, and characteristics of interviewers, but they are unavoidable.

The next few pages describe in detail how interviewers are rated. Since this is somewhat tangential to the main thrust of this chapter, readers who are not especially interested in rating procedures may skip to the next section.

SUBJECTIVE RATING OF INTERVIEWER

Almost all survey organizations make some effort at rating the quality of work of their interviewing staffs. In some cases, this is done on very simple measures such as percentage of assignments completed or meeting of deadlines. Other organizations, including NORC, have field supervisors go through all or a sample of an interviewer's work to judge its quality.

Generally when an interviewer's questionnaires are being checked the supervisor utilizes some sort of check-list (which may at times be a mental one) to rate the interviewer. This rating may take the form of a letter grade, a numerical score, or a descriptive adjective such as "excellent," "above average," or "poor." This rating has traditionally been subjective, depending on the standards set by the individual rater.

Recently the limitations of these subjective ratings have been recognized. Due to turn-over among raters, the level of ratings changes substantially depending on the differing quality expectations of different raters. The length and complexity of the questionnaire as well as the training methods used can also have substantial effects on interviewer ratings for a given study. This makes it difficult to evaluate changes in interviewer performance over periods of several years, or even to have a satisfactory estimate of the average quality of an interviewer's work.

The methods suggested in this section are extremely simple and use only the most basic of elementary statistical techniques. Since, however, most field supervisors are non-mathematicians, these simple but useful techniques may not have occurred to them. It is evident that these are not the only possible methods, but hopefully the discussion of these methods will stimulate those who evaluate interviewers to develop quantitative methods that best suit their own needs.

Use of Coders To Evaluate Interviewers

The first method for quantifying interviewer quality does not use the judgment of the field supervisor, and might therefore be considered as a radical departure from that method. There is some evidence, however, that there is a high correlation between coders' evaluations and the more exact methods that use trained field supervisors. This method is described first because it is a low cost production method that, at very little added cost, can be made part of the coding process.

The simplest use of the coding process to evaluate interviewers is used by the Bureau of the Census. There, a code is established for a missing answer to a question. When the results of the study are tabulated, the missing answers for each interviewer are tabulated. When divided by the number of interviews, this gives a ratio of missing answers per interview. While this is only one type of error that an interviewer can make, it is an important error and does give an indication of how well instructions are being followed.

NORC uses a more detailed method by coders. Coders are supplied with error sheets on which they note the following types of interviewer errors:

Type of Error	Error Weight
1. Answer missing	3
2. Irrelevant or circular answer	3
3. Lack of sufficient detail	2
4. "Don't know" with no probe	2
5. Dangling probe	1
6. Multiple codes in error	1
7. Superfluous question asked	1

As can be seen, error weights are assigned to the types of errors depending on how seriously they lead to coding difficulties. These weights were determined by the coding and field supervisors. The list above does not exhaust all types of errors that can be made by interviewers, but includes only those that coders should be able to spot during the coding process.

Evaluation by Field Supervisors

Certain types of errors can be spotted only by field supervisors who are more familiar with the interviewing process than are coders. The same principle has been used in the supervisor's evaluation of interviewers, however, as that used by coders. A checklist of types of errors has been prepared, and weights have been assigned to errors based on their seriousness. While this list is more comprehensive, it covers much the same ground as does the coder's error list. This supervisor's check-list is shown on the next page.

To the extent that coders are able to pinpoint interviewer errors that made coding difficult, this work need not be duplicated by higher-paid field supervisors. To date, it has been our experience that coders and field supervisors agree reasonably well in their rating of interviewers.

For example, a comparison of twenty-seven interviewers on the NORC Happiness Study (Bradburn and Caplovitz, 1965) indicated a correlation of .47 between coders' and supervisors' ratings, even though the rating methods were entirely different. The supervisor rated four interviews per interviewer on the first wave of the panel study. The coders rated a section of all the questionnaires on the third wave.

Standardization for Difficulty of Study

The simple summing or averaging of error points over several studies could lead to misevaluations of interviewer quality. Studies differ greatly in length and difficulty, and simple averages would penalize those interviewers who worked on the most difficult studies, and might in fact be the better interviewers. Some method of standardizing for difficulty of study is required. One simple approach would merely be to rank interviewers by number of errors and then to translate these ranks into percentiles (to account for the varying number of interviewers on different studies).

A slightly more sensitive method is to use the method of standardized scores that is used in most psychological and educa-

---

Error Forming Criteria for Rating of Interviews

Error Weights	Type of Error
	1. Failure to probe initial:
5	a. Don't know
4	b. Vague answer
5	c. Irrelevant answer
5	d. Uncodeable answer to precoded questions
	2. Use of:
1	a. Dangling probes
1	b. Unpreceded probes
	3. Improper probing:
3	a. Accept partial answers
4	b. Use encouraging probes without using clarifying probes
2	c. Accept first clear answer without probing for additional ideas
5	d. Probe irrelevant answer instead of probing for an appropriate answer, which results in irrelevant response
5	e. Leading probe
1	4. Unexplained changes of code or answers (including erasures)
	5. Circling errors:
5	a. Contradictions
1	b. Failure to code reply when codeable side comment exists
5	c. Multiple coding
1	6. Answer recorded in wrong place
	7. Failure to complete:
5–10	a. Omitting any parts of classification. If race, sex, age or marital status is omitted along with other omissions, score is 10
5	b. Enumeration and/or sampling table
5	8. Evidence of paraphrasing (always check other interviews— given per interview, not per question)
1	9. Unclear parenthetical notes
	10. Omissions and superfluous notes:
5	a. Omitting questions (or portions of questions)
1	b. Excess questions (or portions of questions)

tional achievement tests. For each study, the mean and standard deviation of the error point distribution is computed. A standard score for each interviewer is derived from the formula:

$$\text{Standard Score} = 5 + 2 \frac{(\overline{X} - \text{Actual Score})}{S}$$

where $\overline{X}$ is the mean error score for the study, and S is the standard deviation.

To put this into words, the interviewer who is average gets a standard score of 5 for a given study; if her error score is one standard deviation below average her score is 7; if her error score is higher than average her standard score is below 5.

Standard scores can then be averaged over a series of studies to give a meaningful measure of interviewer quality. This averaging implicitly assumes that interviewer quality is not changing over time.

QUALITY-COST

It is clear that a low quality, high cost interviewer is less satisfactory than a high quality, low cost interviewer, but many cases are mixed. What of the interviewer who is high quality, high cost or low quality, low cost? Arbitrarily, we established two categories using the following definition of better quality-cost interviewers:

> High quality—any cost
> Average quality—average or low cost
> Low quality—low cost

The remaining interviewers were called poorer quality-cost.

NUMBER OF YEARS EMPLOYED AT NORC

While this figure was the easiest to derive, it is the trickiest to analyze. A major problem is due to the new NORC sample which was first used in 1962. This new sample contained some of the same large cities that were in the older sample, and interviewers in these cities were retained, while in all other places new interviewers were hired. Thus there is a confounding between years employed and location. In addition, at the other end of the scale, the most recent employees are also a mixed group. Some of them will remain with NORC for many years while others will soon resign. The only way to know would be to wait for several more years.

Finally, length of service, unlike cost or quality behavior, is to some extent dependent on acts of God. Pregnancies, moves to other areas because the husband has a new job, financial problems that require full-time employment, and increased household responsibilities are all important factors that may cause an interviewer to quit, although at times these reasons are used to hide basic job dissatisfactions.

For these reasons, the relation between personal attitudes and number of years employed is smaller than those between personal attitudes and quality and cost. In addition, the problem of changing attitudes with increasing length of employment is not fully handled. Nevertheless, we present some results to remind the reader of the importance of length of service as a measure of performance.

THE INTERVIEWER QUESTIONNAIRE

The questionnaire used to obtain information from NORC interviewers for this study is given in the Appendix (pp. 204–28). The design of this questionnaire was strongly influenced by the occupational studies which are in progress at NORC and particularly by Alice Rossi's studies of career orientation in women. Initially, we hypothesized that quality of interviewing would be related to education, intelligence, and personality characteristics. We believed that cost behavior would be related to career orientation, education and intelligence, happiness, morality, financial need, guilt about working, enjoyment of interviewing, available spare time, and involvement with other interviewers. The questionnaire attempts to tap these dimensions.

As the results below indicate, not all of the questions were useful. The starred questions on the questionnaire in the Appendix are the ones that we would suggest be tried by other survey organizations who wish to study interviewer quality and costs related to characteristics. One other point should be made clear. No NORC interviewers were ever evaluated by their supervisors based on the results of the questionnaire. The individual results were available only to the author and not to NORC's field supervisors.

THE RELATION BETWEEN QUALITY, COST, AND NUMBER OF YEARS EMPLOYED AT NORC

Before this study was started there was some fear that quality and cost would be inversely related, that the highest quality interviewers would also charge the most. As the study progressed, the reverse appeared to be true, that highest quality interviewers charged least. Now it appears that the relation is more complex. A simple cross-classification of quality and cost reveals no relation, either positive or negative, but this does not mean that the variables are independent. Rather what seems to be happening is that both quality and cost are related to other variables that neutralize each other.

High quality and low cost are both positively related to education and intelligence as will be seen in the next section. From this, one would expect a positive correlation between low cost and high quality. However, most of the career orientation variables are positively related to quality and negatively related to low cost, which results in a negative correlation between high quality and low cost. Thus, intelligence and career orientation cancel each other out. A fuller discussion of this is given in the section on career attitudes. As one might expect, however, number of years employed at NORC is positively correlated with quality and cost. The causation probably goes in both directions. Better quality-cost interviewers stay longer, and the longer an interviewer stays, the better she becomes. Certainly, there is no confirmation of the folklore that long-term interviewers become more and more costly.

Table 8.1 shows the relation between years employed at NORC and cost and quality-cost. Thirty-seven per cent of interviewers who have worked at NORC for one year or less were high cost interviewers as compared to 23 per cent among interviewers who worked at NORC for four or more years. Among interviewers with four or more years at NORC, 65 per cent were better quality-cost compared to 53 per cent of interviewers who worked a year or less.

EDUCATION AND INTELLIGENCE

It should be remembered that the NORC interviewers who are the sample for the study discussed in this chapter have already gone through a rigorous selection process. About 80 per cent have had some college and all have been judged capable of following the sometimes complex instructions which NORC sends its interviewers. It may, therefore, be a little surprising to discover that, even in this group, quality increases with increased education and intelligence, costs go down, and number of years employed goes up.

Quality

Several measures of intelligence and education were available for comparison with quality of interviewing, and since they are all highly correlated with each other they all show about the same magnitude of differences. Table 8.2 relates quality of interviewing to high school grade average, liked science subjects in high school, perceived intelligence, estimated intelligence based on a short nine-item intelligence test, and total years of school completed.

High school grade average was obtained from the interviewer directly on the questionnaire, and there is no reason to doubt the general accuracy of this self-report. Among interviewers whose

Table 8.1 High, Standard, and Low Cost, and Better and Poorer Quality-Cost Interviewers by Years Employed at NORC (Per Cent)

Cost and Quality-Cost	Years Employed		
	One Year or Less	Two–Three Years	Four Years or More
Cost:			
High	37	33	23
Medium	43	54	61
Low	20	13	16
Total	100	100	100
Base N	(103)	(198)	(76)
Quality-Cost:			
Better	53	56	65
Poorer	47	44	35
Total	100	100	100
Base N	(73)	(167)	(49)

grade average was A or A –, 56 per cent were high quality interviewers, while only 43 per cent of those whose high school average was B – or lower were high quality.

Past experience indicated a relationship between intelligence
and liking for science subjects in school which was why this item
was included. The four science subjects included in the question
were biology, chemistry, mathematics, and physics. Among interviewers who really enjoyed two or more of these subjects, 55 per
cent were high quality as compared to 42 per cent high quality
among interviewers who mentioned no science subjects.

A very simple-minded way of determining intelligence is to ask
the interviewer, "On intelligence tests that you took in school,
did you get the impression that you were very much above average, above average, or average in intelligence?" Among interviewers who perceived their intelligence to be above average or
very much above average, 52 per cent were high quality inter-

Table 8.2 Intelligence and Education Variables Related to Quality
of Interviewing (Per Cent)

Intelligence and Education	Quality			Total	Base N
	High	Average	Low		
High school grade average:					
A or A –	56	30	14	100	115
B + or B	44	34	22	100	157
B – or lower	42	38	20	100	55
Science subjects liked in high school:					
High (2 or more)	55	–	45	100	73
Medium (1)	50	–	50	100	100
Low (0)	42	–	58	100	134
Perceived intelligence:					
Very much above average	52	33	15	100	33
Above average	53	33	14	100	167
Average	36	34	30	100	97
Estimated intelligence:					
Above average	55	32	13	100	119
Average	43	39	18	100	89
Below average	45	30	25	100	118
Education level:					
Completed college	53	33	14	100	137
Some college	44	34	22	100	120
High school or less	43	33	24	100	70

viewers and 15 per cent were low quality. Among interviewers who considered themselves to be of average intelligence, only 36 per cent were high quality, and 30 per cent were low quality. This item is probably the best single discriminator of the items in Table 8.2.

Another attempt to determine intelligence was made using a nine-item similarities test adapted with permission from the Wechsler-Bellevue Intelligence Scale. Interviewers were classified into approximately equal thirds based on scores of this test. The groups are called above average, average, and below average, but this should not be confused with any reference to national norms, since almost certainly the average intelligence of interviewers is above the national average. Of the interviewers in the above-average intelligence group, 55 per cent were high quality and 13 per cent low quality. In the other groups, 44 per cent were high quality and 22 per cent low quality.

The final measure in this table is the number of years of school completed. Those interviewers who have completed college are about 10 per cent more likely to be high quality interviewers than are interviewers with some college or high school. A surprising finding here is that there is no difference in quality between those with some college and those with high school or less. Of interviewers who completed college, 53 per cent were high quality and 14 per cent low quality; among other interviewers, 44 per cent were high quality and 23 per cent low quality.

These five highly correlated characteristics were combined into an index which is called the Intelligence-Education Index. One point is given for each of the following: high school grade average A or A−, like science subjects, perceived intelligence above average, estimated intelligence above average, and completed college.

The relation between scores on this index and quality of interviewing is given in Table 8.3. Here interviewers are grouped into two categories of quality and three categories on the scale. Among interviewers who were high on the Intelligence-Education Index with 3–5 points, 60 per cent were high quality interviewers as compared to 43 per cent among interviewers who had only 0–1 points on the index.

Cost

The same variables were investigated for their relation to inter-viewer cost behavior. Some field supervisors fear that more intelligent interviewers charge more either because they might feel they deserve it, or because they are better able to cheat on time records. Just the reverse is the case. The more intelligent inter-viewers are less likely to be high cost interviewers. In retrospect, it seems clear that costs are highly related to how well the inter-viewer does her job. The more efficient she is, the lower her costs, and the more intelligent interviewers are most efficient.

Table 8.4 gives the relation between education and cost. Among interviewers who finished college, only 23 per cent were high cost interviewers, while among the others 40 per cent were high cost. An interesting reversal occurs in this table—interviewers with some college are more likely to be high cost than are interviewers with high school or less. While the reversal may be due to sam-pling variability, it may be due to characteristics of women with some college which have not yet been discovered.

Table 8.5 gives the relation between cost and the interviewer scores on the Intelligence-Education Index. Of interviewers who

Table 8.3   Intelligence-Education Index Related to Quality of Interviewing (Per Cent)

Intelligence-Education Index	Quality		Total	Base N
	High	Low		
High (3–5)	60	40	100	73
Medium (2)	54	46	100	123
Low (0–1)	43	57	100	111

Table 8.4   Education of High, Standard, and Low Cost Interviewers (Per Cent)

Education	Cost			Total	Base N
	High	Standard	Low		
Finished college	23	60	17	100	150
Some college	41	44	15	100	142
High school or less	35	50	15	100	84

are high on the Intelligence-Education Index, 18 per cent are high cost interviewers and 28 per cent are low cost. Among the other interviewers, 34 per cent are high cost and only 15 per cent low cost.

Quality-Cost

Since both quality and cost are separately related to education and intelligence, it is not surprising to see in Tables 8.6 and 8.7 that the interviewers who are high in intelligence and education are more likely to be the better quality-cost interviewers. Table 8.6 gives three of the variables in the Intelligence-Education Index: estimated intelligence, education, and high school grade average. There is also one new index, a language enjoyment index based on

Table 8.5 Intelligence-Education Index Related to High, Standard, and Low Cost Interviewers (Per Cent)

Intelligence-Education Index	Cost			Total	Base N
	High	Standard	Low		
High (3–5)	18	54	28	100	100
Medium (2)	30	55	15	100	196
Low (0–1)	39	47	14	100	134

Table 8.6 Intelligence and Education Variables Related to Better and Poorer Quality-Cost Interviewers (Per Cent)

Intelligence and Education	Quality-Cost		Total	Base N
	Better	Poorer		
Estimated intelligence:				
Above average	63	37	100	94
Average	58	42	100	85
Below average	52	48	100	108
Education:				
Finished college	62	38	100	100
Did not finish college	54	46	100	189
High school grade average:				
A or A –	65	35	100	91
B+ or lower	53	47	100	198
Language liked index:				
High (2)	62	38	100	141
Medium (1)	54	46	100	105
Low (0)	47	53	100	43

the question that asked about subjects really enjoyed in school. If both English and foreign languages were listed, the interviewer received a score of 2 on this index; if only one of the two was mentioned, the score was 1; if neither was mentioned the score was 0.

Among interviewers who were above average on the nine-item intelligence test, 63 per cent were better quality-cost, as compared to 52 per cent of below-average intelligence interviewers. Among interviewers who finished college, 62 per cent were better quality-cost, as compared to 54 per cent of the interviewers who did not finish. Sixty-five per cent of interviewers with an A or A− high school grade average were better quality-cost, compared to 53 per cent of interviewers whose average was B+ or lower.

Among interviewers who liked both English and a foreign language in school, 62 per cent were better quality-cost, while among interviewers who liked neither, only 47 per cent were better quality-cost. This variable is somewhat doubtful, since on either cost or quality separately, the differences, while in the same direction, are smaller.

Finally, Table 8.7 indicates that 72 per cent of interviewers who are high on the Intelligence-Education Index are better quality-cost as compared to 53 per cent of those who score low on this scale.

Years Employed at NORC

As seen in Table 8.1, and as expected, there is a positive relation between quality-cost and years employed at NORC. One would, therefore, expect that there would be a positive relation between

Table 8.7   Intelligence-Education Index Related to Better and Poorer Quality-Cost Interviewers (Per Cent)

Intelligence-Education Index	Quality-Cost		Total	Base N
	Better	Poorer		
High (3–5)	72	28	100	60
Medium (2)	58	42	100	113
Low (0–1)	53	47	100	106

intelligence and education and years employed, and this is the case, but the relation is considerably weaker. Table 8.8 shows that among interviewers who had finished college, 26 per cent had been at NORC for four or more years while only 17 per cent of interviewers who did not finish college had been at NORC for four or more years. Similarly, 25 per cent of interviewers who scored high on the science subjects liked index had been at NORC for more than four years compared to 14 per cent for interviewers who liked no science subject.

In Table 8.9, number of years employed at NORC is related to the Intelligence-Education Index. Of interviewers who were high on the Intelligence-Education Index, 25 per cent had been at NORC for four or more years and 19 per cent for one year or less.

Table 8.8   Intelligence and Education Variables by Years Employed at NORC (Per Cent)

Intelligence and Education	Years Employed			Total	Base N
	One Year or Less	Two–Three Years	Four Years or More		
Education:					
Finished college	26	48	26	100	150
Did not finish college	33	50	17	100	275
Science subjects liked:					
High (2 or more)	15	60	25	100	103
Medium (1)	32	45	23	100	148
Low (0)	39	47	14	100	174

Table 8.9   Intelligence-Education Index by Years Employed at NORC (Per Cent)

Intelligence-Education Index	Years Employed			Total	Base N
	One Year or Less	Two–Three Years	Four Years or More		
High (3–5)	19	56	25	100	111
Medium (2)	33	47	20	100	165
Low (0–1)	37	48	15	100	149

Of interviewers who were low on the Intelligence-Education Index, 15 per cent had been at NORC for four or more years and 37 per cent for one year or less.

NEED ACHIEVEMENT

The next variable is labeled Need Achievement as a shorthand way of describing its components; it is actually based on a question that asks interviewers which of a list of thirteen characteristics they believe are most important and least important for children to have. The question was taken from Greeley and Rossi (1966), where it served the function of measuring the degree to which Catholics support the Protestant ethic. While we expected some relation, we did not expect that this would be the variable most strongly related to quality of interviewing.

Quality

Tables 8.10 and 8.11 give the results, first in detail by question, and then summarized in a Need Achievement Index. The items included in the index are the seven characteristics shown in Table 8.10. One point was given for each of these qualities listed as most desirable:

> That he tries hard to succeed,
> That he is interested in how and why things happen.
> That he gets along well with other children,
> That he has good sense and sound judgment, and
> That he is considerate of others.

One point was also given for each of these qualities listed as least important:

> That he has good manners, and
> That he is neat and clean.

Interviewers with three or more points were classified high, those with two points were medium, and those with zero or one point were low. Among interviewers who were high on the Need Achievement Index, 66 per cent were high quality and 11 per cent low quality. On the other hand, of interviewers who were low on this scale, 41 per cent were high quality and 35 per cent were low quality.

Table 8.10 Attitudes toward Children Related to Quality of Interviewing (Per Cent)

Attitudes toward Children	Quality			Total	Base N
	High	Average	Low		
All interviewers	48	33	19	100	377
Should try hard to succeed	63	26	11	100	35
Should have good sense and sound judgment	50	33	17	100	159
Should get along well with other children	53	35	12	100	60
Should be considerate of others	49	36	15	100	119
Should be interested in how and why things happen	50	34	16	100	155
Least important that they have good manners	53	29	18	100	113
Least important that they be neat and clean	52	34	14	100	192

Quality-Cost

There is no apparent connection between need achievement and cost behavior, so that the relation between quality-cost and need achievement is the same as between quality and need achievement. This is seen in Table 8.12, where 71 per cent of the interviewers high on need achievement are better quality-cost as compared to 46 per cent of interviewers low on need achievement. Finally, there is no evidence of any relation between need achievement and number of years employed at NORC.

CAREER ATTITUDES

One of our initial hypotheses in preparing the questionnaire was that career-oriented women would be higher cost interviewers than traditional women. We used a series of items developed by A. Rossi for a study now in progress from which the following ten items were combined into three subindexes: household attitudes, marital attitudes, and child-rearing attitudes. These three subindexes were then combined to form the Career Orientation Index. The items used on the indexes are given on the next page.

Table 8.11   Need Achievement Index Related to Quality of Interviewing (Per Cent)

Need Achievement Index	Quality			Total	Base N
	High	Average	Low		
High (3 or more)	66	23	11	100	59
Medium (2)	53	26	21	100	113
Low (0–1)	41	24	35	100	132

Table 8.12   Need Achievement Index of Better and Poorer Quality-Cost Interviewers (Per Cent)

Need Achievement Index	Quality-Cost		Total	Base N
	Better	Poorer		
High (3 or more)	71	29	100	55
Medium (2)	62	38	100	109
Low (0–1)	46	54	100	125

Household Attitudes

1. Answered "No" to, "During the past few weeks, have you ever felt that you were not the kind of wife you would like to be?"

2. Answered "No" to, "During the past few weeks have you ever felt that you were not the kind of mother you would like to be?"

3. Answered "Moderate amount or quite a lot" to, "On the whole would you say that you spend quite a lot of time, a moderate amount of time or relatively little time doing things together with your husband?"

4. Answered "Strongly in favor" to, "Generally, how does your husband feel about your work as an interviewer?"

These four items all ask the interviewer about her guilt feelings because she is employed. The other two subindexes deal with more general attitudes on career and marriage:

Marital Attitudes

1. Agree that one of the most important things for a happy marriage is for a man and woman to be equal in intelligence.

2. Disagree that if a wife earns more money than her husband, the marriage is headed for trouble.

3. Disagree that a married woman can't make long-range plans for her own career because they depend on her husband's plans for his.

Child-rearing Attitudes

1. Agree that a preschool child is likely to suffer emotional damage if his mother works.

2. Agree that even if a woman has the ability and interest she should not choose a career field that will be difficult to combine with child rearing.

3. Agree that a working mother cannot establish as warm and secure a relationship with her children as a mother who does not work.

While these last two indexes are highly correlated, the relationship is inverse. That is, a high career orientation is indicated by a high score on the Marital Attitudes Index and a low one on the Child-rearing Attitudes Index.

For all indexes one point is given to each response. The Career Orientation Index is obtained by summing the first two subindexes and subtracting the Child-rearing Index score.

Quality

Tables 8.13 and 8.14 give the relation between quality of interviewing and the Child-rearing Attitudes items and subindex, and Table 8.15 gives the relation between quality of interviewing and the Career Orientation Index. These tables say that high quality interviewers are more likely to have high career orientation. Of interviewers who score low on the Child-rearing Attitude Index and are thus high in career orientation, 62 per cent are high quality interviewers, as compared to 42 per cent of those scoring high on this index. The same relations are observed on the other

Table 8.13 Child-rearing Attitudes Related to Quality of Interviewing (Per Cent)

Child-rearing Attitudes	Quality			Total	Base N
	High	Average	Low		
All interviewers	48	33	19	100	328
A pre-school child is likely to suffer emotional damage if his mother works.	44	25	31	100	116
Even if a woman has the ability and interest she should not choose a career field that will be difficult to combine with child-rearing.	43	34	23	100	184
A working mother cannot establish as warm and secure a relationship with her children as a mother who does not work.	43	29	28	100	68

Table 8.14 Child-rearing Index Related to Quality of Interviewing (Per Cent)

Child-rearing Index	Quality			Total	Base N
	High	Average	Low		
High (2–3)	42	25	33	100	103
Medium (1)	50	26	24	100	116
Low (0)	62	21	17	100	84

two subindexes, but the differences are small. On the combined index, the relationship is seen even more clearly. Of interviewers with a high score (4 or more) on the Career Orientation Index, 61 per cent were high quality interviewers while only 36 per cent of those scoring low on this index were high quality.

Cost

Thus far, high career orientation is related to high quality interviewing, but, unfortunately, it is also related to high costs, as we hypothesized. The results are given in Tables 8.16–8.18, which first give the relation between cost and the individual items, then between cost and the subindexes, and finally between cost and Career Orientation. The relation may be seen most clearly in Table 8.18 where the Career Orientation Index is cross-classified with cost. Of interviewers who are high on the Career Orientation Index, 46 per cent are high cost interviewers as compared to 30 per cent of those who are medium or low on Career Orientation. The same differences are found on the Household Attitudes sub-index and the Marital Attitudes subindex in Table 8.17, but no differences are seen on the Child-rearing Attitude Index.

Quality-Cost

Since quality and cost are both positively related to career orientation, one would expect that these would cancel each other and that there would be no apparent relation between career orientation and the combined quality-cost characteristic. This is confirmed in Table 8.20, but strangely Table 8.19 suggests that there is still some correlation between quality-cost and two of the

Table 8.15 Career Orientation Index Related to Quality of Interviewing (Per Cent)

Career-orientation Index	Quality		Total	Base N
	High	Low		
High (4 or more)	61	39	100	54
Medium (2–3)	52	48	100	141
Low (1 or less)	36	64	100	112

Table 8.16 Child-rearing, Household, and Marital Attitudes Related to High, Standard, and Low Cost Interviewers (Per Cent)

Attitudes	Cost			Total	Base N
	High	Standard	Low		
All interviewers	32	52	16	100	377
Household Attitudes:					
Felt that I was the kind of mother I would like to be	37	46	17	100	161
Felt that I was the kind of wife I would like to be	36	53	11	100	172
Spend more than a moderate amount of time doing things together with my husband	34	52	14	100	309
My husband strongly in favor about my work as an interviewer	39	52	9	100	140
Marital Attitudes:					
One of the most important things for a happy marriage is for a man and a woman to be equal in intelligence	35	52	13	100	252
Disagree—if a wife earns more money than her husband, the marriage is headed for trouble	38	48	14	100	141
Disagree—a married woman can't make long-range plans for her own career because they depend on her husband's plans for his	36	51	13	100	236
Child-rearing Attitudes:					
A pre-school child is likely to suffer emotional damage if his mother works	40	41	19	100	172
Even if a woman has the ability and interest she should not choose a career field that will be difficult to combine with child-rearing	35	52	13	100	217
A working mother cannot establish as warm and secure a relationship with her children as a mother who does not work	33	52	15	100	84

Table 8.17 Child-rearing, Household, and Marital Attitude Indexes
Related to High, Standard, and Low Cost Interviewers (Per Cent)

Attitude Indexes	Cost			Total	Base N
	High	Standard	Low		
Household Attitude Index:					
High (3–4)	40	50	10	100	145
Medium (2)	28	56	16	100	105
Low (0–1)	26	53	21	100	127
Marital Attitude Index:					
High (2–3)	43	43	14	100	104
Medium (1)	29	57	14	100	169
Low (0)	27	52	21	100	104
Child-rearing Attitude Index:					
High (2–3)	33	50	17	100	127
Medium (1)	31	57	12	100	142
Low (0)	32	49	19	100	108

Table 8.18 Career Orientation Index Related to High, Standard,
and Low Cost Interviewers (Per Cent)

Career-orientation Index	Cost			Total	Base N
	High	Standard	Low		
High (4 or more)	46	42	12	100	67
Medium (2–3)	30	55	15	100	168
Low (1 or less)	29	52	19	100	143

Table 8.19 Child-rearing and Household Attitude Indexes Related
to Better and Poorer Quality-Cost Interviewers (Per Cent)

Attitude Indexes	Quality-Cost		Total	Base N
	Better	Poorer		
Child-rearing:				
High (2–3)	52	48	100	96
Medium (1)	54	46	100	113
Low (0)	66	34	100	80
Household:				
High (3–4)	52	48	100	118
Medium (2)	57	43	100	82
Low (0–1)	63	37	100	89

subindexes. Since the Child-rearing Attitude Index was unrelated to cost while related to quality, it is not too surprising to find that 66 per cent of those interviewers who were low on this index (where a low score meant high career orientation) were better quality-cost interviewers as compared to about 53 per cent of other interviewers.

For the Household Attitudes Index, where one might expect that the cost and quality relations would cancel each other, we now find a negative relation between quality-cost and score. Of interviewers scoring high on this index, 52 per cent are better quality-cost, while of interviewers scoring low, 63 per cent are better quality-cost. Here, the cost behavior seems to dominate, although this difference could certainly be due to sampling error.

Years Employed at NORC

As might be expected from the preceding discussion, there is hardly any relation between years employed at NORC and career orientation. The Career Orientation Index shows no differences by length of time employed. The only one of the subindexes that shows anything is the Household Attitude Index, which we suggested measures guilt feelings about interviewing. Table 8.21 indicates that interviewers who have been at NORC for four or more years are somewhat more likely to have higher guilt feelings; 25 per cent of interviewers who are low on the index (high in guilt) have been at NORC for four or more years, as compared to 15 per cent of interviewers high on this index. While there is no way of knowing the cause-effect direction, it is more likely that guilt increases somewhat with length of employment rather than length of employment increasing as interviewers feel guiltier.

Table 8.20 Career Orientation Index Related to Better and Poorer Quality-Cost Interviewers (Per Cent)

Career-orientation Index	Quality-Cost		Total	Base N
	Better	Poorer		
High (4 or more)	57	43	100	53
Medium (2–3)	61	39	100	131
Low (1 or less)	51	49	100	105

While the career orientation items are interesting to analyze, because of their mixed behavior they are not very useful for predicting the value of an interviewer. Only the Child-rearing Attitude Index seems to be of much use, since it is positively related to quality and does not seem to be related to cost behavior.

ATTITUDES TOWARD INTERVIEWING AND INTERVIEWING ACTIVITIES

Most of the variables we have discussed so far were probably not influenced by our interviewers' job experiences, but some such as guilt feelings about working may be. Attitudes toward interviewing, on the other hand, may be present at the time the interviewer is first hired, but are more likely to develop through experience. If this is so, then these are not good variables for measuring interviewer value, since after the interviewer is hired there are direct measures of cost and quality behavior. We discuss them here, however, since we are not certain that these attitudes were not present when the interviewer was hired.

As with career attitudes, enthusiasm for interviewing is seen both in high cost and in high quality interviewers, but seems to be more related to cost than to quality. There seem to be two factors which are only slightly correlated. The first is an enjoyment of interviewing activities. This is related to both high cost and quality. The other is an attitude toward interviewing that views interviewing as a stepping-stone to another job or as a high prestige part-time occupation. This factor is positively related to high cost and negatively to quality. Neither of the factors are strongly related to number of years employed.

Table 8.21 Household Attitudes Index Related to Years Employed at NORC (Per Cent)

Household Attitudes Index	Years Employed			Total	Base N
	One Year or Less	Two– Three Years	Four Years or More		
High (3–4)	32	53	15	100	162
Medium (2)	31	48	21	100	116
Low (0–1)	29	46	25	100	147

The first factor is described in an Interviewing Activities Index. One point is given on this index for each of the following answers:

Prefer a questionnaire that has a great many open-ended questions,

Like study and training very much,

Like editing very much,

Like field counting very much,

Like listing very much, and

Find maps very easy to read.

The second factor is described in an Attitudes toward Interviewing Index. One point is given for each of the following responses:

See interviewing as a stepping-stone to another job,

Interviewing provides an excellent opportunity to be helpful to others,

Love interviewing and look forward to every assignment,

No other employment now besides interviewing,

Would like a full-time career if I had the opportunity,

Not nervous at all when someone first opens the door at an assigned household,

Plan to continue interviewing indefinitely, and

Interviewing provides me an excellent opportunity to use my special abilities or aptitudes.

Quality

Tables 8.22 and 8.23 show the relation between quality and attitudes toward interviewing and interviewing activity. It may be seen in Table 8.22 that of interviewers who were low on the Inter-

Table 8.22 Enjoyment of Interviewing Activities Index Related to Quality of Interviewing (Per Cent)

Interviewing Activities Index	Quality		Total	Base N
	High	Low		
High (3 or more)	52	48	100	88
Medium (2)	54	46	100	84
Low (0–1)	41	59	100	125

viewing Activities Index, 41 per cent are high quality interviewers, as compared to 53 per cent for those who were medium or high on this index. The reverse is the case on the Attitudes toward Interviewing Index. Table 8.23 suggests that the least enthusiastic respondents are likely to be the higher quality interviewers. Of interviewers low on the Attitudes toward Interviewing Index, 59 per cent are high quality as compared to about 50 per cent for those who are medium or high on this index.

Cost

Tables 8.24 and 8.25 indicate that the relation between high cost and enjoyment of interviewing activities is stronger than the relation between high quality and interviewing activities. Of inter-

Table 8.23 Attitudes toward Interviewing Index Related to Quality of Interviewing (Per Cent)

Attitudes toward Interviewing Index	Quality		Total	Base N
	High	Low		
High (5 or more)	52	48	100	105
Medium (3–4)	47	53	100	120
Low (0–2)	59	41	100	82

Table 8.24 Enjoyment of Interviewing Activities by High, Standard, and Low Cost Interviewers (Per Cent)

Attitude	Cost			Total	Base N
	High	Standard	Low		
All interviewers	32	52	16	100	377
Like field counting very much	37	51	12	100	59
Like listing very much	35	52	13	100	85
Like editing very much	46	42	12	100	113
Like study and training very much	36	48	16	100	220
Prefer questionnaire with great many open-ended questions	37	48	15	100	146
Find maps very easy to read	38	47	15	100	136

viewers who are high on the Interviewing Activities Index, 43 per cent are high cost interviewers as compared to 25 per cent of interviewers low on this index. As is seen in Table 8.24 where the separate items of this index are presented, the single item most highly related to high cost is enjoyment of editing a questionnaire for clarity after the interview is completed.

A stronger relation is found between attitudes toward interviewing and costs, as shown in Tables 8.26 and 8.27. Among interviewers who are high on the Attitudes toward Interviewing Index, 45 per cent are high cost interviewers, as compared to 19 per cent of interviewers who are high cost among those who are low on this index. The separate items are given in Table 8.26, and it may be seen that the strongest relation is on the item "see interviewing as a stepping-stone to another job."

Quality-Cost

Since both quality and cost are positively related to the Interviewing Activities Index, they cancel each other and there is no net effect. The relation between attitudes toward interviewing and quality-cost is still present, although weaker than the relation with costs alone. Table 8.28 shows that 48 per cent of interviewers scoring high on the Attitudes toward Interviewing Index are better quality-cost, as compared to the 61 per cent who are better quality-cost among those who are low on this index.

Another item that seems related to quality and cost, but not much related to each separately is the interviewer's perception of the prestige of being an interviewer. The respondents were asked whether they believed that interviewing was higher, lower, or

Table 8.25 Enjoyment of Interviewing Activities Index by High, Standard, and Low Cost Interviewers (Per Cent)

Enjoyment of Interviewing Activities Index	Cost			Total	Base N
	High	Standard	Low		
High (3 or more)	43	43	14	100	132
Medium (2)	29	55	16	100	96
Low (0–1)	25	58	17	100	149

about the same in prestige as artist, public school teacher, playground director, waitress, nurse, singer in night club, clothes presser in a laundry, saleslady in a store, welfare worker, chemist, and owner-operator of a lunch stand. An answer for a given occupation was scored two if the respondent rated interviewing higher

Table 8.26 Attitudes toward Interviewing Related to High, Standard, and Low Cost Interviewers (Per Cent)

Attitude	Cost			Total	Base N
	High	Standard	Low		
All interviewers	32	52	16	100	377
I would like a full-time career if I had the opportunity	36	51	13	100	157
Interviewing provides an excellent opportunity to use my special abilities or aptitudes	35	51	14	100	217
Interviewing provides an excellent opportunity to be helpful to others	40	44	16	100	121
No other employment now besides interviewing	37	48	15	100	245
Plan to continue interviewing indefinitely	35	51	14	100	297
See interviewing as a stepping-stone to another job	44	38	18	100	67
Not nervous at all when someone first opens the door at assigned household	37	53	10	100	188
I love interviewing and look forward to every assignment	39	49	12	100	132

Table 8.27 Attitudes toward Interviewing Index Related to High, Standard, and Low Cost Interviewers (Per Cent)

Attitudes toward Interviewing Index	Cost			Total	Base N
	High	Standard	Low		
High (5 or more)	45	43	12	100	130
Medium (3–4)	30	55	15	100	152
Low (0–2)	19	59	22	100	95

than most other interviewers, zero if interviewing was rated lower than most respondents rated it, and one if rated the way other respondents rated it. Of interviewers who were high on the Interviewer Prestige Index, 52 per cent were better quality-cost interviewers as compared to 64 per cent who were better quality-cost among interviewers who were low on this index. These results are given in Table 8.29.

Years Employed at NORC

Only the Attitudes toward Interviewing Index seems related to years employed at NORC. Table 8.30 shows that among interviewers who are high on this index, 82 per cent have been with NORC for more than one year and 24 per cent for four years or more. On the other hand, of interviewers low on this scale, 64 per cent have been with NORC for more than a year and 17 per cent for more than four years. Again the direction of the cause-effect relation is unclear. Does longevity cause enthusiasm, or does enthusiasm cause longevity?

In general, none of the measures in this section gives a clear-cut

Table 8.28 Attitudes toward Interviewing Index Related to Better and Poorer Quality-Cost Interviewers (Per Cent)

Attitudes toward Interviewing Index	Better Quality-Cost	Poorer Quality-Cost	Total	Base N
High (5 or more)	48	52	100	100
Medium (3–4)	61	39	100	115
Low (0–2)	61	39	100	74

Table 8.29 Interviewer Prestige of Better and Poorer Quality-Cost Interviewers (Per Cent)

Interviewer Prestige	Quality-Cost		Total	Base N
	Better	Poorer		
High (14 or more)	52	48	100	101
Medium (11–13)	55	45	100	114
Low (10 or less)	64	36	100	74

prediction of the value of an interviewer. Enjoyment of interviewing tasks as opposed to the glamour and prestige of being an interviewer is likely to mean that the interviewer will be high quality, but also high cost. The applicant who is attracted by the glamour of the job is likely to be a poorer quality-cost interviewer, but may be more likely to remain an interviewer. To confirm this, it will be necessary to ask these questions of applicants, rather than experienced interviewers.

PREVIOUS EXPERIENCE AND KNOWLEDGE OF OTHER INTERVIEWERS

Many field organizations have strong policies on hiring or not hiring interviewers with experience at other organizations. It is either argued that experienced interviewers will be more skillful or that they will be more costly because they have had different training and have acquired bad habits. Sheatsley (1950) found little relation between past experience and quality, nor do we in this study. We do find, however, that interviewers who have worked for other organizations are somewhat more likely to be high cost interviewers, as shown in Table 8.31. Among interviewers with past experience, 38 per cent are high cost as compared to 28 per cent high cost among interviewers with no past experience.

There is also some tendency for interviewers who know other interviewers to be high cost. The measure of interviewer contact with other interviewers is obtained by summing the number of other NORC interviewers with whom the respondent gets together

Table 8.30 Attitudes toward Interviewing Index by Years Employed at NORC (Per Cent)

Attitudes toward Interviewing Index	Years Employed			Total	Base N
	One Year or Less	Two–Three Years	Four Years or More		
High (5 or more)	18	58	24	100	101
Medium (3–4)	33	47	20	100	189
Low (0–2)	36	47	17	100	135

socially and the number of interviewers for other survey organizations whom she knows.

Table 8.32 shows that 40 per cent of interviewers who know five or more other interviewers are high cost as compared to 29 per cent high cost among interviewers who know only one or no other interviewers. Essentially the same thing is seen in Table 8.33 where only the number of non-NORC interviewers known is related to cost.

Since interviewers known is not related to quality, the relation still holds comparing interviewers known to quality-cost. Table 8.34 shows that 54 per cent of interviewers who know five or more

Table 8.31 Previous Interviewing Experience by High, Standard, and Low Cost Interviewers (Per Cent)

| Previous Experience | Cost | | | Total | Base N |
	High	Standard	Low		
Yes	38	52	10	100	158
No	28	52	20	100	219

Table 8.32 Total Interviewers Known by High, Standard, and Low Cost Interviewers (Per Cent)

| Total Interviewers Known | Cost | | | Total | Base N |
	High	Standard	Low		
5 or more	40	51	9	100	107
2–4	32	53	15	100	143
0–1	29	51	20	100	127

Table 8.33 Non-NORC Interviewers Known by High, Standard, and Low Cost Interviewers (Per Cent)

| Non-NORC Interviewers Known | Cost | | | Total | Base N |
	High	Standard	Low		
4 or more	37	54	9	100	113
1–3	32	53	15	100	137
0	29	49	22	100	127

other interviewers are better quality-cost, while 63 per cent of those who know only one or no other interviewer are better quality-cost interviewers.

FAMILY RESPONSIBILITY

The common practice among survey research organizations is to avoid hiring applicants with heavy family responsibilities because of the fear that they will not have the time to complete assignments, and will be more likely to quit. While our results confirm this, they also indicate that interviewers with heavy family responsibilities are less likely to be high cost interviewers and more likely to be better quality-cost. This would suggest that heavy family responsibilities not be an automatic cause of rejection.

The Family Responsibility Index was obtained by counting one point for each child in the household and adding one point for a yes answer to the question, "Do you feel obliged to spend substantial amounts of time with relatives other than your husband or children?" Clearly, number of children and family responsibility are very highly correlated. This may be seen in Tables 8.35 and

Table 8.34 Total Interviewers Known by Better and Poorer Quality-Cost Interviewers (Per Cent)

Total Interviewers Known	Quality-Cost		Total	Base N
	Better	Poorer		
5 or more	54	46	100	85
2–4	54	46	100	108
0–1	63	37	100	96

Table 8.35 Family Responsibility by High, Standard, and Low Cost Interviewers (Per Cent)

Family Responsibility	Cost			Total	Base N
	High	Standard	Low		
High (4 or more adults or children)	22	61	17	100	94
Medium (2–3)	36	49	15	100	214
Low (0–1)	35	51	14	100	69

8.36, which relate first family responsibility, then number of children to cost. Twenty-two per cent of interviewers with responsibility for four or more adults or children are high cost interviewers as compared to 35 per cent high cost for those with responsibility for one or no persons.

Since family responsibility is not related to quality, one would expect to see a relation to quality-cost. This is given in Table 8.37, which shows that 66 per cent of interviewers with high family responsibility are better quality-cost as compared to 50 per cent with low family responsibility.

The fly in the ointment is that interviewers with heavy responsibilities are more likely to resign. Table 8.38 shows that among interviewers with high family responsibilities, only 21 per cent have been with NORC for four or more years while 34 per cent have been here a year or less. Among interviewers with low family responsibilities, 34 per cent have been at NORC for four or more years and 19 per cent for less than a year. Thus, differential resignation rates counteract reduced costs, so that family responsibility is not a good measure of the value of an interviewer.

Table 8.36 Number of Children by High, Standard, and Low Cost Interviewers (Per Cent)

Number of Children	Cost			Total	Base N
	High	Standard	Low		
0–1	35	48	17	100	82
2–3	34	50	16	100	224
4 or more	22	65	13	100	68

Table 8.37 Family Responsibility by Better and Poorer Quality-Cost Interviewers (Per Cent)

Family Responsibility	Quality-Cost		Total	Base N
	Better	Poorer		
High (4 or more adults or children)	66	34	100	65
Medium (2–3)	58	42	100	165
Low (0–1)	50	50	100	48

EFFICIENCY AND SELF-SUFFICIENCY

Efficiency in planning should be reflected by lower interviewing costs, and our results confirm this. An efficiency index was developed based on one point for each of the following responses:

Self-rating of more efficient when asked, "Compared to most other women you know how efficient would you say you are?"

Generally plan week's menus in advance;

Prefer to do everyday cooking myself all the time;

Prefer to do cooking for special occasions myself all the time;

Prefer hired help all the time for weekly household cleaning; and

Prefer to read a road map rather than ask someone how to get there when going some place new.

It can be seen that the items measure not only efficiency, but also self-sufficiency with these two characteristics being highly correlated.

While neither quality nor cost alone are highly related to this index, Table 8.39 shows that there is a relation between efficiency and the quality-cost variable. Of interviewers who are high on this index, 63 per cent are better quality-cost interviewers as compared to 50 per cent among those low on the Efficiency Index.

Table 8.40 suggests that there is a relation between years employed at NORC and efficiency. Among interviewers high on the Efficiency Index, one-third have been at NORC for four or more

Table 8.38 Family Responsibility by Years Employed at NORC (Per Cent)

Family Responsibility	Years Employed			Total	Base N
	One Year or Less	Two–Three Years	Four Years or More		
High (4 or more adults and children)	34	45	21	100	100
Medium (2–3)	33	52	15	100	248
Low (0–1)	19	47	34	100	77

years and 27 per cent for a year or less. Among interviewers low on the Efficiency Index, 21 per cent have been at NORC for four or more years and 43 per cent for a year or less. Again, it is possible that greater efficiency is due to the demands of interviewing, rather than efficiency causing longevity.

ACTIVITIES ENJOYED

Interviewers were asked for a list of sixteen activities—either that they personally enjoyed or that they thought they would enjoy if they had the opportunity to engage in them. An Activities Enjoyed Index, which correlated highly, was developed from the items. As will be seen, most of the items deal with outdoors activities, which seems reasonable since a part of interviewing requires walking from house to house. The items on the index each given one point are: mountain climbing, skiing, gardening, tennis, golf, making a speech, gossiping, and building furniture.

A Sports Activities Enjoyed subindex was also derived using only the first five items on the list.

Table 8.39 Efficiency Index by Better and Poorer Quality-Cost Interviewers (Per Cent)

Efficiency Index	Quality-Cost		Total	Base N
	Better	Poorer		
High (4 or more)	63	37	100	83
Medium (2–3)	56	44	100	156
Low (0–1)	50	50	100	50

Table 8.40 Efficiency Index by Years Employed at NORC (Per Cent)

Efficiency Index	Years Employed			Total	Base N
	One Year or Less	Two–Three Years	Four Years or More		
High (4 or more)	27	50	33	100	125
Medium (2–3)	29	53	18	100	233
Low (0–1)	43	36	21	100	67

Quality

Tables 8.41 and 8.42 show that there is a positive, but rather weak relation between quality and the Activities Enjoyed and Sports Enjoyed indexes. Among interviewers who enjoyed more than five of the activities, 51 per cent were high quality as compared to 43 per cent of interviewers who enjoyed four or fewer of the activities. Similarly, among interviewers who enjoyed four or five sports activities, 55 per cent were high quality as compared to 44 per cent high quality among interviewers who enjoyed three or less sports.

Cost

For a pleasant change, the Activities Enjoyed Index is negatively related to cost so that it adds to rather than cancelling the quality measure. As seen in Table 8.43, of interviewers who were high on the Activities Enjoyed Index, 24 per cent were high cost as compared to 37 per cent among interviewers low on this index.

Table 8.41   Activities Enjoyed Index Related to Quality of Interviewing (Per Cent)

Activities Enjoyed Index	Quality		Total	Base N
	High	Low		
High (7 or more)	51	49	100	68
Medium (5–6)	52	48	100	110
Low (4 or less)	43	57	100	129

Table 8.42   Sports Activities Enjoyed Index Related to Quality of Interviewing (Per Cent)

Sports Enjoyed Index	Quality		Total	Base N
	High	Low		
High (4–5)	55	45	100	114
Medium (2–3)	43	57	100	127
Low (0–1)	44	56	100	66

Quality-Cost

Table 8.44 relates activities enjoyed to quality-cost. Of interviewers who enjoyed five or more of the activities on the index, 63 per cent are better quality-cost interviewers as compared to 48 per cent of those who enjoyed four or less activities. Again, most of this is related to enjoyment of sports. Table 8.45 shows that 64 per cent of interviewers who enjoy four or more sports are better quality-cost interviewers as compared to 53 per cent of those who enjoy three or less sports.

Although there is no relation between activities enjoyed and

Table 8.43 Activities Enjoyed Index by High, Standard, and Low Cost Interviewers (Per Cent)

Activities Enjoyed Index	Cost			Total	Base N
	High	Standard	Low		
High (7 or more)	24	56	20	100	91
Medium (5–6)	32	52	16	100	125
Low (4 or less)	37	50	13	100	161

Table 8.44 Activities Enjoyed Index by Better and Poorer Quality-Cost Interviewers (Per Cent)

Activities Enjoyed Index	Quality-Cost		Total	Base N
	Better	Poorer		
High (7 or more)	61	39	100	66
Medium (5–6)	65	35	100	103
Low (4 or less)	48	52	100	120

Table 8.45 Sports Activities Enjoyed Index by Better and Poorer Quality-Cost Interviewers (Per Cent)

Sports Enjoyed Index	Quality-Cost		Total	Base N
	Better	Poorer		
High (4–5)	64	36	100	62
Medium (2–3)	53	47	100	121
Low (0–1)	52	48	100	106

number of years employed at NORC, this variable does seem useful in discriminating between better and poorer quality-cost interviewers.

POLITICAL PARTY PREFERENCE

Survey organizations have sometimes attempted to control for party preferences of their interviewers, particularly on political surveys where this is a relevant factor. There is no reason to believe that party preference would be useful as a selection device, but our measures of interviewer value are all related to party preference, although none of the relations are particularly impressive. Since party preference is known to depend heavily on geographic and socioeconomic variables, we would like to explore these, but our sample size and questionnaire design do not permit this. The results of this section should be treated cautiously—we are certainly not suggesting that Democrats not be hired as interviewers.

The relations between party preference and the measures of interviewer value are given in Tables 8.46–8.49. Table 8.46 relates party preference and quality. Among Democrats, 43 per cent are high quality interviewers as compared to 52 per cent among Re-

Table 8.46 Political Party Preferences Related to Quality of Interviewing (Per Cent)

| Party Preference | Quality | | Total | Base N |
	High	Low		
Democratic	43	57	100	150
Republican and others	52	48	100	157

Table 8.47 Political Party Preferences Related to High, Standard, and Low Cost Interviewers (Per Cent)

| Party Preference | Cost | | | Total | Base N |
	High	Standard	Low		
Democratic	37	48	15	100	188
Republican and others	27	56	17	100	186

publicans and others. In Table 8.47, which relates party preference and cost behavior, it can be seen that 37 per cent of the Democrats are high cost as compared to 27 per cent of the Republicans and others.

Combining these two results, Table 8.48 indicates that 63 per cent of Republicans and others are better quality-cost interviewers, while 50 per cent of the Democrats are better quality-cost. Finally, Table 8.49 relates party preference to number of years employed. A mixed picture is seen, with Democrats more likely to be new interviewers or those who have worked for NORC for four years or more. Our sample is too small to determine the reasons for this distribution but these facts should be considered. Those interviewers who have worked for four years or more are most likely from the largest cities that were in the old NORC sample and are in the current sample. These largest cities are probably more likely to have a higher proportion of Democrats. Among interviewers who were recruited for the new sample, the ones who have remained longer seem more likely to be Republicans, but this too

Table 8.48 Political Party Preferences Related to Better and Poorer Quality-Cost Interviewers (Per Cent)

Party Preference	Quality-Cost		Total	Base N
	Better	Poorer		
Democratic	50	50	100	139
Republican and others	63	37	100	150

Table 8.49 Political Party Preferences Related to Years Employed at NORC (Per Cent)

Party Preference	Years Employed			Total	Base N
	One Year or Less	Two–Three Years	Four Years or More		
Democratic	39	23	38	100	203
Republican and others	23	54	23	100	222

may be due to size of community. The smaller towns and rural areas, which are the easiest to interview in and where opportunities for other employment are limited, are more likely to be Republican. Possibly, the same sort of reasoning explains the quality and cost differences related to party preference, and some of the other relations in earlier sections.

MACHIAVELLIANISM

The Machiavellian scales have been developed by Christie and Merton (1958) as a measure of the tendency to manipulate other people. The first two questions of the interviewer questionnaire form the basis for two scales known as Mach I and Mach II. Mach I does not discriminate well on highly educated groups, nor did it discriminate between any of the measures of interviewer value. Mach II, the second question, is based on a series of forced choice items. In general, respondents dislike these kinds of questions, and this one caused the most complaints among interviewers, but it did produce an interesting finding.

We had thought that interviewers high on the Mach scales would be high cost interviewers since they might attempt to manipulate NORC. Just the reverse turned out to be true as can be seen in Table 8.50. Of interviewers high on the Mach II Scale, 66 per cent were better quality-cost as compared to 51 per cent who were better among interviewers low on the Mach II.

Since differences in quality are slight, this is mostly due to differences in cost. In other words, if any one is being manipulated, it is the respondent and not the research organization.

Table 8.50 Machiavellianism by Better and Poorer Quality-Cost Interviewers (Per Cent)

Machiavellian Scale	Quality-Cost		Total	Base N
	Better	Poorer		
High (5 or more)	66	34	100	83
Medium (3–4)	54	46	100	105
Low (2 or less)	51	49	100	101

PERCEIVED QUALITY AND COST

The final two tables demonstrate a strong relation between perception and behavior. The best interviewers know it, and the high cost interviewers know it too. These perceptions are obtained from contact with supervisors and with other interviewers. It is possible, however, that applicants may be able to predict their quality and cost behavior when hired, and if so then self-perception might be the best predictor of interviewer value.

The quality perception question asked, "How good an interviewer do you think you are?" Of interviewers who said "One of the very best," 75 per cent were high quality as compared to 41 per cent among those who were average or below, as is shown in Table 8.51. Note, however, the small case base for interviewers claiming to be one of the very best.

The cost perception question asked, "How do you think your costs compare to those of other interviewers in your area?" Table 8.52 indicates that 77 per cent of interviewers who thought that their costs were above average were high cost interviewers as compared to 14 per cent who thought their costs below average.

Table 8.51 Perceived and Actual Quality of Interviewing (Per Cent)

Perceived Quality	Quality			Total	Base N
	High	Average	Low		
I am one of the very best	75	8	17	100	24
I am above average	49	41	10	100	156
I am average or below	41	30	29	100	143

Table 8.52 Perceived Costs by High, Standard, and Low Cost Interviewers (Per Cent)

Perceived Cost	Cost			Total	Base N
	High	Standard	Low		
My costs are above average	77	23	0	100	22
My costs are average	32	52	16	100	268
My costs are below average	14	60	26	100	42

Again, however, the case bases for both above and below average are small.

SOME VARIABLES THAT DON'T WORK

In this section we list the other variables included in the questionnaire that did not appear to be related to any of the measures of interviewer value.

Happiness.—We had thought that less happy interviewers would charge more than happy ones or be lower quality interviewers, but there were no differences.

Financial need.—An attempt was made to measure financial need with the idea that interviewers with strong financial needs would charge more than those without these needs, or that need might be related to length of service. We found, however, that hardly any NORC interviewers have pressing financial needs or admit to working for this reason. Nor are any differences seen in the interviewer value measures when total family income or husband's occupation is used.

Membership in other organizations.—Almost all interviewers are active in many other organizations so this variable cannot be related to anything else.

Religious behavior.—We could find no differences in quality or cost related to either denomination or religiousness.

Perfectionism.—No table is given, but there is a weak relation between perfectionism and cost. Of interviewers who like to see the job done perfectly, 37 per cent are high cost interviewers as compared to 29 per cent among interviewers who are satisfied if the job is done well but less than perfectly.

Size of place where raised.—There was no relation between the value measures and whether the interviewer was brought up mostly on a farm, in a town, in a small city, in a large city or in a suburb of a large city.

COMBINATIONS OF VARIABLES

If the sample size were larger, the next step in the analysis would be to cross-classify our interviewing variables with combinations of the independent variables. Since this is not possible, a multiple regression procedure is used. This procedure is used, not because it solves the problems of the small samples, but because the computer programs are well developed and regression lines can be computed quickly and cheaply.

The problem of discriminating between groups on the basis of a series of items is far from solved theoretically. Readers with some mathematics background will be interested in Solomon's *Studies in Item Analysis and Prediction* (1961) and particularly in the detailed discussion of Anderson's *W* statistic, which is related to the multiple regression technique.

Further, most of the variables we consider are qualitative rather than quantitative, and there are serious doubts that the normality and linearity assumptions are met. Finally, the small size and the peculiarities of our sample and our search procedure for explanatory variables would certainly keep the results from holding exactly true for other populations.

For this reason, we merely present in this section the combinations of variables that seem to best predict the various interviewer values. We do not give beta coefficients since, given the limitations mentioned above, they are more likely to be confusing than helpful. At this stage, we have merely tried to identify those variables that should be studied by other survey groups who wish to evaluate their interviewer applicants.

The regression procedures also give estimates of the amount of variation explained among interviewers by the independent variables. While we shall give these estimates, they are subject to the same limitations mentioned. It should be noted that for all our interviewer variables, the independent variables explain only a minor part of the variance. While these variables are useful, they should never be used in place of supervisor judgment.

Quality

As one would expect from looking at the indexes separately, the combination of variables that best predict high quality are (in probable order of importance):

> Need achievement
> Career orientation
> Education and intelligence
> Attitudes toward interviewing (negative)

Interviewing activities

Activities enjoyed

Using these variables gives a multiple R of .4 which means that about 15 per cent of the variation is explained. The first three of the variables account for the major part of the explanation in the regression model, as is generally the case.

Cost

The variables most useful for predicting high cost behavior are:

Career orientation

Attitudes toward interviewing

Interviewing activities

Family responsibility (negative)

Activities enjoyed (negative)

Education and intelligence (negative)

Total interviewers known

Previous interviewing experience

Using these variables gives a multiple R of about .45, which means that about 20 per cent of the variation in costs is explained. Note the high degree of overlap in the independent variables between quality and cost with only Need Achievement and Family Responsibility as exceptions. Total Interviewers Known and Previous Interviewing Experience explain only a small part of the cost variables and have some small relation to quality.

We are faced with what some social scientists call the "fully-only" problem. Are we pleased that according to our regression procedures fully 15 to 20 per cent of the variance is explained, or are we disappointed that only 15 to 20 per cent is explained? The reader must decide for himself. The author finds these results to be promising, although there is certainly the possibility that they could be improved. For example, if self-perceptions of quality and cost proved to be as highly correlated with actual behavior of applicants as they are with experienced interviewers, then the predictions would be improved considerably.

It should also be remembered that costs and quality may depend to a large extent on the local supervisor. In hiring and in training and controlling interviewers, her behavior may be responsible for much of the variation between interviewers. We are, however, unable to measure this since only a single supervisor is used in a sampling area, and thus supervisor characteristics are confounded with the sampling area.

Quality-Cost

Combining cost and quality, the better quality-cost variable is best explained by the following independent variables:

> Need achievement
> Activities enjoyed
> Education and intelligence
> Mach II
> Attitudes toward interviewing (negative)

Because of the mixed relations of some of the variables with both cost and quality, the estimated multiple R is about .35, which means that about 12 per cent of the variance is explained.

Other survey organizations testing these variables may wish to omit the Mach II scale because of the earlier discussed difficulties that respondents have in answering the questions.

Years Employed at NORC

The most difficult of the variables to predict is longevity, for reasons discussed earlier. It is not too surprising to learn that the best combination of variables yields a multiple R of only .25, which means that only about 5 per cent of the variance in longevity is explained. The independent variables used are:

> Education and intelligence
> Attitudes toward interviewing
> Family responsibility (negative)
> Efficiency

As a general concluding remark, the combinations of variables that seem most important on the regressions are pretty much what one would have predicted from looking at the separate indexes. This is because none of the indexes are highly correlated with each other. Since this work has been exploratory, the tendency has been to include variables even if they are only weakly related to the interviewing value variables, and to leave the winnowing of the best predictors for the future. Of course, it may turn out that variables that were not considered in this chapter are even better predictors than the ones included here. We suspect, however, that the most critical attributes of an interviewer cannot be captured in a questionnaire, but must be uncovered by a sensitive high quality field supervisor.

9

The Use of Computers To Code Free Response Answers in Survey Research

INTRODUCTION

Asking respondents to give verbal or written statements to questions has long been a major method of gathering data in survey research. This form of gathering data has most often been used instead of precoded forms when precoding is too complicated or cumbersome, or when types of responses cannot be determined in advance. For example, a detailed listing of occupational titles is simply too complicated and cumbersome; one should not expect an interviewer or respondent to handle it. Nor is it possible to construct codes in advance for a question such as, "What kinds of things do you worry about most?"

Typical procedures for coding open-ended questions have inhibited their full usefulness. On the basis of a very limited sample of the responses, the analyst must determine how he wishes to categorize all responses. Most often categories are one-dimensional and occasionally two-dimensional, but the codes can seldom be more complicated. After a set of codes has been established and used to categorize natural language response, time and money pressures almost always prevent recoding, no matter how brilliant or insightful an idea the analyst may have as he examines the tabulated results.

Many ways in which data might be summarized have not been used because it was assumed that they were beyond the technical

Bruce Frisbie was the senior author of this chapter.

capacity of survey procedures. For example, it has not been feasible to use free response information to evaluate a respondent's state of psychological well-being or his attitude toward his life situation. It is unrealistic to ask interviewers or students to make such judgments because they lack sufficient training. On the other hand, there is little likelihood that trained psychologists will read and evaluate two or three thousand interviews along such dimensions; the task would be laborious, and the expense prohibitive.

THE GENERAL INQUIRER

This chapter describes some experimental work at NORC on the use of computers in coding responses to open-ended questions. Because of the progress made in the speed of processing data, the amounts of data that can be handled, and the variety of ways in which the same raw data can be analyzed, much work has been done on processing and summarizing natural language data by computer (Doyle, 1965; Iker and Harway, 1965; Simmons, 1965). One very important system for analyzing or summarizing the content of natural language text has been developed at Harvard, principally by Philip Stone, and is called the General Inquirer (Stone *et al.,* 1962; Stone and Hunt, 1963; Dunphy *et al.,* 1965). Since our ideas and methods evolved from attempts to use the General Inquirer (Harvard III dictionary), it may be useful to give some of its history.

In this system the input information, or the data to be processed by machine, is natural language text, such as that which you are now reading, composed of words and phrases, sentences and paragraphs, divided into sets of texts or sets of respondents. The text is on data processing cards or tapes, rather than on standard sheets of paper. A large list of words—a dictionary of them—defined by an arbitrary number of concepts (usually of current usage in the behavioral sciences) is stored in the computer, which compares each word or phrase in the data with this dictionary. All words listed in the dictionary which have been defined as representing a given concept are assigned a number representing it. (For example, concept SELF is defined as I, me, mine, all of which have the number 01, the numeric meaning of SELF.) A sentence is read into the computer, and each word and phrase in the text is compared with each word and phrase in the dictionary. A sequence of numbers representing the concepts found by matching the text and dictionary words and phrases is then assigned to the sentence. All words and phrases occurring in the text but not in the dictionary are sent to a different tape so that the untagged words can be reviewed later. Since the concepts or codes are always devised by the analyst, all the criteria for coding or summarizing the data are explicit and predetermined—the machine merely does the work.

The General Inquirer system has often been compared to a dictionary. The format in which the system is used by the computer does indeed look like a dictionary (as previously described). As an idea, however, it is most similar to a thesaurus; it is a set of concepts by which words are grouped as similar or dissimilar. Each concept is defined by a list of words and phrases and the list of concepts defining the words comprises the dimensions of the thesaurus. The system only resembles a dictionary in that a list of words and phrases and their thesaurus definitions exists. Not all words are defined by the concepts. The thesaurus does not necessarily include all words and phrases or all categories of meaning in the natural language. The concepts used to categorize words are merely those of interest to the analyst.

The history of the General Inquirer's origins and development began at Harvard University as an extension of Interaction Process Analysis, devised by Robert F. Bales (1950). The Bales technique is used for description and analysis of small group interaction and measures how people relate to each other, but not the substance of their conversations. It soon became apparent that it would be helpful to know something about the substance as well as the form of interaction in small groups. From this desire for such summary information grew the idea of automated procedures for analysis of natural language text. The idea of using a constant set of categories for analyzing discrete words within a sentence—the sentence forming the smallest unit for an action-oriented description and analysis—is quite consistent, if not a logical outgrowth of the initial Bales system. Philip Stone was intrigued by Bales' idea and began working on ways to implement the idea operationally. Although a host of people here and abroad have expressed interest in the system and have worked with it, the primary orientation of almost all users of the system has been psychological or has usually involved extensive analysis of small, or homogeneous, groups of people or texts (Dunphy, 1964; Paige, 1964; Smith *et al.,* 1965). To the best of our knowledge, this study represents the first and most extensive attempt to modify and use any such automated procedure for analysis and summary of survey materials.[1]

The chief difference between other approaches and the NORC approach is that, while other data have been small in size or highly homogeneous in nature, NORC data are neither small nor homogeneous. In the study to be discussed later, the sample was 540 respondents who spoke about 35,000 words. The analysis was multivariate, involving at least twenty different ways of analyzing the text from the viewpoint of independent and control variables.

Many of the issues and problems discussed in this chapter have emerged because of the heterogeneous nature of the sample and the heterogeneity of variables used in multivariate analysis. This is especially true in regard to developing and operationally defining lists of idioms and homographs and in regard to developing a general procedure for construction of any dictionary. To solve these problems, the system has been reoriented to a general method applicable to a wide variety of data.

The next section will discuss and show the usefulness of the General Inquirer for existing survey research procedures in processing and analyzing natural language information. This will involve the types of data that can be handled, a discussion of the comparative cost of manual and non-manual techniques for data processing, and benefits for analysis. The following section will discuss possible uses of the General Inquirer in extending analysis in survey research. The final section describes the general process for building any type of dictionary and the problems involved in using a dictionary-based system for coding natural language text.

---

[1]E. Scheuch, then at Harvard and now at the University of Cologne, has studied the possibilities of using the system for help in summarizing, storing, and retrieving questions asked in surveys for data archive purposes (Scheuch and Stone, 1964).

CURRENT USES IN SURVEY RESEARCH

The types of information which are not precoded, in which the respondent must answer a question in his own language, are legion. The purposes for asking a question as well as the ways information may be summarized are no less various or complicated. A respondent may be asked to list all jobs he has held, companies for which he has worked, schools he has attended, or different cities in which he has lived. He may be asked questions requiring more complicated responses, such as how he feels about having leisure time, what it means to him, what he has been concerned about recently, how he reacted to the Cuban crisis, what is good or bad about his marriage, or the duties of his job. Both types of questions are commonly asked in surveys, and responses to each type may be summarized in several ways, all potentially useful. We shall consider only two examples, one involving a simple "information"-seeking question and another involving a "thematic" question.

Information Responses

As our first example, let us take the responses to the question, "What kind of work do you do?" The coding scheme for this type of data is usually composed of three units of information: kind of occupation (farmers, managers, officials, proprietors, clerical workers, etc.), kind of employing organization, and perceived status of the occupation. The occupations may be divided into twelve to eighteen different categories and the perceived status of the occupation into decile rankings, either ninety-nine or ten discrete units, depending on the complexity of analysis and sample size. Assume that a list of about one thousand titles has been extracted from a much larger source, distributed to the coders, and explained to them. Armed with the list, the coders then receive bundles of questionnaires. Each one must find the appropriate page on which the information about occupation is written, read the title, search for this title in the summary list, find the occupational title's appropriate numeric equivalent, transcribe this number sequence to the questionnaire, and close the questionnaire. The process is repeated over and over. Generally, this type of coding task is extremely tedious. Boredom tends to create a high frequency of random error and unproductive use of time. The specific ways in which errors occur are in associating the wrong number sequence with the occupational title, incorrectly transcribing the number sequence, and making keypunch errors due to illegibility of the transcribed number.

Analysts who must resolve the problem of processing list information, such as occupational titles, usually resolve it in one of two ways: If the information is not considered crucial for the study, it is simply ignored and becomes part of the stockpile of unprocessed items of information remaining in questionnaires. If, however, the information is a direct and important part of the analysis, it is coded. Codes used are general and broad, easy to code, but sometimes of limited use for detailed analysis. The issues of time, money, and staff dictate that complicated coding procedures not be used, resulting in a great deal of lost information, much of which could be useful.

Examples of list information other than occupational titles are ethnic backgrounds, religious affiliations, cities, nations, colleges or universities, fraternal or professional organizations, business corporations, titles of books, magazines, and newspapers, etc. The lists are usually quite long, but the responses are usually quite short. The types of coding schemes or categories used to summarize the data are, optimally, large enough to be cumbersome both in construction and use, but, relatively speaking, not nearly so unmanageable as non-list types of information. They are usually summarized along two to six dimensions.

How can a computer coding system such as the General Inquirer help code this type of data? Basically the job to be done is to match a short set of words with an identical set and translate the matched set into a numeric equivalent. Rather than have people do this tedious search-and-find task, the machine can search, compare, and categorize symbols with great speed. Further, the list of titles which can be compared is much larger than those which can be efficiently used by manual coders. A list of particular titles stored in the computer for comparison against a sample can be 6,000 or more titles long, and the computer is indifferent to the number of dimensions used to categorize the data.

Indeed, several completely different or opposing theoretically based coding schemes can be used at the same time, with no loss of speed or information.

We do not contend that the entire job can be handled by automated procedures, nor even that it should be done this way. We estimate that between 85 and 90 per cent of the coding jobs pertaining to list information do not require an interpretation on the part of the coder. A great deal of list data is quite unambiguous.

The General Inquirer has two properties extremely useful for coding list information: (1) All information not matched or found within the computer dictionary of titles is separately stored and summarized and automatically becomes one type of output (including all ancillary information, such as respondent identification number) for the analyst to review. (2) The types of categories used by the computer are absolutely arbitrary, being completely at the analyst's discretion. This latter attribute allows one to automatically pre-edit. For example, there may be many general job titles or specific industries in which job titles are known to be difficult to classify unambiguously. There may be many conditional uses of the same job title, and the criteria for deciding how the job should be summarized cannot be handled easily by the computer. Those titles that might cause problems in automated summarizing can have a separate code of their own, one which does not code them, but automatically feeds them back to the analyst or coder for manual inspection and evaluation. The list information known to need human evaluation for correct classification is automatically sorted out, in its original form, and is arranged for further manual processing. Thus new information is automatically summarized for further evaluation, and ambiguous information is also summarized for manual coding procedures. Another useful aspect of this system is that the dictionary can quite readily be updated or changed. If a new or unexpected job title occurs frequently, it can be placed within the dictionary and the person who next uses the list will not have to worry about it.

As with any computer operation, the initial costs are large. Thus it would not be economical to build a dictionary of occupations or, indeed, any dictionary of list information for a small one-time sample. But the costs of keypunching and computer coding the information once the dictionary is established would probably be substantially less than the costs of manual coding. Furthermore, such a dictionary would be of considerable value to other survey houses, who could either borrow, rent, or purchase it. It should be stressed that the initial costs are not exorbitant. Dictionary construction of occupational or organizational titles would make sense for large samples, for smaller continuing studies, or for information routinely sought in a wide variety of studies.

Thematic Responses

However, list information is only one type of open-ended information. Open-ended questions are also asked of respondents when the analyst does not know what types of responses he will get, when he does not know exactly how he will want to summarize the responses, or when the types of summaries he wants are not amenable to precoding. Part of our initial interest in computer techniques was to see if complicated forms of language analysis could be machine coded. To do this we selected a study and question designed to offer as many open-ended responses as possible and which contained other information directly relevant to such a comparative analysis of measurement techniques. Further, the responses to the open-ended questions had already been manually coded. We had to simulate the task of manual coding within the framework of a previously determined set of codes.

The respondents form part of the basis for a study of behavior related to mental health, now in progress at NORC under the direction of Norman Bradburn. The question we selected from this study asked about the concerns or worries people had had in the last two weeks: "Everybody these days has some things he worries about—some big and some small. What about the big things? What would you say has worried you or been on your mind most *in the past few weeks?*"

Three coding schemes were used to summarize the written information:

1. The substantive area about which the respondent expressed concern,
   a. marital problems,
   b. financial concerns or unemployment,

    c. health or medical worries,
    d. national or international tensions,
    e. problems with children, and
    f. work or job problems (not unemployment),
  2. The referent of the worry (whom the respondent was concerned about), and
  3. The total number of different worries the respondent had.

We chose to simulate three of the substantive areas of concern (b, c, and d), as they differ considerably in size and complexity of coding task. The verbatim responses from the questionnaires were punched onto data processing cards.

The dictionary we constructed to test these data and codes is far from perfect. Our first intention was to build a slightly modified version of the Harvard III General Inquirer dictionary. After this plan failed (it had no idioms and was too "high class"), we decided to build an idiomatic language dictionary encompassing a wide range of dimensions (based again on the General Inquirer), hoping it would be of general use in the field of survey research. Isolating and defining idioms and homographs was done by using a wide variety of idiom and slang dictionaries, H. L. Mencken's *American Language,* and some of the warehouse of raw text gathered from responses to any number of open-ended questions. After several months of extremely frustrating work we realized that no single general dictionary would ever be very useful, and that our time would be best spent in constructing specialized dictionaries designed to be of quick and meaningful use for a particular study problem, such as race relations, or a particular geographic area, such as Appalachia.

The dictionary, as used here, is much less "well educated" or formal than others, is highly oriented toward idiomatic expressions and contexts for differentiating homographs, has not been edited or checked for errors, and is based on *a priori,* non-empirical word inclusions and exclusions.

We first compared the machine and manual codes to see if the machine coding procedure could equal or surpass the accuracy of manual coding. Remembering that the dictionary we used was quite primitive, we were encouraged to find that generally the

machine and manual coding methods gave about the same overall results. Each method had some advantages and some disadvantages which are worth discussing.

Variability of specific topic and vagueness of speech used to
describe a subject of concern are major problems in using a
computer to code natural language data. It is in these areas that
the machine does less well than the manual coder. The manual
coder is more sensitive to abuses and nuances of speech. Our lack
of knowledge of the diversity of idiomatic expressions and homographs was the most critical area for the success or failure of
computer coding.

On the other hand, a topic that has relatively specific or finite
word lists associated with it can be better handled by computer.
The most succinct example of this is the theme of employment
or money. A single word can easily be overlooked by a coder
scanning a page of words. This is not true of the computer. It
systematically processes all the text and it never gets bored or
tired while doing so. Further, random error is found only in
manual coding, not in computer coding. Each and every misclassification can be and is accounted for when using computer methods. This is hardly the case for any manual coding method.

A detailed examination of the three themes will clarify these
generalizations. The results are given in Table 9.1. Overall, it can
be seen that both the computer and the manual coders were right
92 per cent of the time, but the computer overestimated the number of worries while manual coders underestimated worries. The
text of the respondents (who were differentially coded) was read
and judged to determine which scheme was correct.

When the computer missed a worry it was primarily because the
computer did not recognize the idiom used. Thus in the search for
worries about financial concerns, the computer missed items such
as "enough to live on," "paid off," and "out of the hole." On the
theme of national or international tensions, the computer missed
responses such as "that Alabama thing," "I'm sorry for the people
in Dallas," "Communism frightens me," or "our gold standard
is shaky." These expressions were not in the dictionary. Manual
coders were not so noticably systematic in their errors. They were
likely to miss an expression of worry if it was stated as a single

word or if the response could be interpreted in more than one way. Thus such words as "money," "debts," "bills" were occasionally missed in coding financial concerns, and a mother complaining of her problems with a sick but attention-seeking child could be coded as either a "medical" or a "children" problem. However, there was usually no such reason for inaccurate manual coding.

Both the computer and manual coders did about equally well in coding the absence of worries. Only on the item dealing with national and international tensions did the computer misclassify more respondents than did the manual coders, and this was primarily due to the inclusion of worries about local and city affairs. This is not a major problem, since with rare worries such as those connected with national and international tensions it is better to make the classification broad, then to cut back later. This presents no problem to the computer or to the analyst, although it would mean complete recoding if done manually.

Consider, now, the comparative costs of manual and machine

Table 9.1 Correct and Incorrect Classification of Three Types of Worries by Computer and Manual Coding (NORC Happiness Study)

Topic	Both Computer and Manual Correct		Computer Correct— Manual Incorrect		Manual Correct— Computer Incorrect		Total	
Employment, money, job problem worries:								
Yes	81%	(203)	12%	(30)	7%	(18)	100%	(251)
No	88	(255)	6	(17)	6	(17)	100	(289)
Total	85	(458)	9	(47)	6	(35)	100	(540)
Health, medical concerns:								
Yes	80	(229)	16	(47)	4	(10)	100	(286)
No	72	(183)	5	(12)	23	(59)	100	(254)
Total	76	(412)	11	(59)	13	(69)	100	(540)
National, international tensions:								
Yes	62	(15)	25	(6)	13	(3)	100	(24)
No	93	(481)	2	(8)	5	(27)	100	(516)
Total	93	(496)	3	(14)	6	(30)	100	(540)
Total, three questions	84%	(1,366)	8%	(120)	8%	(134)	100%	(1,620)

coding. For the very specific types of questions, such as those that deal with worry, some setup time will be required for each new question and study. It is the professional time involved in setting up (or modifying) the computer dictionary that will almost always make this a more expensive procedure. If setup costs were omitted, then the computer would probably be no more expensive, and perhaps a little cheaper, than manual coding. Computer coding requires substantial keypunching and machine processing, but these costs are less than typical coding costs if one includes the hiring, training, and supervision of coders plus the overhead expenses of space, organizational size, etc.

The important difference is the time that the survey analyst and his assistants spend in dictionary construction. Determining which codes or sets of codes might be most appropriate for analysis never has and never will be a predictable task. Sometimes preconceived notions about responses are analytically correct, sometimes they are not; new ways of thinking about analysis often are generated from the raw data itself, and these ideas must be molded and honed and clarified for use in analysis and coding. However, once the categories for coding have been defined, any reasonably intelligent clerk can place the appropriate words and phrases within the categories. Anyone who can code open-ended information can place words and phrases into a scheme of prearranged categories, especially if all the words and phrases are alphabetized and appear within the context of a sentence.

Transcribing the verbatim responses is easily done by keypunch operators; both operators and machines punch written and numeric information. The cost of transcribing verbatim information is the proportion of extra keypunching that operators must do to transcribe all the information contained in the questionnaire. Thus, if it takes an operator three-quarters of an hour to do all but the written information and two minutes to do the written information, the additional cost of keypunching is 4 per cent.

In conclusion, we have shown that computer methods can be as efficient as manual methods in the coding of free response information; that the computer method can be very expensive if put only to limited use, but less expensive than manual methods if used repeatedly; and that there are several advantages in the computer method not available by manual coding methods. For example, the computer method offers far greater flexibility in the use of codes for open-ended responses and allows access to the data at all times. By increased flexibility we mean that the analyst can use any variety of codes, either detailed or refined aspects of some large theme or completely different ways of coding the same data. For example, he can differentiate respondents who worry about financial concerns and those who worry about unemployment; he can separate those who are concerned about getting more money from those who are concerned about not having enough to make ends meet; he can separate those who have serious medical problems from those who have only routine medical worries, etc. This flexibility offers the analyst the opportunity to determine empirically the coding scheme that will maximize his understanding of the responses and his analysis of the data. Furthermore, the analyst can have—if he chooses—first-hand contact with the data whenever he desires; previous technology tended to inhibit the analyst's contact with and understanding of the information. This method eliminates the technical middlemen who stand between the analyst and his data. The analyst can now proceed sequentially, using earlier codes and results to suggest still more useful codes, to arrive, finally, at a more complete understanding of the data, with confidence in the validity of these codes.

Latent Response

As was mentioned earlier, another purpose of our inquiry was to see if computer content analysis could be used to tap latent dimensions in respondent answers to open-ended questions. In this section we report our attempts to measure latent social psychological dimensions using open-ended responses. The data are far from optimal for such a test—all responses were recorded by interviewers. We do not know the interviewer's effect on the kinds of words used by respondents or the choices of topics which they mention in response to the question. It is not surprising, however, that we were unsuccessful in tapping latent dimensions other than those of the crudest type, as it seems reasonable that the area of content in which we are interested—the style of words used to describe a worry—would be the one most likely to be altered by an interviewer. Yet the results indicate that further work in analyzing verbatim responses might well be worth the effort (Cronbach, 1960; Dohrenwend, 1965; Payne, 1965).

Social psychologists have been concerned with measuring (developing scales for) personal orientations such as optimism *vs.* pessimism, fatalistic *vs.* manipulative views of the universe or environment, open- *vs.* closed-mindedness, authoritarian *vs.* non-authoritarian personalities, anxious *vs.* non-anxious orientations, high *vs.* low affectivity levels, etc. All such measures have been based on sets of responses to a variety of checklist questions asking respondents for their perceptions of potential or real feelings and behavior. Clinicians have used projective techniques for describing similar orientations in individual personalities. They tend to treat the responses as real behavior; the person is doing something in the act of responding. We intend to apply these clinical techniques (needless to say in a very limited way) to open-ended responses. We hope to open a new avenue for the social psychologist using survey methods to tap basic or latent personality dimensions or orientations.

We will compare responses to open-ended questions with responses to related checklist items. We may ask, for example, if people who state they worry "a lot" (opposed to those who state they never worry) actually talk more about their worries in an open-ended context.

The question used to measure verbal responses, as transcribed by interviewers, is, "What have you been concerned about recently?" The concept used to summarize the natural language information was derived, by and large, from the Harvard III General Inquirer dictionary. The kinds of tags or concepts used, ninety-three in all, cover several sets of general themes. The names of the concepts used to classify words and phrases are shown on the following page.

One example of latent themes we measured was orientation toward financial problems. Some people worry about expenses: paying their bills, finding money to make ends meet, or in general adapting themselves to an inflexible economic situation. Other people are more active in changing their economic circumstances. They may try to earn more money to gain economic security. We tried to measure these orientations by arranging words and

National Opinion Research Center Idiomatic Dictionary

Persons	*Emotions* [+]	*Institutional Contexts (cont.)*
Self	Arousal	Technical
Selves	Urge	Job roles
Others	Affection	Family roles*
	Pleasure	Domestic concerns*
Male roles	Distress	Legal
Female roles	Anger	Medical
Neuter roles	Regnancy, import*	Military
		Polity
Groups	*Thought*	Recreation
Small groups	Perception, sense	Religion
Large groups	Cognition	
	Condition	*Status Connotations* [+]
Physical Objects	Comparison*	High
Body parts	Sameness-Differentness*	Peer group
Physically normal states*	Not	Low
Tools	Cause	
Natural objects		*Psychological Themes* [+]
Non-specific objects	*Action States*	Overstate
	Communicate	Understate
Physical Qualifiers	Approach	
Sensory	Attempt	Strong actor
Time	Achieve	Weak actor
Duration*	Consume	
Frequency*	Attack	Ego accepts
Space	Control	Ego rejects
Quantity	Guide	
	Work	Closeness*
Environments	Stasis	Distance*
Social place	Decline*	
Natural world	Avoid	Ascend themes
	Follow	Authority themes
Culture	Expel	
Ideal values		*Miscellaneous Concepts*
Deviations	*Institutional Contexts*	Danger themes
Physical deviations*	Academic	Death themes
Normative actions	Artistic	
Message forms	Community	*Editorial Tags* *
Economic forms*	Economy	Ambiguous words, phrases
Thought forms	Security* [+]	Idiomatic, homographic
	Expense* [+]	expressions

*Indicates tags added to the Harvard III General Inquirer dictionary.
[+] Indicates latent themes this study tried to tap.

phrases pertaining to financial concerns into two lists, which are presented below:

ECONOMIC SECURITY

abl	busines	deposit	honest	luxury	proces	skill(ed)
accomplish	buy	dollar	honesty	manag	produc	sold
account	capabl	earn	hospitalizat	manufactur	product	stor
adjust	capital	effectiv	humane	merchandis	profit	suppli
appointment	career	efficient	import	nest egg	promot	techniq
assignment	cent	employ	incom	occupat	property	tenant
auto	charg	employment	industrial	offic	purchas	trad
automobil	check	estat	industry	on (the) road	rais	treasur
balanc	coin	exchang	insur	out (of) hol	repair	unite
benefit	commiss	experienc	invent	partnership	reward	wag
bid	construct	expert	job	pay off	rich	wealth
blue collar	contact	fall back	labor	penni	salary	welfar
bought	count on	fortun	leadership	penny	sal(e)	white collar
break even	creat	fund	lend	performanc	shop	worker
build	credit	generou	lent	plan	skil	
built	day off	hir	luxuri	procedur		

ECONOMIC EXPENSE

afford		expens	lock out	poor
bargain		expensiv	loos everything	pric
beg		fal apart	lost everything	rate
bil		fall(ing) apart	on strike	recession
bill		fees	out (of) job	seasonal
borrow		financ	out (of) money	shortag
budget		financial	out (of) work	spent
cash		hand out	overhead	su
cheap		hospitaliz	ow	tax
cost (of) living		inflat	overwork	taxat
deal		insuranc	paid	taxpayer
dealt		laid off	paid off	unemploy
debt		lay off	pay	unemployment
du		let go	pay up	worn out
economic		loan	payment	

Table 9.2 presents a comparison between people who explicitly indicated they worried a lot, not very much, or never worried and the tagged natural language responses to the question, "What would you say has worried you or been on your mind most. . .?" In terms of content, people who say they are "worried a lot" are only slightly more worried about everything in general than are those people who say they are not worried. The four themes generally mentioned—economic concerns, medical problems, domestic or family concerns, and job demands—barely differentiate between people who do and do not worry. The people who are not worried explicitly also indicate in the open-ended response

that they are a little less worried. (Tags for "not very worried" are Not, Overstate, and Distress.) The differences in proportions of speech given to any one theme between respondents who worry a lot and not at all are quite small, but people who explicitly indicate they are worried talk more on the average than people who say they are not worried, when they describe what they are concerned about. They do not use more sentences per person to describe their situation, but they do use more words per sentence,

Table 9.2 Intensity of Reported Worry and Selected Concepts Mentioned by Respondents Answering the Free Response Question, "What Have You Been Concerned about Recently?" (Per Cent of Speech Occuring in Each Category within Each Intensity Level)

Concepts Mentioned	Respondents Who Stated They Worried		
	A Lot	Not Very Much	Never Worried
Roles, status, authority:			
Selves	9%	9%	9%
Male roles	17	11	8
Female roles	12	10	6
Lower status	13	12	6
Family roles	24	20	11
Authority	11	8	4
Social, physical things:			
Social places	13	11	3
Special references	19	17	11
Quantity references	31	31	24
Message forms	14	11	7
Social areas, behavior:			
Consuming behavior	22	19	10
Economic concerns	16	14	10
Work behavior	14	14	7
Domestic concerns	10	9	3
Medical concerns	10	8	4
Psychological themes:			
Distress	17	16	23
Overstate	31	34	40
Strong action	16	14	10
Closeness, nearness	72	71	64
Denial:			
Not	22	24	32
Words per sentence	9.0	8.3	7.0
Sentences per person	7.5	6.8	7.2
Words per person	68.0	57.0	51.0
N	192	334	13

resulting in an average of many more words per person to describe their concerns.

To summarize, except for the word counts, the concepts developed thus far did not distinguish well between people who worried a lot and those who worried not very much. This is clearly not the fault of the computer, but rather of the concepts. which were not sufficiently well defined. While these results are disappointing, they do indicate the direction of future research. The computer will make it possible to test empirically concepts that are theoretically derived. Unfortunately, as in this case, many an attractive conceptualization will probably fade in the bright glare of the empirical results.

The same kinds of results are seen in Table 9.3, which compares the results of computer tagging with the results of three indexes

Table 9.3 Selected Computer Concepts for Question, "What Have You Been Concerned about Recently?" and High and Low Positive Feelings, Negative Feelings, and Affect Level (NORC Happiness Study)

Concepts	Positive Feelings[a]		Negative Feelings[b]		Affect Level[c]	
	High	Low	High	Low	High	Low
Family roles	23%	18%	24%	18%	25%	15%
Male roles	14	11	16	10	16	9
Female roles	11	8	13	9	12	6
Peer group status	11	7	12	8	13	4
Message forms	12	12	15	8	16	9
Non-specified objects	27	29	26	34	25	35
Not	22	29	24	24	22	30
Positive emotional states	18	16	18	18	18	15
Sentences per person	7.4	6.5	7.2	6.5	7.4	6.0
Words per sentence	8.5	8.3	8.8	8.4	8.6	8.0
Words per person	62.3	53.5	63.5	55.0	64.2	47.6
N	271	141	252	131	137	50

[a]There were three categories for this index: high (N = 271), medium (N = 128), and low (N = 141).
[b]The same is true for the Negative Feelings Index. The "medium" category contains 157 respondents.
[c]Five categories were used to build this index. "High affect" means people who scored high on both positive and negative feelings; "low affect" means people who scored low on both. The remaining groups are positive high—negative low (N = 55), positive low—negative high (N = 55) and both medium (N = 243). These groups fall between high and low affect respondents.

prepared by Bradburn and Caplovitz (1965, Chapter 2) for the Happiness Study: the Positive Feelings Index, the Negative Feelings Index, and the Affect Level Index. These indexes are derived from a twelve-item checklist. People were asked, for example, if they were often restless, bored, depressed, or very unhappy, and these formed the basis for the negative feelings cluster. Further analysis by Bradburn and Caplovitz indicated that some respondents scored high on both negative and positive feelings. The authors suggested that there is a dimension of sheer affect as well as types of affect (positive and negative) essential for our understanding of human emotions and well-being. We might interpret affect level as a willingness of ability to be responsive, regardless of the context. (This includes willingness to respond to open-ended questions.) We reasoned that some of the concepts used for summarizing the responses to, "What have you been concerned about recently?" might be differentiated on the basis of Bradburn and Caplovitz's measures of positive and negative feelings and affect level.

Differences may occur in one of three ways: (1) People may be concerned about different types of problems in their lives; (2) The emotional impact of these problems may be more or less verbally expressed; and (3) People may use more or fewer words to express their concerns or worries.

Table 9.3 shows the results of these three ways of measuring the responses to open-ended questions controlling for positive feelings, negative feelings, and affect level. Few meaningful tag or thematic differences are found between people categorized as high and low on positive or negative feelings. This is not true for the differences in themes among people who are high and low on affectivity. It seems that respondents categorized as high on affectivity are a great deal more "people"-oriented than those who are low on this dimension. They are more often concerned about other people, as indicated by the greater use of nouns having sex, status, or family connotations. The subject of their concern is people who have some role relationship to the respondent, rather than some particular theme or worry. This is accentuated by the relatively high proportion of people showing a low affect level who use words classified as unspecified referents or objects.

("Anything," "nothing," "item," "object," "problem," "situation" are words of this type.) They are less specific in their speech than people of high affect.

To determine the validity of this tentative conclusion we sought other measures which might give us some clue to kinds of contact respondents might have with other people. Three questions were asked that directly measure frequency of reported contact with other people—how many relatives they get together with, how often they get together with friends, and how often they chat on the phone each day.

It has been suggested earlier by Bradburn and Caplovitz (1965, pp. 41–49) that only positive feelings are associated with sociability. On the basis of the analysis of the open-ended responses, we have suggested that affect level, or willingness to be responsive, is of greater import than either the negative or positive aspect of feelings—that it is most important to be able to feel at all.[2]

It also seemed possible that people who had higher positive feelings might be more likely to use words denoting such a feeling state, the opposite being true for people who had higher negative feelings. The free responses were checked for words indicating emotional states. Included under this general category were words and phrases indicating arousal, urge, affection, and pleasure. The proportions of speech that fell into these categories, controlling for feelings and affect, are given in Table 9.3. There are no differences in the proportions of these types of words by positive or negative feeling levels or by affect level.

We also suspected some differences might occur in the volume of speech used by people of differing affect and feeling levels. This is confirmed in Table 9.3. People of high positive and negative feelings do indeed talk more than those with low positive and negative feelings. In both cases of feelings, those classified as high responded to the open-ended question by giving one more sentence of information than those classified as low on feelings. When the average number of sentences is six or seven this difference in response rate is considerable. Comparing respondents of

---

[2]Tabulations made to test which hypothesis was correct indicated that affect level is considerably more associated with the above "social" measures than positive affect and that this holds true controlling for socioeconomic status.

high and low affect, the difference in average speech patterns is even more marked. The low affect group is lowest of all in the average number of words per sentence and in the average number of sentences they used to describe their concerns and problems.

Bradburn and Caplovitz (1965, pp. 21–24) have shown that both sex and socioeconomic status are correlated with positive and negative feelings as well as with affect level. It might then be possible that the differences in Table 9.3 are due to sex and socioeconomic level instead of affect level. Tables 9.4 and 9.5 show, however, that even when socioeconomic status and sex are controlled, people of high affect still use more words. In fact, socioeconomic status does not appear to be related at all to number of words used, and sex is less important than affect level, although women do respond more freely than men.

Table 9.4   Length of Response to Question, "What Concerns Have You Had?" by Socioeconomic Status and Affect Level

Response	High Socioeconomic Status			Low Socioeconomic Status		
	Affect Level					
	Total	High	Low	Total	High	Low
Sentences per person	7.1	7.2	5.5	7.1	7.2	6.2
Words per sentence	8.6	8.4	9.0	8.5	9.0	7.5
Words per person	61.0	61.0	50.0	61.0	65.0	47.0
N	261	79	17	279	58	33

Table 9.5   Length of Response to Question, "What Concerns Have You Had?" by Sex and Affect Level

Response	Male			Female		
	Affect Level					
	Total	High	Low	Total	High	Low
Sentences per person	6.5	7.1	5.6	7.5	7.6	6.7
Words per sentence	8.3	8.3	8.3	8.7	8.8	7.6
Words per person	54.0	59.0	46.0	66.0	67.0	51.0
N	250	49	32	290	88	18

While the above findings are not conclusive, they certainly are strongly consistent with the notion that Bradburn and Caplovitz's measures of feeling and affect levels are valid. However, it is still difficult to say what they mean. If we assume that a person's response to an open-ended question is an actual unit of behavior we find that the measure developed by Bradburn and Caplovitz from information based on explicit self-perception of feelings actually does discriminate about what people do—how they tend to respond—even in such a minute circumstance as answering a question. The problem of deciding whether activity level determines affect level or vice-versa, or whether both are determined by a cognitive process, cannot be decided here.

The rather sparse results reported here can be used to justify either a pessimistic or an optimistic view of the future use of computers for developing latent concepts. On the pessimistic side, almost none of the concepts used in this study differentiated very much between people who worried a lot or not very much, or between people with positive and negative feeling states. On the more optimistic side, there is the interesting finding that respondents with high affect are more likely to be "people"-oriented and to have specific worries, while those with low affect are more general and use more negative words. The optimist can also hope that the computer will stimulate the analyst to search for and develop concepts which provide a better fit for actual instead of theoretical human behavior. In the long run, the building of concepts must remain the major responsibility of the man who tells the machine what to do, and not of the machine.

DICTIONARY CONSTRUCTION

This section describes a general procedure for dictionary construction. It should be noted that the procedure recommended here is only one way to accomplish dictionary construction. Several other methods have been used. For example, Colby *et al.* (1963) adapted Kluckhohn's value categories system for analyzing cultures; McPherson (1964) adapted several of Parsons' categories;

and Bales *et al.* (1962) adapted a multitude of theories or concepts to this system. All used ad hoc, impressionistic techniques for assigning words most current in the types of texts they planned on analyzing. On the other hand, Ogilvie (1964, and personal communications) followed a much different procedure in his analysis of Icarian imagery—he was trying to use the automated procedures for simulation of results achieved by manual means. This latter type of dictionary is constructed largely on the basis of trial and error. Another approach was used by Holsti (1965), who adapted Osgood's three types of word meaning (derived from factor analysis procedures) to this system.

To build any dictionary, a vocabulary consisting of a finite number of words and phrases is needed. Depending on the purposes for which the dictionary is to be used, all words or only those which are of significant or consistent meaning can be defined.

The one major problem we have had to confront is that in defining words and phrases on an arbitrary basis (usually done by individual people), word meanings—particularly the secondary meanings—are often a function of personal preference and conviction and are not empirically or systematically derived. Because of this, we tried to find some way to reduce personal biases of the persons who decide dominant meanings of words. We are not saying or even implying that the concepts which form the classification scheme should or must be empirically determined. There must be some way the placing of words and phrases under a given concept can be reasonably replicated.

There are two approaches one can use to determine the vocabulary and its definitions, whether the vocabulary is composed of book titles, occupations, responses to open-ended questions, or whatever. One can take all the titles of occupations from a book on occupational titles or all the words in a concise natural language dictionary, or one can sample texts from the data and build an empirically based dictionary. The first method is extremely thorough in its listings but is open to error in that the definitions may be wrong. A pattern of words or individual words are not necessarily defined by respondents the same way in which they are formally defined. This applies to occupational titles almost as much as it applies to ordinary verbal text. The latter method may be in error because the list is incomplete, but the definitions of the words and phrases will be correct.

Preference is given to the latter of the above two approaches because of the variability of word usage and meaning. Many words shown to have several dominant meanings in formal dictionaries are not in fact used informally in any but one way, and vice versa. It is also true that our knowledge about idiomatic expressions is very limited—both in accurately defining known idioms and in isolating commonly used idiomatic phrases.[3] Furthermore, trying to decide beforehand or to anticipate conditional meanings and usage of words and phrases is an academic, endless, expensive, and frustrating task, often resulting in elaborate schemes which are never used because they never occur. Another reason for preferring the empirical approach is that once the raw data have been transferred to tape, sampling procedures of any level of complexity may be used to copy selected sentences from it for use in determining vocabulary and definitions. The machines can handle all the routine clerical tasks quickly, accurately, and inexpensively.

After some reflection we decided that at least three basic dimensions must be considered to accurately define words and phrases.

1. *The meaning of a word depends on the social context in which it is used:* In an academic background, words such as "problem," "situation," and "solution" indicate modes of thought, but when used in a non-institutional setting they are far more likely to refer to vague, undefined, non-specific areas.

2. *Word meaning and usage depend on the mode (written versus verbal, formal versus informal) of presentation:* Verbal communication is simply not the same thing as written unless the speaker is highly educated, highly formal in his speech, or a child of ten or less who has not learned to separate his verbal and written speech habits. For example, we have found that some verbs are "underchosen"; rather than use the most

---

[3]We do not distinguish between idioms, colloquial speech, slang, homographs, etc. For our purposes, any word that must be defined in context of other words is an idiom.

appropriate verb, a familiar and "overchosen" verb will be flanked by a preposition or two, and a small number of verbs will thus be made to suffice for a much larger variety of verbal ideas. For example:

straighten out = correct
keep up   = maintain
talk into   = convince

3. *Words are redefined due to inclusion in compound words or groups.* There are for example several classes of compound word groups: adjective-noun compounds (e.g., vacuum cleaner); auxiliary verbs (e.g., keep going); idioms (e.g., babysit); cliches (e.g., heart of gold).

Perhaps one way of seeing the difference between the individual tagged words and the intended meaning of the combination is to juxtapose them.

get over = recover

These are tagged as Get and Spatial Referent but should be tagged as Sign Strong, Medical, and Get.

talk into = convince

These are tagged as Communicate, Female Theme, and Spatial Referent but should be tagged as Authority Theme and Communicate.

fix up = repair

These are tagged as Technological, Work, Ascend Theme, and Spatial Referent, but should be tagged as Technological, Work.

One special group of compounds that should be mentioned involves "to." These compounds are much more commonly used in verbal communication than their formal equivalents. These are four:

have to   = must
going to   = future tense
use(d) to   = customary, past tense
suppose(d) to = ought

4. *Word usage and meaning vary by region.* We have not yet had occasion to confront this problem, but we have been warned by people in different sections of the country and by students of American language, especially Raven I. McDavid, Jr. (1958), that regional variance of usage and meaning is substantial and significant.

The dictionary that formed the basis for our NORC dictionary was entirely without idiomatic expressions. Our first attempts to build lists of idioms were based on phrases derived from two or three published idiomatic dictionaries. These attempts were completely abortive. The phrases they contained were not used by our respondents, and the meanings of the idioms we had were different from those contained in the standard dictionaries. Further, while there may be in theory several different meanings to a word, many words, as used in response to a specific question, have only one meaning. We also found that many words have a new meaning, not listed in any dictionary and not belonging to an idiomatic phrase.

We know of no better way to avoid the problem of not having crucial words listed under a given concept or to avoid incorrectly defining terms than the use of sampling texts and processing by a computer system named Key Word in Context (KWIC) developed by IBM. The manual states that "KWIC indexes constitute a new approach to the problem of how to furnish information promptly about new literature." Part of the program takes any set of sentences and organizes the key words alphabetically, printing out all instances in which any given word occurs and also printing the context of each sentence.[4] Further, all key words found in a set of sentences are listed separately by frequency. The program is extremely fast and very economical to use.

Let us assume, for example, that we have a set of 3,500 sentences and want to determine the presence or absence of the word "back" and its derivatives as well as its meaning in the texts. We would get from KWIC a listing such as:

> I don't want to get back at him for it though.
> We are so backed up at work I get overtime.
> I wish my baby would get back to normal.
> I have to get back to work one of these days.
> My back hurts all the time.

---

[4]The program has been used mainly with titles of books and articles. The reader has probably seen indexing of journal articles by this system. Several journals in the behavioral sciences use it, among them *The American Political Science Review* and *The American Scientist.*

I have a bad back.
The ceiling in the back of the house is falling in.
I called her back and said I was sorry.
I had to go back to the store and get the food.
This morning the cars were backed up for miles and I was late for work.
I never had these problems back in Alabama.

In a separate listing we would get all key words occurring in the data, arranged alphabetically and indicating the number of times the word was counted.

Thus we have an organized list of all words in the text to be analyzed, and we have an organized listing of contexts in which any given word occurs. The listing of the contexts allows us to determine the meaning or meanings of a word as well as the idiomatic phrases of which it may be a part.

In the above example we have several meanings of the word "back." It means, "to return," "body part," "quantity referent," "space referent," and "attack." Almost all these meanings may be accurately isolated. "Call," "get," and "go back" all mean "return"; "get back at" means "attack"; "my" and "bad back" mean "body part"; "back(ed) up" means "quantity"; "back of" means "spatial referent." "Back," without a conjunctive word, is ambiguous in meaning and might cause problems.

The creation of concepts to be defined by word and phrase lists cannot be discussed here in detail. What concepts can and cannot be operationally defined by words and phrases is a function of the concept as well as the cleverness of the analyst. We feel that the kinds of concepts used in any scheme ought to be as concretely related as possible to the explicit purposes of the analysis. It is extremely easy to create elaborate conceptual schemes—to become involved with subtle multilevel orientations and classifications at the expense of the obvious and straightforward ways of categorizing natural language data. For example, we spent a great deal of wasted time trying to develop different ways of categorizing words denoting time and space and quantity references. The problem we tried unsuccessfully to resolve was that respondents often use one kind of referent when they mean another. "My big boy is having trouble in school," means "my eldest boy." For a while we were so engrossed with these types of problems (which can be great fun) that we forgot about the simple, more pressing problem of past, present, and future time—an issue of greater relevance for responses to a question about current problems and concerns.

Another problem was deciding how to determine the dimensions used in a conceptual scheme. Should each word have only one concept or should we define a word multidimensionally, using as many concepts to define the word within the conceptual framework decided upon as are deemed necessary? We did learn that no one technique, at least at this time, can do all the different types of coding or categorizing we might want. We had hoped to measure some hard-to-tap psychological orientations by use of word and phrase counts, but were not successful using this technique.

Assume that we have a set of concepts we want to define operationally. Let us take a small example and present the steps in some detail. We are interested in ROLES (sex and family), EMOTIONAL STATES, and ECONOMIC CONCERNS. The words that we want to define are classified into seven categories:

01 MALE ROLES: son, father, carpenter, son-in-law
02 FEMALE ROLES: mother, secretary, wife
03 FAMILY ROLES: baby, son, kid, mother, father, brat, son-in-law, wife
04 AROUSAL: edgy, surprised, hate, angry, hope
05 AFFECTION: close to, pleased, happy
06 ECONOMIC CONCERNS: pay, pay back, debts, pay off, laid off, finances, raise, money, nest egg
07 AMBIGUOUS WORDS: want, like, broke, hike

An IBM card containing the word and the numeric codes assigned to the concepts is punched (SON = 0103). When all the words and idioms have been assigned concept codes, the dictionary is finished and ready to be incorporated into the program that tells the machine what to do with the dictionary of words and phrases. Once these steps have been taken, it only remains to process the data through the dictionary.[5]

---

[5]For a detailed discussion and description of the input formats and types of output one can get from the computer and for the possible types of manipulation

Two forms of reference material usually accompany the dictionary, both extremely useful in analysis and for describing the dictionary. The first is an alphabetical listing of all the words and their definitions in the dictionary.

> baby = FAMILY ROLE
> back = NOT DEFINED ALONE/PAY BACK = ECONOMY
> brat = FAMILY ROLE
> broke = AMBIGUOUS

The second listing arranges the words by concept. Use of these two listings allows one to find all the meanings of any one word and its idiomatic contexts or qualifications as well as the operational meaning of any given concept.

In interpreting any given concept in the analysis of data, there are several pitfalls that must be avoided. A concept is defined by the list of words that comprise it, not by the general descriptive title or explanation of the title. General definitions for various concepts used in the behavioral sciences can be found in any textbook, and these definitions are commonly held, but consensus about these descriptive titles and definitions may or may not have anything to do with the word lists supposed to represent these concepts, and the same concept may have a different definition, depending on one's theoretical orientation.

Just as it is necessary to have some idea of the general properties, the attributes, and the limitations of a method used for analysis, it is also helpful to have some idea of its limitations when applied to data. When data are processed through the system and the analyst has summaries of the number and proportion of times a category was scored in the body of text, a strange kind of problem arises. As was mentioned before, the total list of

---

of the processed data, the reader should refer to Stone *et al.* (1966). The General Inquirer has been programmed in BALGOL, SLIP FORTRAN, and COMIT. The most advanced symbolic language we know of is SNOBOL, a very high-powered programing language that offers immense and immediate advantages for anyone using a computer (7090 series) to process natural language text. Apparently, it is easily understood by the layman, is especially flexible for building idiomatic or contextually based definitions of words and for larger categorization procedures not necessarily based on the sentence as the unit of analysis (Farber *et al.*, 1964). For all the foregoing information and references, we wish to thank Patrick Page, formerly of NORC's data processing staff.

words defines the concept, but the frequency distribution of the words in the text listed under a concept affects the interpretation of the concept's meaning as it is derived from the text. In any given set of texts it is quite feasible to find only one or two words responsible for a very high frequency of a particular concept. We tried to measure words that indicated people who tended to overstate issues and problems, people who were concerned with physical and emotional closeness and people who were concerned about distressful emotional states and situations. Almost the only word found in the OVERSTATE category was "very"; in the CLOSENESS category the word was "I," and in the DISTRESS category the word was "worry." We did not feel that the sole occurrence of the words "very" and "I" warranted interpreting these concepts as they were originally intended. We did feel, however, that when people said they were not "worried," they did mean they had no stress or distressful concerns, and we did interpret this concept as it was intended on the basis of this one word.

Thus some concepts may be validly interpreted if any word listed as representing the concept occurs, while other concepts are only reliably interpreted if there is a reasonable distribution, in the text, of the words that form the general concept.

Every method has its peculiar and special quirks. In this section of the chapter we have tried to describe a general procedure for resolving some of the potential problem areas in using this method for content analysis in survey research. Further, we have discussed some of the interpretive problems that can and do arise in its use. It is hoped that by presenting the material in a practical fashion the interested reader will have some idea of the issues he must consider in using a computer system for analyses of natural language texts.

10

The Use of
Optical Scanners To
Code Survey Results

INTRODUCTION

The use of optical scanners for coding survey results has been pioneered by the Census Bureau with great success, using FOSDIC (Film Optical Sensing Device for Input to Computers). The basic process consists of a scanning beam transmitting light through a circle. If the circle has been darkened, the amount of light transmitted is reduced and a code indicating a mark is recorded on magnetic tape. The FOSDIC models have been specially built by the National Bureau of Standards and require a very large volume of input to be economical. The Current Population Survey, with a monthly sample of 35,000 households, is processed using FOSDIC, as well as the decennial censuses and other special censuses.

There are two major reasons for considering the use of optical scanners in surveys—a reduction in time required to process information and an increase in accuracy. The Census Bureau, using almost entirely precoded forms, has been able to eliminate both coders and keypunchers with obvious cost reductions as well as increases in accuracy, since it is axiomatic that errors occur with each handling of data.

Typically, the sample sizes on surveys are far smaller than those used by the Census Bureau. Is there an optical scanner which is economical for smaller surveys? This chapter describes NORC's experiences with the IBM 1230 Optical Mark Scoring Reader, probably the smallest of the scanners. We were pleasantly surprised at the efficiency and accuracy of this machine in handling a simple form. The major usefulness of this machine may be for the researcher at a university which already has it for test grading use. (At most universities the 1230 has replaced the earlier IBM grading machines that required the use of special pencils with magnetic lead.) While it may not be economical to rent a 1230 solely for survey work, its joint use for test grading and survey coding may be quite efficient.

In the next section we describe the procedures of the experiment, and in the following section, the results. After a discussion of some special problems, the chapter concludes with some suggestions for other uses of scanners.

EXPERIMENTAL PROCEDURES

In Chapter 3, the advantages of advance listing for a special population are discussed. It occurred to us that the form used for this purpose might be read on an optical scanner. The form that was developed, called the Non-respondent Data Sheet, is shown in the Appendix (p. 235). Several important factors should be noted about this form:

1. The IBM optical mark scoring readers read only marks in specific locations. There are one thousand response positions arranged in fifty rows and twenty columns, on an eight and one-half by eleven inch sheet.

2. Stray marks or writing on the form may cause errors. It is possible, however, to designate certain areas of the form to be used for writing. In these areas, the machine will ignore all marks. On our form, there is an area in the middle for describing the job of the person being listed.

3. The lines located on the right-hand margin of the data sheet are for control and timing of the sheets as they are fed through the IBM 1230. There is a mark associated with each possible answer.

4. The form was printed by IBM, after we had designed the layout. While the location of the possible answers is somewhat restrictive, it is possible with some planning to arrange the questionnaire in a way in which it can be easily handled by an interviewer. Specific paper requirements are given in IBM's reference manual for the 1230. Careful attention must be paid to the quality of paper for feeding reasons and to the exact printing of the timing lines.

5. The form can be printed on both sides, but for our experiment we used only one side of the sheet.

6. While no special pencil is required, errors are less likely if a No. 2 pencil is used. No. 1 pencils are hard to erase, and others are too light. Pens should not be used.

7. For survey uses, the scoring reader is connected to a card punch machine. It is possible on the IBM 1231, which is an advanced version of the 1230, to read information directly into the central processing unit of a computer and then onto tape, but this would not generally be an efficient use of most computers.

The field test for this form was conducted during the spring of 1966. Fifteen hundred forms were returned as part of the normal interviewer assignment for that study. Interviewers had some difficulty with the form, and it will probably be revised a little for new uses. The major problem was that interviewers wrote comments on parts of the form where this could lead to errors. This was not surprising, since generally NORC interviewers have been instructed to write comments next to the question when any sort of explanation is necessary. Additional training and use of the form would probably eliminate this, but even so, it caused only a few errors, as will be seen in the next section.

EXPERIMENTAL RESULTS

Accuracy

The 1230 results were compared to those obtained from an above-average keypunch operator. There were about 290 errors in 38,000 punches from the 1230, or an error rate of 0.8 per cent. These errors were due to extra marks on the forms, erasures, and machine errors. The manual keypunching resulted in about 700 errors, or an error rate of 1.9 per cent. These comparisons are not completely valid, since the form was not set up for manual keypunching and some columns were hard for the puncher to follow. On the other hand, an experienced puncher with an especially high level of accuracy was used. It seems reasonable to expect that, with proper interviewer instructions, and with proper machine methods for editing, the 1230 can read with sufficient accuracy for survey needs, and with greater accuracy than a keypuncher.

Time and Costs

Even with some feeding difficulties, to be discussed in the next section, the 1230 read the fifteen hundred forms in about three hours at a rate of about five hundred per hour. Although the rated maximum of this machine is twelve hundred forms per hour, the five hundred per hour rate seems likely to be nearer the attainable level. Keypunching of the cards took fourteen hours at a rate of slightly better than one hundred cards per hour. For this type of material, the scanner works between four and five times faster than a keypuncher.

Several different factors need to be considered in evaluating relative costs:

Forms.—For 10,000 forms, the printing cost was $250 or 2.5¢ each for the special IBM form used. Regular forms would cost about 1¢ each in about the same quantities. On the other hand, the IBM form would not need to be spread out to reduce keypunch error, so fewer sheets would be needed. The cost differences may be small for forms, but it should be remembered that using special forms requires additional time for preparation, printing, and delivery, which should be included in the schedule of the study.

Machine costs.—The 1230 rents for approximately four times the rental of a keypunch machine. It is obviously expensive to have it standing idle. As suggested earlier, current users of such machines may have available time for rent, particularly on second or third shifts.

Personnel.—The 1230 requires only limited training to operate and can probably be operated by clerical or tabulating personnel as a part-time activity. The hiring, training, and supervision of additional keypunch operators can be avoided, although it is unlikely that all processing will avoid manual punching. In this area, the 1230 is clearly superior, when feasible.

Problems

The 1230 scanner was designed to handle test sheets that do not normally become wrinkled or damp. Once forms are sent into the field they face the vicissitudes of the weather and the interview situation, and may sometimes be difficult to feed. A misfeed will cause the machine to stop and sometimes to jam. Jams are relatively easy to correct and generally the sheet may be fed again, but this process obviously slows down the feeding. If the sheet becomes too wrinkled in the jam, it can always be manually punched.

Our experience suggests that extra marks are not a severe problem. Erasures will not normally be accepted, and most stray marks will be treated the same way. In addition, the computer can be programmed to edit and eliminate most remaining errors.

OTHER USES OF SCANNERS

Coding

The 1230 is directly useful only for precoded questions. It cannot read written or printed words. (There are currently some special machines that can be programmed to read special type faces, but their usefulness is for document reading and not for surveys. Machines that can read a variety of writing and printing styles are somewhere in the future, although the census FOSDIC machine can read numbers that follow a given set of dots.) Many survey questions require written answers and need to be processed when they return from the field. One procedure for processing open-end questions is given in the previous chapter, but another method could be to use manual coding, but to code on optical scanning sheets. This eliminates costs and errors associated with keypunching.

Self-administered Questionnaires

With reasonably simple questionnaires, there is no reason why the respondent cannot use an optical scanner form. The Census Bureau expects to use FOSDIC forms for the 1970 census, which will be primarily self-administered. In addition to the cost and accuracy reasons, the scanner forms can give the respondent an even greater sense of privacy in answering possibly embarrassing questions.

Time Records

Since time records kept by interviewers and by internal office personnel are relatively simple forms, it would seem efficient to use scanner sheets and eliminate the keypunching of these records, assuming that time records have been mechanized.

SUMMARY

Although most survey organizations use samples of only a few thousand cases, they may find it useful to consider optical scanners such as the IBM 1230 for eliminating coding and keypunching costs and errors. The 1230 works at a high level of accuracy with errors of less than 1 per cent and at speeds four to five times those of keypunchers. Although scanner forms are more expensive than multilith or printed forms, probably fewer will be needed. Even where forms cannot be coded for scanning by the interviewer or respondent, it may still be efficient to use such forms in coding to eliminate keypunching.

The major problems with the 1230 optical scanner are feeding and stray marks. The machine jams because of wrinkled or damp forms, but even with time lost, it still operates far faster than a keypuncher. Stray marks may cause errors in reading, but these errors can be avoided by training of interviewers, and by proper machine editing of forms.

11

The Schedule
of a Survey

INTRODUCTION

In this final chapter, the flow of a study is discussed. The results are based on sixteen NORC studies since 1962 for which information could be obtained. There is no claim that these results are typical of all survey organizations regarding average times for various parts of the project. What is almost certainly typical is the large variability between different studies. Of almost every study it can probably be predicted that some parts will take longer than average, although which parts cannot be predicted in advance.

What does this mean for the study director attempting to plan his schedule most efficiently? We would suggest the following three procedures for minimizing scheduling problems:

1. After making best estimates for the total time of a project based on realistic estimates of the subparts, allow a substantial additional period of time for uncertainty. As a rough rule of thumb, an additional 25 per cent should be allowed on studies lasting a year or more and even higher amounts on shorter studies.

2. Wherever possible during the course of the study, plan for parallel activities so that delays in one area do not stop the project completely. While this advice is undoubtedly easier to give than to put into effect, there are sometimes parts of a study that are relatively independent. For example, in their study of adult education, Johnstone and Rivera simultaneously studied a large national sample of participants and planned a study of adult education facilities in four communities.

3. As will be seen in the tables, the major delays in a survey occur at the beginning and end. This, of course, suggests that projects overlap. While one study is being completed another study can be in the planning stage.

These remarks are so banal that one hesitates to express them. Nevertheless, in practice it is common to see study lengths grossly underestimated with considerable periods of frustrating inactivity for the project director.

The basic information of this chapter is summarized in two tables—Table 11.1 and Table 11.2. Table 11.1 gives the mean and median times for the NORC probability with call-back studies and the standard deviation and range as measures of variability. The table is divided into the following five periods, which are also discussed in the text:

1. *Planning and writing the proposal.*—This covers the period from the time planning started for the writing of the proposal to the time funds are made available. Arbitrarily, we start the planning period with some written memo describing the proposed project, although this is probably a minimum estimate. In many cases a study director will have been thinking about a project for some time and may even have had informal discussions with colleagues and possible sources of funds before anything is ever written.

2. *Planning the project.*—This covers the period from the time funds were made available to the start of the field period. During this period

Table 11.1 Time Required for a Survey

The Five Phases of a Survey	Months				Number of Studies
	Mean	Median	Standard Deviation	Range	
1. Planning and writing the proposal	6.1	6.0	5.2	1–18	11
2. Planning the project	5.5	5.0	3.3	2–12	11
3. Field period	3.0	3.0	1.0	2– 5	10
4. Preliminary processing	4.5	3.0	4.2	1–14	9
5. Final processing, analysis, and report writing	9.2	9.0	5.9	2–21	9
Total*	26.6	25.5	13.4	5–50	10

*These totals, based on ten studies, are not the sums of the subparts of the table, but are derived directly from the basic data.

the sample is designed, the questionnaire constructed and pretested, and the basic analytic procedures are developed.

3. *Field period.*—From the start of the field period to the date that the last acceptable questionnaire is received.

4. *Preliminary processing of data.*—From the end of the field period to the time the first marginal tabulations are received. This includes coding, punching, cleaning, and editing of data.

5. *Final processing, analysis, and report writing.*—From the first marginal tabulations to the final paper, report or monograph. Since requests for tabulations, analysis and report writing generally go on simultaneously, these are combined into the final category.

Table 11.2 gives information for NORC Survey Research Service (SRS) projects. Note that the first and last phases of Table 11.1 are omitted since these are not normally part of the service.

The reader may wonder why national, regional, and local surveys are not separated in Tables 11.1 and 11.2. They are not separated because the geographic scope of the study does not seem to have any important effect on its length. Very simple surveys are sometimes done nationally, and complicated studies are often done locally. Nor is there any difference in the field period required. If anything, unlike what might be expected, a local study may take longer if interviewers are not available and need to be hired or trained.

The remainder of the chapter is devoted to a brief commentary on the two tables.

Table 11.2 Time Required for NORC SRS Surveys Using Probability with Quota Samples

The Three Phases of Survey Research Service Surveys	Months				Number of Studies
	Mean	Median	Standard Deviation	Range	
1. Planning the project	3	3	3	0.25– 9.00	6
2. Field period	0.75	0.75	0.3	0.25– 1.00	6
3. Preliminary processing	1.5	1.5	1.5	0.50– 4.00	6
Total	5	5	4	2.00–12.00	6

NORC PROBABILITY SAMPLE WITH CALL-BACKS

Planning and Writing the Proposal

Two factors determine the length of this part of a project. The more complex the project, the longer it will take to search the literature and prepare a proposal. Far more important, however, is the availability of funds. At one extreme, a funding agency may take the initiative and ask to have a study conducted, in which case the time between the initial consideration of the project and the time funds are made available may be a month or less. On the other hand, a controversial project, or one that does not fit very well the criteria of funding agencies, requires a long search procedure that may well end with the proposal being abandoned. On the average, six months is generally spent in this phase of the study.

Planning the Project

While this phase also averages five or six months, there is somewhat less variability. Standard national probability samples with a single questionnaire take the least time to prepare, while samples of special populations using several questionnaires take longer. The habits of the director of the project and his other commitments are also a factor, as they are in all parts of a study.

Field Period

Since this is the shortest of the periods, it is most subject to measurement and rounding errors, and the average of three months may be slightly biased on the high side because we were not able in all cases to split out parts of a month. Still, it is clear that the average is greater than two months. The major part of any sample will probably be interviewed within six weeks, but the stragglers and problem cases stretch this period considerably. These results include several mail questionnaires that take as long as or longer than personal interviews if a high cooperation rate is to be achieved. Also included are two studies where the field work was done by other survey organizations, although the study was planned and analyzed at NORC. As in planning the project, the field period is shortest for a standard national probability sample that takes about two months. Special samples, particularly those requiring new interviewers, take longer.

The time of year during which a study is conducted is also a factor. Field work takes longer in summer, when more respondents and interviewers are on vacation. The field period must also be extended if it covers the period between Thanksgiving and New Year, since almost all field operations are suspended in the latter half of December.

It is possible to reduce the total length of a study a little by starting preliminary processing when the questionnaires first return from the field. Theoretically, this would mean that final processing could start almost immediately after the final questionnaires were returned. This parallel operation has only been partly successful in the past at NORC, with several additional months for additional processing required after the close of the field period. The period of preliminary processing would be even longer, however, if some of the work had not been done in parallel.

Preliminary Processing

The major factor in preliminary processing is the machine and hand editing required. Coding and keypunching do not cause major time delays, since even with large samples or long questionnaires it is possible, at least in a university community, to expand and contract the coding staff relatively quickly, and keypunching can be farmed out to a service agency. Editing, however, can become enormously complicated if various parts of a questionnaire must be reconciled against each other, as is usually the case with any kind of financial data. Even greater complications arise in attempting to reconcile data from various waves of a panel study, but panel studies are so complex in all ways that they are omitted from Tables 11.1 and 11.2.

Final Processing, Analysis, and Report Writing

The final phase of a project averages about nine months, and as in other areas of human endeavor, it is not possible, generally, to shorten this period by having nine analysts spend one month each. The typical analytic procedure is sequential with the earlier findings pointing the direction for the later probing. Note, however, that, as in nature, the gestation period for a report varies considerably, depending on the nature of the beast. Some of the reports of projects were later published in book form, but the time required for publishing is not included in this final phase.

Total Time
The total time for an average NORC probability sample with call-backs is slightly more than two years, with a standard deviation of thirteen months. Some of this variation can be anticipated in planning the study, but the unanticipated variation should be anticipated by allowing for an uncertainty factor.

SRS SURVEYS USING PROBABILITY WITH QUOTA SAMPLES

Considering only the three comparable phases—planning, field, and preliminary processing—the Survey Research Service studies take only 40 per cent of the time taken by the regular NORC projects. It is not only the field period that is reduced; planning and preliminary processing are cut down just about as much. The SRS samples have simple designs and simple questionnaires, with rare exceptions. As has been pointed out in Chapter 2, a major advantage of these studies is the ability to field them quickly in special situations, such as the Kennedy assassination, or the power failure in the East. The variability in the total time of these projects is also considerably lower, except in the planning phase. Although no data are presented on analysis of results, informal discussions suggest that NORC's clients spend about as much time in data analysis as do NORC study directors.

Is there a relationship between how long a study takes and its quality? The answer is a qualified yes. Some studies need to be fielded quickly; others have basically faulty designs which no amount of ex post facto analysis can correct. But most well-designed studies benefit from a looseness in the time schedule that provides the study director with a chance to reconsider what has been done and to plug the gaps.

Appendix

Survey Questionnaires and Data Records

DEMOGRAPHIC QUESTIONS EXCERPTED FROM NORC ADULT EDUCATION STUDY

3 2		3 3		Page 7 3

NORC column 1		NORC column 2		NORC column 3	
NAME: _____		NAME: _____		NAME: _____	
RELATION TO HOUSEHOLD HEAD:		RELATION TO HOUSEHOLD HEAD:		RELATION TO HOUSEHOLD HEAD:	
_____	8-	_____	8-	_____	8
AGE.............. _____	9-10	AGE.............. _____	9-10	AGE.............. _____	9-10
SEX..............Male........	11-1	SEX..............Male........	11-1	SEX..............Male........	11
Female......	2	Female......	2	Female.....	
CODE IF LIVING:		CODE IF LIVING:		CODE IF LIVING:	
In school residence..........	8	In school residence..........	8	In school residence.........	
On Armed Forces base........	9	On Armed Forces base........	9	On Armed Forces base........	
Married.....................	29-1	Married.....................	29-1	Married.....................	29
Single.....................	2	Single.....................	2	Single.....................	
Widowed.....................	3	Widowed.....................	3	Widowed.....................	
Separated..................	4	Separated..................	4	Separated..................	
Divorced...................	5	Divorced...................	5	Divorced...................	
D.K.	Y	D.K.	Y	D.K.	
Work full-time	30-1	Work full-time..............	30-1	Work full-time..............	30
Work part-time only.........	2	Work part-time only.........	2	Work part-time only........	
Work part-time/keep house....	3	Work part-time/keep house....	3	Work part-time/keep house...	
Work part-time/school.......	4	Work part-time/school.......	4	Work part-time/school.......	
Keep house only............	5	Keep house only............	5	Keep house only............	
Go to school only...........	6	Go to school only...........	6	Go to school only..........	
Retired.....................	7	Retired.....................	7	Retired.....................	
D.K.	Y	D.K.	Y	D.K.	
Other (Specify)		Other (Specify)		Other (Specify)	
TYPE OF WORK		TYPE OF WORK		TYPE OF WORK	
_____	31-	_____	31-	_____	31
BUSINESS OR INDUSTRY		BUSINESS OR INDUSTRY		BUSINESS OR INDUSTRY	
_____	32-	_____	32-	_____	32
CODE IF SELF-EMPLOYED	0	CODE IF SELF-EMPLOYED.........	0	CODE IF SELF-EMPLOYED........	
Protestant...................	33-1	Protestant...................	33-1	Protestant...................	33
(Specify denomination)		(Specify denomination)		(Specify denomination)	
Catholic....................	2	Catholic....................	2	Catholic....................	
Jewish......................	3	Jewish......................	3	Jewish......................	
None........................	4	None........................	4	None........................	
D.K.	Y	D.K.	Y	D.K.	
Other (Specify)		Other (Specify)		Other (Specify)	
Never attended school........	34-1	Never attended school.........	34-1	Never attended school	34
1-4 years....................	2	1-4 years....................	2	1-4 years....................	
5-7 years....................	3	5-7 years....................	3	5-7 years....................	
8 years.....................	4	8 years.....................	4	8 years.....................	
9-11 years..................	5	9-11 years..................	5	9-11 years..................	
12 years (Finished high school)	6	12 years (Finished high school)	6	12 years (Finished high school)	
Some college.................	7	Some college.................	7	Some college.................	
Completed college...........	8	Completed college...........	8	Completed college...........	
Graduate training...........	9	Graduate training...........	9	Graduate training...........	
D.K.	Y	D.K.	Y	D.K.	
Other schooling in addition (Specify)		Other schooling in addition (Specify)		Other schooling in addition (Specify)	
INTERVIEWED THIS PERSON......	35-1	INTERVIEWED THIS PERSON.......	35-1	INTERVIEWED THIS PERSON.......	35
36- 37- 38- 39-		36- 37- 38- 39-		36- 37- 38- 39-	

HOUSEHOLD INFORMATION

14. HAND RESPONDENT INCOME CARD.

Now to finish up, in which of these general groups did your total family income (did NAME'S total income) fall last year--before taxes, that is?

RECORD SEPARATELY FOR EACH FAMILY IN HOUSEHOLD

	"YOUR" FAMILY (If more than one family list members)	2ND FAMILY (List members)	3RD FAMILY (List members)
INCOME ... Under $1,000.........	A....66-X	A....67-X	A....68-X
$1,000-1,999.........	B.... 0	B..ʌ.. 0	B.... 0
$2,000-2,999.........	C.... 1	C.... 1	C.... 1
$3,000-3,999.........	D.... 2	D.... 2	D.... 2
$4,000-4,999.........	E.... 3	E.... 3	E.... 3
$5,000-5,999.........	F.... 4	F..... 4	F.... 4
$6,000-6,999.........	G.... 5	G.... 5	G.... 5
$7,000-7,999.........	H.... 6	H.... 6	H.... 6
$8,000-9,999.........	I.... 7	I.... 7	I.... 7
$10,000-14,999.........	J.... 8	J.... 8	J.... 8
$15,000 or over.......	K.... 9	K.... 9	K.... 9
D.K.	D.K. .. Y	D.K.. Y	D.K.. Y
IF REFUSED, CHECK HERE AND ESTIMATE......	Refused.. ☐	Refused.. ☐	Refused.. ☐
	Estimate	Estimate	Estimate

15. SUMMARY OF HOUSEHOLD COMPOSITION:

ENTER NUMBER OF ADULTS IN HOUSEHOLD....................TOTAL ADULTS: _____ 69-

ENTER NUMBER OF YOUTH IN HOUSEHOLD....................TOTAL YOUTH: _____ 70-

ENTER NUMBER OF CHILDREN 3 TO 16......................TOTAL CHILDREN: _____ 71-

ASK UNLESS OBVIOUS: Are there any other children under the age of 3 living here?........................NUMBER: _____ 72-

TOTAL PERSONS IN HOUSEHOLD: _____ 73-

16. May I please have your telephone number in case I have to call back for any reason?

TELEPHONE NUMBER: _____

Refused...........☐

No telephone......☐

COMPLETE THESE ITEMS AS SOON AS INTERVIEW IS FINISHED

17. RACE OF RESPONDENT: White..........74-1
Negro.......... 2
Oriental...... 3

18. CHECK ONE OF THE FOLLOWING TO SHOW TYPE OF DWELLING UNIT:

Located on farm...................75-1

Non-farm: single family house.... 2

Non-farm: duplex or two family structure............. 3

Non-farm: multi-unit structure (e.g. apartment)...... 4

19. CIRCLE ONE OF THESE TO SHOW LOCATION OF DWELLING UNIT:

Inside the largest city in the primary unit.76-1

In a suburb of the largest city in primary sampling unit............................ 2

In the outskirts (including nearby small towns of the primary sampling unit)....... 3

In open country............................ 4

INTERVIEWER'S SIGNATURE _____

DEMOGRAPHIC AND BOOK READING QUESTIONS
EXCERPTED FROM NORC CRIME STUDY

Now to change the subject for a minute.

20. About how often do you read a newspaper--every day, almost every day, just on weekends, or not at all?

Every day 1   62

Almost every day 2

Just on weekends 3

Not at all 4

---

21. Have you read any book, either hardcover or paperback, within the past six months? (If you've started but not finished a book, that counts too.)

Yes . . . (ASK A) 7   63

No . . (GO TO Q. 22) . . 8

A. IF YES: How many books have you read?

One 1   64

Two to five 2

Six to ten 3

Eleven to twenty 4

Twenty-one or more . . . 5

22. Now a few more questions.

FOR OFFICE USE ONLY	PERSON NUMBER (CIRCLE THE NUMBER OF THE PERSON WHO IS YOUR RESPONDENT ON THIS SCREENER.)	A. I'd like to list the full name of all persons who have lived in this household during the last 12 months--that is, from July 1, 1965, to July 1, 1966. Let's start with the head. Who else lives here? (PROBE: Have we missed anyone--new babies, a roomer, anyone who was here then but is away now?) RECORD BELOW AND ASK B-G.	B. ASK FOR EACH PERSON: What is (name's) relation to (head)?	C. ASK FOR EACH PERSON: What is (name's) age, please?	D. CODE SEX FOR EACH PERSON. (11/3)
(6/1)	(7-8)	FIRST AND LAST NAME		(9-10/99)	M F
4	01		HEAD		1 2
4	02				1 2
4	03				1 2
4	04				1 2
4	05				1 2
4	06				1 2
4	07				1 2
4	08				1 2
4	09				1 2
4	10				1 2

E. ASK FOR EACH PERSON: Was (name) living here during all or only part of the last 12 months? (12/8)		F. ASK FOR EACH PERSON--UNLESS OBVIOUS: Is (name) now married, widowed, divorced, separated, or was (he/she) never married? (13/6)					G. ASK FOR EACH PERSON: What was the last grade that (name) completed in school? (14/y)									
							No formal schooling . 0 One to four years . . 1 Five to seven years . 2 Eight years--completed grammar school. 3 Nine to eleven years. 4					12 years--completed high school . . . Some college . . . . Completed college . Graduate or professional school . Don't know				
All	Part	M	W	D	Sep	NM										
6	7	1	2	3	4	5	0	1	2	3	4	5	6	7	8	9
6	7	1	2	3	4	5	0	1	2	3	4	5	6	7	8	9
6	7	1	2	3	4	5	0	1	2	3	4	5	6	7	8	9
6	7	1	2	3	4	5	0	1	2	3	4	5	6	7	8	9
6	7	1	2	3	4	5	0	1	2	3	4	5	6	7	8	9
6	7	1	2	3	4	5	0	1	2	3	4	5	6	7	8	9
6	7	1	2	3	4	5	0	1	2	3	4	5	6	7	8	9
6	7	1	2	3	4	5	0	1	2	3	4	5	6	7	8	9
6	7	1	2	3	4	5	0	1	2	3	4	5	6	7	8	9
6	7	1	2	3	4	5	0	1	2	3	4	5	6	7	8	9

BEGIN DECK 02

23.

(1-5)

	A. What is (head's) religious preference? CODE BELOW.	B. IF HEAD IS CURRENTLY MARRIED: What is the religious prefer- ence of (head's spouse)?
Protestant . (ASK [1]) . .	1 06/6	1 07/6
Roman Catholic	2	2
Jewish	3	3
Other (SPECIFY) _____	4	4
None	5	5

[1] IF PROTESTANT: What denomination?

Baptist	1 08/8	1 09/8
Methodist	2	2
Episcopalian	3	3
Presbyterian	4	4
Lutheran	5	5
Congregational	6	6
Other (SPECIFY) _____	7	7

24. What does (head) usually do--work full time, work part time (keep house, go to school),
or something else?

```
Works full time . . . . . . (ASK A-C) . . . . . . 1   10/0
Works part time only . . . (ASK A-C) . . . . . . 2
Works part time and keeps house  (ASK A-C) . . . 3
Works part time and goes to school  (ASK A-C) . . 4
Keeps house only . . . . (GO TO Q. 25) . . . . . 5
Retired . . . . . . . . . (ASK A-C) . . . . . . 6
Don't know . . . . . . (GO TO Q. 25) . . . . . 7
Other (SPECIFY)_____ 8
```

IF HEAD WORKS AT ALL OR IS RETIRED:

A. Exactly what type of work (does/did) (head) do?

OCCUPATION: _____ 11-13/

B. In what type of business or industry (does/did) (head) work?

INDUSTRY: _____ 14-16/

C. (Is/Was) (head) self-employed?

Yes 1   17/3
No 2

25. HAND RESPONDENT CARD 2. In which of these general groups did your total family income
fall last year--before taxes, that is?

```
A.  Under $2,000 . . . . . . . . . 0   18/y
B.  $2,000 to $2,999 . . . . . . . 1
C.  $3,000 to $4,999 . . . . . . . 2
D.  $5,000 to $5,999 . . . . . . . 3
E.  $6,000 to $6,999 . . . . . . . 4
F.  $7,000 to $7,999 . . . . . . . 5
G.  $8,000 to $9,999 . . . . . . . 6
H.  $10,000 to $14,999 . . . . . . 7
I.  $15,000 to $19,999 . . . . . . 8
J.  $20,000 or over . . . . . . . 9
K.  Don't know; refused . . . . . . X
    ESTIMATE: $ _____
```

THE INTERVIEWER QUESTIONNAIRE

national opinion research center⸻⸻⸻⸻ — **NORC**

UNIVERSITY OF CHICAGO
5720 Woodlawn Avenue
Chicago, Illinois 60637
PLaza 2-6444   Area Code 312
Peter H. Rossi, Director
December, 1964

Dear Interviewer:

   Will you help us in an important NORC methodological study in which we are trying to find out what kinds of people are attracted to interviewing and make good interviewers? This questionnaire is being sent to all of NORC's interviewers since we feel that you all are among the best interviewers in the United States. We plan to ask at least some of the same questions of all future applicants and also to compare NORC interviewers to those of other survey organizations.

   From these results we hope to learn what background and attitudes you have in common with other successful interviewers so that in the future there will be a more scientific basis for the selection of new interviewers. In other words, we are trying to develop a questionnaire which will predict interviewer success. If we can do this, we shall publish these results (in statistics and percentages, of course).

   As of now, we don't know what answers will help us predict that an applicant is suited for interviewing. There are no "right" answers on this questionnaire. The "right" answers will be the ones that you give.

   The questionnaires are to be returned directly to me. Your answers will not be used by the Field Department in making any judgments about specific interviewers.

   Please fill this out as completely as you can, and feel free to make any additional comments which you think will help improve this questionnaire. Could we have this back in the next week or so?

   Thanks very much!

                                        Cordially,

                                        Seymour Sudman

                                        Seymour Sudman
SS   Senior Study Director
453   Interviewer Research Project

P. S.   We realize that this is a long questionnaire, and to repay you for the
        time you spend, we shall be pleased to send you $4.00 for your completed
        questionnaire.

NATIONAL OPINION RESEARCH CENTER

University of Chicago

INTERVIEWER RESEARCH PROJECT

BEGIN DECK 1

First, let's start off with some attitude questions. (You may remember king some of these questions on other NORC studies.)

For each statement, circle the answer which gives your first reaction.

		Agree Strongly	Agree Somewhat	Can't Decide	Disagree Somewhat	Disagree Strongly	
A.	Next to health, money is the most important thing in life	1	2	3	4	5	11/y
B.	Most people can still be depended upon to come through in a pinch . . .	5	6	7	8	9	12/y
C.	There is no excuse for lying to someone else .	1	2	3	4	5	13/y
D.	It is all right to ask an insurance company for more money than you deserve after an auto accident if you think they might cut your claim . .	5	6	7	8	9	14/y
E.	You sometimes can't help wondering whether anything is worthwhile any more	1	2	3	4	5	15/y
F.	When you ask someone to do something for you, it is best to give the real reasons for wanting it rather than giving reasons which might carry more weight	5	6	7	8	9	16/y

1. Continued

		Agree Strongly	Agree Somewhat	Can't Decide	Disagree Somewhat	Disagree Strongly	
G.	Most people are basically good and kind	1	2	3	4	5	17
H.	Most men forget more easily the death of their father than the loss of their property	5	6	7	8	9	18
I.	If you try hard enough, you can usually get what you want	1	2	3	4	5	19
J.	A salesman has the right to exaggerate the quality of his product to make a sale he might otherwise lose	5	6	7	8	9	2C
K.	Generally speaking, men won't work hard unless they're forced to do so	1	2	3	4	5	21
L.	Most people will go out of their way to help someone else	5	6	7	8	9	22
M.	The best way to handle people is to tell them what they want to hear .	1	2	3	4	5	23
N.	Anyone who completely trusts anyone else is asking for trouble . . .	5	6	7	8	9	2C
O.	One should take action only when sure it is morally right	1	2	3	4	5	25
P.	It would be wrong for an employee to take considerable time off while working for a large company, even though the company would not be hurt by it at all	5	6	7	8	9	2(
Q.	Even today, the way that you make money is more important than how much you make	1	2	3	4	5	27
R.	It is hard to get ahead without cutting corners here and there	5	6	7	8	9	2(

We've just asked whether you agree or disagree with some statements.

Now we're going to ask a different type of question. Here are some groups of three statements each.

This time it won't matter how much you agree or disagree with them. We just want you to <u>compare</u> the statements with each other.

We want you to indicate which one of them is <u>closest</u> to your own feelings, and which one you think is the most <u>opposite</u> to what you really feel.

Again, we're interested in your first impressions.

Mark a + in front of the statement in <u>each</u> group which is closest to your own feelings.

Mark a - in front of the statement in <u>each</u> group which is most opposite to what you really feel.

Please consider and mark each group separately.

Group ____ Men are more concerned with the car they drive than with the   29/
A   clothes their wives wear.

    ____ It is very important that imagination and creativity in chil-
dren be cultivated.   30/

    ____ People suffering from incurable diseases should have the choice
of being put painlessly to death.   31/

Group ____ Never tell anyone the real reason you did something unless
B   it is useful to do so.   32/

    ____ The well-being of the individual is the goal that should be
worked for before anything else.   33/

    ____ Once a truly intelligent person makes up his mind about the
answer to a problem he rarely continues to think about it.   34/

Group ____ Most people who get ahead in the world lead clean, moral
C   lives.   35/

    ____ Any man worth his salt shouldn't be blamed for putting his
career above his family.   36/

    ____ People would be better off if they were concerned less with
<u>how</u> to do things, and more with <u>what</u> to do.   37/

Group ____ The world would be a much better place to live in if people
D   would let the future take care of itself and concern themselves only with enjoying the present.   38/

    ____ It is wise to flatter important people.   39/

    ____ Once a decision has been made, it is best to keep changing
it as new circumstances arise.   40/

2. Continued

Group ____ It is a good policy to act as if you are doing things you do
E   because you have no other choice.   ℓ

      ____ The biggest difference between most criminals and other people
           is that criminals are stupid enough to get caught.   ℓ

      ____ Even the most hardened and vicious criminal has a spark of
           decency somewhere within him.   ℓ

Group ____ All in all, it is better to be humble and honest than to be
F   important and dishonest.   ℓ

      ____ A man who is able and willing to work hard has a good chance
           of succeeding in whatever he wants to do.   ℓ

      ____ If a thing does not help us in our daily lives, it isn't very
           important.   ℓ

Group ____ A man's first responsibility is to his wife, not his mother.   ℓ
 G
      ____ Most men are brave.   ℓ

      ____ It's best to pick friends that are intellectually stimulating
           rather than ones it is comfortable to be around.   ℓ

Group ____ It is best to give others the impression that you can change
H   your mind easily.   ℓ

      ____ It is a good working policy to keep on good terms with everyone. ℓ

      ____ Honesty is the best policy in all cases.   ℓ

Group ____ It is possible to be good in all respects.   ℓ
I
      ____ To help oneself is good; to help others is even better.   ℓ

      ____ War and threats of war are unchangeable facts of human life.   ℓ

Group ____ Barnum was probably right when he said that there's at least
J   one sucker born every minute.   ℓ

      ____ Life is pretty dull unless one deliberately stirs up some ex-
           citement.   ℓ

      ____ Most people would be better off if they controlled their
           emotions.   ℓ

*3. For each of the following statements, circle the answer that best describes your agreement. (Circle one in each row.)

	Strongly Agree	Mildly Agree	Neutral	Mildly Disagree	Strongly Disagree	
A. A man can make long-range plans for his life, but a woman has to take things as they come	1	2	3	4	5	59/y
*B. A pre-school child is likely to suffer emotional damage if his mother works	5	6	7	8	9	60/y
C. A wife should respond to her husband's sexual overtures even when she is not interested	1	2	3	4	5	61/y
*D. Even if a woman has the ability and interest, she should not choose a career field that will be difficult to combine with child-rearing	5	6	7	8	9	62/y
E. We fool ourselves if we think we can control the course of our own lives .	1	2	3	4	5	63/y
*F. One of the most important things to a happy marriage is for a man and woman to be equal in intelligence	5	6	7	8	9	64/y
G. Men who object to women colleagues and supervisors are probably insecure about their own masculinity	1	2	3	4	·5	65/y
*H. A working mother can establish just as warm and secure a relationship with her children as a mother who does not work	5	6	7	8	9	66/y
*I. If a wife earns more money than her husband, the marriage is headed for trouble	1	2	3	4	5	67/y

	Strongly Agree	Mildly Agree	Neutral	Mildly Disagree	Strongly Disagree	
J. Women should stop expecting special privileges because of their sex . . .	5	6	7	8	9	68/y
K. A husband should respond to his wife's sexual overtures even when he is not interested	1	2	3	4	5	69/y
L. Nowadays married couples put too much of their income into insurance of all sorts	5	6	7	8	9	70/y
*M. A married woman can't make long-range plans for her own career because they depend on her husband's plans for his	1	2	3	4	5	71/y

4. Different people see different kinds of similarities between things.
In what way do you think that these pairs of things are <u>alike</u>?

A. North -- West   1

B. Eye -- Ear   1

C. Air -- Water   1

D. Table -- Chair   1

E. Egg -- Seed   1

F. Poem -- Statue   1

G. Wood -- Alcohol   1

H. Praise -- Punishment   1

I. Fly -- Tree   1

Next, the questions deal with your life, and your family.

5. What is your current marital status? (Circle one)

$$\begin{array}{ll}
\text{Single} & 1 \cdot 20/\text{y} \\
\text{Divorced or separated} & 2 \\
\text{Widowed} & 3 \\
\text{Married} & 4
\end{array}$$

IF YOU ARE NOT NOW MARRIED, PLEASE SKIP TO QUESTION 11.

6. What kind of work does your husband do?

Occupation _____

21-22

Industry _____

7. Generally, how does your husband feel about your work as an interviewer?

$$\begin{array}{ll}
\text{Strongly in favor of my work} & 1 \quad 23/\text{y} \\
\text{Mildly in favor of my work} & 2 \\
\text{Neutral} & 3 \\
\text{Mildly opposed to my work} & 4 \\
\text{Strongly opposed to my work} & 5
\end{array}$$

8. On the whole, would you say that you spend quite a lot of time, a moderate amount of time, or relatively little time doing things together with your husband?

$$\begin{array}{ll}
\text{Quite a lot} & 1 \quad 24/\text{y} \\
\text{Moderate amount} & 2 \\
\text{Little time} & 3
\end{array}$$

9. Generally speaking, do you tell your husband about what went on during your day?

$$\begin{array}{ll}
\text{Always} & 1 \quad 25/\text{y} \\
\text{Usually} & 2 \\
\text{About half the time} & 3 \\
\text{Seldom} & 4 \\
\text{Never} & 5
\end{array}$$

*10. During the past few weeks, have you ever felt that you were not the kind of wife you would like to be?

Yes . (ANSWER A) . . . 1 26/y

No X

IF YES:	A. Did you feel that way often or only once or twice?

Often 4 27/9

Once or twice 5

*11. IF MARRIED, WIDOWED, DIVORCED OR SEPARATED: How many children do you now have? (COUNT A CURRENT PREGNANCY AS ONE CHILD.)

(ANSWER A) _____ 28/y

IF NO CHILDREN, SKIP TO QUESTION 14.

IF CHILDREN:	A. Please list them, giving their sex, their ages, and the number of years of school which they have finished so far.

Sex	Age	Years of School Completed	29-48

*12. During the past few weeks, have you ever felt that you were not the kind of mother you would like to be?

Yes . (ANSWER A) . . . 1 49

No X

IF YES:	A. Did you feel that way often or only once or twice?

Often 4 50

Only once or twice . . . 5

13. Here is a list of things people generally like when they see them in young children.

    A. Which <u>three</u> qualities listed would you say are the most desirable for children to have? (Circle three in Column A.)

    B. Which <u>one</u> of these three is the most desirable of all? (Circle one in Column B.)

    C. All of these may be desirable, but which three would you consider <u>least important</u>? (Circle three in Column C.)

    D. And which one of these three is <u>least important</u> of all? (Circle one in Column D.)

	A. Three Most	B. One Most	C. Three Least	D. One Least	
1) that he has good manners	1	0	3	4	51/y
2) that he tries hard to succeed	1	0	3	4	52/y
3) that he is honest	1	0	3	4	53/y
4) that he is neat and clean	1	0	3	4	54/y
5) that he has good sense and sound judgment	1	0	3	4	55/y
6) that he has self-control	1	0	3	4	56/y
7) that he acts like a boy (she acts like a girl)	1	0	3	4	57/y
8) that he gets along well with other children	1	0	3	4	58/y
9) that he obeys his parents well	1	0	3	4	59/y
10) that he is responsible	1	0	3	4	60/y
11) that he is considerate of others . . .	1	0	3	4	61/y
12) that he is interested in how and why things happen	1	0	3	4	62/y
13) that he is a good student	1	0	3	4	63/y

THE FOLLOWING QUESTIONS SHOULD BE ANSWERED BY EVERYONE:

14. Do you feel obliged to spend substantial amounts of time with relatives other than your husband or children?

                                           Yes (ANSWER A & B) . 1 64/y

                                           No X

IF YES:	A. What is the relationship? 65+66
	B. About how much time do you spend each week?

15. Taken all together, how would you say things are these days--would you say you're <u>very happy</u>, <u>pretty happy</u>, or <u>not too happy</u>?

                                    Very happy 1 67/y

                                    Pretty happy 2

                                    Not too happy . . . 3

16. Do you belong to any organization such as church and school groups or social, civic and fraternal clubs?

Yes (ANSWER A & B) . 1 68/y

No X

IF YES: A. List the names of the organizations to which you belong.

B. How actively do you participate in the activities of each organization? (Circle one on each line under B below.)

A.	B			
List Name of Organization	Very Active	Usually Attend Meetings	Just Belong	
	1	2	3	69/
	1	2	3	70/
	1	2	3	71/
	1	2	3	72/
	1	2	3	73/
	1	2	3	74/

BEGIN DECK 3

17. Do you find you have quite a bit, some, very little, or no spare time?

Quite a bit 1   11/y

Some 2

Very little 3

None 4

18. What is your religious preference?

None 1   12/y

Protestant (ANSWER A). . 2

Catholic 3

Jewish 4

Other SPECIFY _____ 5

IF PROTESTANT: A. What denomination?

_____   13/

19. How religious would you say you are at the present time?

Very religious 0   14/y

Somewhat religious . . . 1

Not too religious 2

Not at all religious . . 3

20. In national politics, do you consider yourself a Democrat or Republican?

                                    Democrat 0   15/y
                                    Republican 1
                                    Independent ⌉ 2
                                    Other . . . ⟩(ANSWER A) 3
                                    Don't know ⌋. X

IF INDEPENDENT, OTHER OR DON'T KNOW:	A. In general, would you say you are closer to the Democratic or Republican party in national politics?
	
	                    Democratic 7
	                    Republican 8
	                    Neither 9
	                    Don't know 6

21. Have you ever served as an election official or precinct worker for a political party?

                                    Yes 1   16/y
                                    No X

22. Circle YES for each activity listed below that you personally enjoy or think you would enjoy if you had an opportunity to engage in it. Circle NO for those you would not enjoy. Circle either YES or NO for each activity.

	Yes	No	
Attending concerts	1	2	17/3
Bowling	4	5	18/6
*Building furniture	7	8	19/9
Fishing	1	2	20/3
*Gardening	4	5	21/6
*Gossiping	7	8	22/9
*Making a speech	1	2	23/3
*Mountain climbing	4	5	24/6
Painting and drawing pictures.	7	8	25/9
Painting the house	1	2	26/3
*Playing golf	4	5	27/6
*Playing tennis	7	8	28/9
Reading	1	2	29/3
Shoveling snow	4	5	30/6
*Skiing	7	8	31/9
*Washing the car	1	2	32/3

*23. Assuming you were financially able to employ household help, circle the category which best describes the extent to which you would like to handle each of the following activities yourself, or hire someone to do it for you. (Circle one in each row.)

	Do Myself All the Time	Do Myself Most of the Time	Share or Alternate with Hired Help	Hired Help Most of the Time	Hired Help All the Time	
*Everyday cooking	5	6	7	8	9	33/
*Cooking for special occasions	X	0	1	2	3	34/
Daytime supervision and care of children . .	5	6	7	8	9	35/
*Weekly household cleaning .	X	0	1	2	3	36/
Special spring or fall cleaning	5	6	7	8	9	37/
Washing, ironing the clothes	X	0	1	2	3	38/
Mending, alterations	5	6	7	8	9	39/
Gardening . . .	X	0	1	2	3	40/

24. About how many trips do you make to the grocery store each week?

_____ 41/

*25. Do you generally plan your week's menus in advance or day by day?

In advance . . . 1 42/

Day by day . . . X

Compared to most other women you know, how efficient would you say you are? (Circle one.)

Much more efficient 1 43/y
Somewhat more efficient . . 2
Average 3
Somewhat less efficient . . 4
Much less efficient 5

Some people like things done perfectly, while others don't care provided the job is done well but less than perfectly. How about you? Do you generally want to see a job done perfectly or would you be satisfied if it were done well but less than perfectly?

Like to see the job done perfectly 1 44/y
Satisfied if done well but less than perfectly X

Do you consider yourself overweight, underweight, or just about right?

Quite a bit overweight . . 5 45/4
Somewhat overweight 6
Just about right 7
Somewhat underweight . . . 8
Quite a bit underweight . . 9

Now let's turn to some questions which deal with interviewing. Remember, there are "right" answers. Just give us your reactions.

Do you ever get together socially with other NORC interviewers?

Yes . . . . (ANSWER A) . . . 1 46/y
No X

IF YES: | A. About how many? _____   47/y

Do you know any people who interview for any other survey or research groups besides NORC?

Yes . . . . (ANSWER A) . . . 1 48/y
No X

IF YES: | A. About how many do you know? _____   49/y

*31. Do you now interview for any other survey or research groups besides NORC?

                                Yes . . (ANSWER A & B) . . . 1 50/y

                                No X

| IF YES: | A. Which ones? | 51-54 |
| | B. About how many hours a month on the average, do you work for other organizations? | 55-56 |

*32. Had you ever interviewed for any survey organization before you started interviewing for NORC?

                                Yes 5 57/9

                                No 6

33. How many years have you been interviewing on a fairly regular basis for NORC or any place else?

                                                        58/y

*34. Here is a list of other occupations. How do you suppose most people would rate the prestige of interviewing as compared to these other occupations? Would you say that, in general, interviewing would be ranked higher than, lower than, or about the same as each of these? (Circle one on each line.)

Compared with...	Interviewing Is Higher	Interviewing Is Lower	Interviewing is About the Same	
Artist who paints pictures.	1	2	3	59/y
Public school teacher . . .	4	5	6	60/y
Playground director	7	8	9	61/y
Waitress	1	2	3	62/y
Nurse	4	5	6	63/y
Singer in night club . . .	7	8	9	64/y
Clothes presser in a laundry	1	2	3	65/y
Saleslady in a store . . .	4	5	6	66/y
Welfare worker for a city .	7	8	9	67/y
Chemist	1	2	3	68/y
Owner-operator of a lunch stand	4	5	6	69/y

35. What do you see as the major advantages of interviewing as compared to other jobs?

70-71

36. What are the disadvantages, if any, of interviewing as compared to other jobs?

72-73

37. What are your major reasons for working?

74-75

BEGIN DECK 4

38. Do you think that interviewing pays better, as well or not as well as other jobs which you would be qualified for?

Better 6	11/9
As well 7	
Not as well 8	

39. Would you be in favor of a sliding pay scale which depends on the difficulty of the study?

Yes . . . .(ANSWER A) . . . 1	12/y
No X	

IF YES:	A. What parts of a study should be considered?
	13/

40. Do you think bonuses should be paid to interviewers who obtain above-average cooperation rates for their areas?

Yes 1 14/

No X

41. Do you think bonuses should be paid to interviewers whose costs are below average in their areas?

Yes 1 15/y

No X

*42. How do you think that your costs compare to those of other interviewers in your area?

My costs are considerably above average . . 1 16/y

My costs are slightly above average 2

My costs are average 3

My costs are slightly below average 4

My costs are considerably below average . . 5

43. How about the hours you work? Do you think that these are better, as good, or worse than the hours on other jobs?

Better 1 17/y

As good 2

Worse 3

44. How about the working conditions of interviewing? In your opinion, are they better, as good, or worse than working conditions on other jobs?

Better 5 18/9

As good 6

Worse 7

*45. Here is a list of some of the things you do as an interviewer. Which of these do you like <u>very much</u>? Which <u>somewhat</u>? Which do you <u>dislike</u>? (Circle one in each row.)

	Like Very Much	Like Somewhat	Dislike	
Study and training	1	2	3	19/y
Clerical (time sheets, forms) . .	6	7	8	20/9
Editing	1	2	3	21/y
Traveling	6	7	8	22/9
Interviewing	1	2	3	23/y
Knocking on doors	6	7	8	24/9
Telephoning	1	2	3	25/y

*46. Do you prefer a questionnaire which has a great many open-ended questions or one which has just a few?

A great many . . . 1 26/y

Just a few 2

*47. How well do you like to do map reading, field counting and listing? (Circle one in each row.)

	Like Very Much	Like	Don't Mind	Dislike	Dislike Very Much	Have Never Done This	
Map reading . . .	1	2	3	4	5	0	27/y
Field counting .	5	6	7	8	9	0	28/y
Listing	3	4	5	6	7	0	29/y

*48. Do you find the maps we send you easy or hard to read?

Very easy 1 30/y

Pretty easy 2

Not too easy 3

Hard 4

*49. When going some place new either while interviewing or for personal reasons do you prefer to read a road map or ask someone how to get there?

Read a road map 7 31/9

Ask someone 8

50. What do you think about the understandability of the specifications you get from us? Do you find the specifications easy or hard to understand?

Very easy 1 32/y

Pretty easy 2

Not too easy 3

Hard 4

*51. If you had the opportunity, would you like a full-time career?

Yes 7 33/9

No 8

*52. A. What characteristics do you think an <u>ideal</u> job would have?
(Circle the items you consider most important in Column A.)

B. Regardless of how important they are to you, please rate interviewing
in terms of the opportunities it gives you for achieving each of the
following. [Circle a number for each item in either Column (a), (b),
or (c).]

A. Ideal Job	Items	B. Opportunities in Interviewing			
		Excellent (a)	Average (b)	Poor (c)	
1	Provide an opportunity to use my special abilities or aptitudes .	1	2	3	35/y
2	Provide me with a chance to earn a good deal of money	6	7	8	36/9
3	Permit me to be original and creative	1	2	3	37/y
4	Give me social status and prestige	6	7	8	38/9
5	Give me an opportunity to work with people rather than things . .	1	2	3	39/y
6	Enable me to look forward to a stable, secure future	6	7	8	40/9
7	Leave me relatively free from supervision by others	1	2	3	41/y
8	Give me a chance to exercise leadership	6	7	8	42/9
9	Provide me with adventure	1	2	3	43/y
0	Give me an opportunity to be helpful to others	6	7	8	44/9

34/y

53. Do you have any other part-time or full-time employment now besides interviewing?

Yes, part-time . (ANSWER A). . 7 45/y
Yes, full-time . (ANSWER A). . 8
No . . . . (ANSWER B). . 9

IF YES:	A. What sort of work do you do?
	46/
IF NO:	B. Would you like other employment?
	Yes 1 47/
	No 2

54. The money you earn interviewing--does it generally go for your ordinary living expenses, or do you use it as extra money for things you wouldn't otherwise buy, or do you save it up for some special purpose?

Ordinary expenses 1   48/y

Extra luxuries 2

Special purpose 3

55. A. What NORC study did you most enjoy working on as an interviewer?

49-50

B. Why was that?

51-52

56. A. What NORC study did you least enjoy working on as an interviewer?

53-54

B. Why was that?

55-56

*57. How long do you plan to continue interviewing?

Less than a year . . 1   57/y

1-2 years 2

3-5 years 3

6-10 years 4

Indefinitely 5

*58. Do you see interviewing as a stepping-stone to another job?

Yes . (ANSWER A & B). 1   58/y

No X

IF YES: | A. What kind of job?

59/

B. How will interviewing prepare you for it?

60-61

*59. How good an interviewer do you think you are?

One of the very best. 1   62/y
Above average 2
Average 3
Below average 4

*60. How nervous are you when someone first opens the door at an assigned household?

Very nervous   . . 5   63/
Pretty nervous . . 6
Not too nervous . 7
Not nervous at all 8

61. Do you prefer to interview people like yourself, or people of a different age, sex, race, or social background? (Circle one in each row.)

	People Like Myself	People Different from Me	Doesn't Matter	
Age	1	2	3	64/
Sex	6	7	8	65/
Race	1	2	3	66/
Social background . . .	6	7	8	67/

62. What is your reaction when a respondent refuses to be interviewed?

68-69

63. In general, how do you think most people feel about being interviewed?

They enjoy it 1   70/
They don't mind 2
They dislike it 3

4. Do you feel that people in general are more willing or less willing to be interviewed than they used to be?

More willing 6	71/9
Less willing (ANSWER A) . . 7	
No difference 8	

IF LESS WILLING: | A. Why do you think this is happening?

72-73

65. Which one of the following statements best expresses your attitude toward interviewing? Code the one that comes closest.

A. I love interviewing and look forward to every assignment 1   74/y

B. I like interviewing, even though it's difficult and frustrating sometimes 2

C. Interviewing to me is a job, and I simply try to do my best . . . 3

D. I find interviewing unpleasant in many ways, but there are compensations 4

BEGIN DECK 5

Finally, here are some questions about your background:

66. What is your age?

Less than 25 1	11/y
25-34 2	
35-44 3	
45-54 4	
55-64 5	
Greater than 64 6	

67. Were you brought up mostly on a farm, in a town, in a small city, in a large city, or suburb of a large city?

Farm 1	12/y
Town 2	
Small city 3	
Large city 4	
Suburb 5	

68. What was the last grade that you completed in school?

8 years or less 1	13/y
9-11 years 2	
12 years (finished high school) 3	
Some college 4	
Completed college 5	
Graduate training 6	
Other schooling in addition . X	

(SPECIFY)_____

*69. A. What was your high school grade average? (If you were not graded using
         A as the highest grade, please circle the grade which most closely
         corresponds.)

                                                      A 1   14/y
                                                      A- 2
                                                      B+ 3
                                                      B 4
                                                      B- 5
                                                      C+ 6
                                                      C 7
                                                      C- 8
                                                      D+ 9
                                                      D 0
                                                      D- X

      B. If you attended college: What was your college grade average?

                                                      A 1   15/y
                                                      A- 2
                                                      B+ 3
                                                      B 4
                                                      B- 5
                                                      C+ 6
                                                      C 7
                                                      C- 8
                                                      D+ 9
                                                      D 0
                                                      D- X

*70. On intelligence tests which you took in school, did you get the impres-
      sion that you were above average or average in intelligence?

                                                      Average 1   16/y
                                                      Above average 2
                                                      Very much above average 3

*71. Which of the following subjects did you really enjoy when you were in
school? Which did you actively dislike? (Circle all that apply.)

	Really Enjoyed	Disliked
Art	1	1
Biology	2	2
Chemistry	3	3
English	4	4
Foreign languages	5	5
Geography	6	6
History	7	7
Home economics	8	8
Mathematics	9	9
Music	0	0
Physical education	X	X
Physics	y	y
None	R	R

         17/   18/

---

72. How many people including yourself are now living in your household?

       _____ 19/y

---

73. How many rooms do you have in your house or apartment?

       _____ rooms 20/y

---

74. Do you own or rent?

       Own . . . (ANSWER A) . . 1 21/y

       Rent . . . (ANSWER B) . . 2

IF OWN: | A. What is the approximate value of the house?

       $ _____ 22/

IF RENT: | B. How much is the rent a month?

       $ _____ 23/

75. If you decided to pay off all of your debts in the next month or so, would you be able to do so without borrowing money, even if it meant selling everything you own?

Yes	. . . .(ANSWER A)	. . . 1	24/y
No	. . . .(ANSWER B)	. . . 2	
Don't have any debts	 X		

IF YES: | A. Would it take just about everything you have or would you have something left over?

Take everything	 1	25/y
Something left	 2	
Don't know	. . . ., . . . 3	

IF NO: | B. About how much would you be able to pay off--less than half of what you owe, just about half, more than half, or just about everything?

Less than half 6

Half 7

More than half 8

Just about everything 9

---

76. Adding up the income from all sources, what was your total family income in 1963?

A. Under $2,000 0	26/y
B. $ 2,000 to $ 2,999 1	
C. $ 3,000 to $ 3,999 2	
D. $ 4,000 to $ 4,999 3	
E. $ 5,000 to $ 5,999 4	
F. $ 6,000 to $ 6,999 5	
G. $ 7,000 to $ 7,999 6	
H. $ 8,000 to $ 9,999 7	
I. $10,000 to $14,999 8	
J. $15,000 and over 9	
Don't know X	

77. Did you find any of the questions on this questionnaire embarrassing in any way? If you did, tell us about it here. You may also wish to suggest additional questions which were not asked.

INTERVIEWER'S TIME REPORT: SURVEY RESEARCH SERVICE

SRS Study No. _____

Page _____ of _____ pages

Is this your final Time Report
to be submitted for this study?

Yes _____   No _____

FOR OFFICE USE ONLY:
Interviews received: _____
Computed: _____
Checked: _____

Check No.: _____

PLEASE PRINT:
Mr., Mrs., or Miss: _____
Street Address: _____

City, Zone No., State: _____

Signature of Interviewer _____

| Date 196 | TOTAL TIME | | TRAVEL | | INTERVIEWING | | OTHER TIME | | | S.U. No. | No. Completed Interviews | EXPENSES | |
Month Day	From (o'clock)	To	Hrs.	Mins.	Hrs.	Mins.	Hrs.	Mins.	Explain				Explain	Amount
TOTALS....													

FOR OFFICE
USE ONLY

HRS. _____   MIN. _____

HRS. _____   TOT. HRS. _____

_____ X _____ RATE = _____ + _____ EXPENSES = _____ PAY

INTERVIEWER'S TIME REPORT: NORC

NORC Study No. _____
SIDE 1: Page _____ of _____ pages

Is this your final Time Report
to be submitted for this study?

Yes _____   No _____

FOR OFFICE USE ONLY:
Interviews received: _____
Computed: _____
Checked: _____
Check No: _____

PLEASE PRINT:
Mr., Mrs., or Miss: _____
Street Address _____
City, Zone No., State _____

_____
Signature of Interviewer

DATE	FROM	TO	TIME WORKED		SEGMENT	EXPLANATION OF TIME NOT SHOWN ON SEGMENT CALL RECORD	EXPENSES	
	(o'clock)		Hrs.	Mins.			Explain	Amount
TOTALS								

FOR OFFICE USE ONLY

HRS. _____   MIN. _____

SEGMENT CALL RECORD

NAME _____ INTERVIEWER _____

S.U. _____ SEGMENT # _____

DATE	TIME		Travel to and from segment	Travel within segment	Waiting for respondent	Seeking or talking with respondent	Actual inter-viewing	Other (EXPLAIN IN "REMARKS")	HOUSE-HOLD #	RESULT	REMARKS
196__	FROM	TO									

TIME AND DISTANCE ESTIMATE RECORD

To help us in planning your future assignments, would you please take few minutes to tell us how far you are from the NORC sampling points listed b and how long it takes you to get to them. If you aren't sure, put down your estimate and a (?) to indicate uncertainty. If you don't drive, would you indicate next to the time the method of transportation you would probably use (Subway, bus, train, etc.)

We <u>don't</u> want you to actually drive there, but just to use your past experience or judgment. A self-addressed envelope is enclosed for your conve ience in returning this form to me.

Segment	One-way Distance (Miles)	One-way Time (Minutes)

LETTER TO INTERVIEWERS ON PAY METHODS

NATIONAL OPINION RESEARCH CENTER
University of Chicago
5720 South Woodlawn Avenue
Chicago, Illinois   60637

Dear Interviewer:

For as long as I can remember, one of the chief complaints of interviewers has been keeping the detailed time sheets. Frankly, at our end, checking these time sheets is also an expensive time-consuming job. We think we have come up with a plan which will make life easier for all.

As part of our study of the costs of survey research, we are conducting an experiment in connection with SRS-760. We are offering you the <u>choice</u> of two pay methods. The first method is the current one, using time sheets, so if you wish, you may be paid just as you have been. The second method is based on our experience over the last three years and can be called the formula pay method.

We have found that interviewer pay depends on the following:

        a)   Length of interview

        b)   Length of time to get from the specific inter-
              viewer's house to the sampling point

        c)   The number of trips the interviewer has to make

        d)   Length of time spent searching for the proper
              respondent

We have come up with a formula which is described in detail on the attached sheet. Using this formula, we compute in advance for each interviewer how much he/she will get for completing his/her assignment. When your assignment is returned to us, we mail you the check with no time sheet needed from you, and no fuss and muss at our end. If you decide to try the formula pay method, and something unusual happens so that you feel that you are not getting enough money, we will adjust your pay if you write and tell us about it.

This is an experiment, and whether or not we adopt this method will depend, in part, on how our interviewers like it. For your convenience space has been provided on the return post card attached to the Warning Notice for you to let us know by which pay method you wish to be paid on SRS-760.

                              Sincerely,

                              (Mrs.) Eve Weinberg
                              Field Director

INTERVIEWER PAY FORMULA

1. <u>Study and Clerical Time</u>

   For this study you will be paid for __2__ hours of study time, and __2__ hours of clerical time at your usual hourly rate.

2. <u>Interviewing</u>

   For this study you will be paid for __1 - 1 1/2__ hours per interview. (Not The exact time per interview has not yet been set since we are still revis the questionnaire. When you receive your assignment, you will be given th standard interview length.)

3. <u>Travel to Segment</u>

   You will be paid for three round trips to each SU. Since you live _____ miles and _____ minutes from the SU, (as you told us recently) you wil receive credit for _____ hours of travel at your usual hourly rate plus $_____ for mileage which is your total miles travelled at 8¢ per mile (Note: These figures will be filled in when we determine in which SU's you will interview.)

4. <u>Travel in SU's to Locate Respondents</u>

   You will be paid for three hours travel time in each SU at your usual hour rate.

5. <u>Total Pay</u>

   For this study you are credited with:

   _____ hours at $_____ per hour, or $_____

   _____ miles @ 8¢ per mile $_____

   Total: $_____

NOTE: Please submit memo for payment of any other expenses.

ON-RESPONDENT DATA SHEET

SURVEY NO.

S.U. NUMBER

RACE:

WHITE ⊐

NEGRO ⊐

OTHER ⊐

RELIGION

NONE ⊐

CATHOLIC ⊐

JEWISH ⊐

BAPTIST ⊐

METHODIST ⊐

REASON N.S.

LUTHERAN ⊐

NON QUOTA ⊐

PRESBYTERIAN ⊐

NOT AVAILABLE ⊐

OTHER ⊐

TOTAL ADULTS _____

FOR EACH ADULT (21 AND OVER)

①	②	③	④
SEX: MALE ⊐ FEMALE ⊐	SEX: MALE ⊐ FEMALE ⊐	SEX: MALE ⊐ FEMALE ⊐	SEX: MALE ⊐ FEMALE ⊐
SCHOOL: 8 OR LESS ⊐ 9-12 ⊐ 13-16 ⊐ 17+ ⊐	SCHOOL: 8 OR LESS ⊐ 9-12 ⊐ 13-16 ⊐ 17+ ⊐	SCHOOL: 8 OR LESS ⊐ 9-12 ⊐ 13-16 ⊐ 17+ ⊐	SCHOOL: 8 OR LESS ⊐ 9-12 ⊐ 13-16 ⊐ 17+ ⊐
AGE -25 25-29 30-34 35-39 40-44 45-49 50-54 55-59 60-64 65+	AGE -25 25-29 30-34 35-39 40-44 45-49 50-54 55-59 60-64 65+	AGE -25 25-29 30-34 35-39 40-44 45-49 50-54 55-59 60-64 65+	AGE -25 25-29 30-34 35-39 40-44 45-49 50-54 55-59 60-64 65+
EMPLOYED: YES ⊐ NO ⊐	EMPLOYED: YES ⊐ NO ⊐	EMPLOYED: YES ⊐ NO ⊐	EMPLOYED: YES ⊐ NO ⊐
IF YES, DESCRIBE JOB:	IF YES, DESCRIBE JOB:	IF YES, DESCRIBE JOB:	IF YES, DESCRIBE JOB:
OCCUPATION CODE	OCCUPATION CODE	OCCUPATION CODE	OCCUPATION CODE

NAME (HEAD OF HOUSEHOLD)_____ ADDRESS _____PHONE_____

References

AKIN, KATHERINE. Time study of Georgia public health nurses. *Nursing Outlook,* 1962, **10**, 544–46.

BALES, R. F. *Interaction process analysis.* Cambridge, Mass.: Addison-Wesley, 1950.

BALES, R. F., STONE, P. J., and PRATT, R. W. Proposal to the division of social sciences. Washington, D.C.: National Science Foundation, 1962. (Mimeographed.)

BIRMBAUM, Z. W., and SIRKEN, MONROE. On the total error due to non-interview and to random sampling. *Intl. J. opinion and attitude Res.,* 1950, **4**, 179–91.

BRADBURN, NORMAN, and CAPLOVITZ, DAVID. *Reports on happiness.* Chicago: Aldine, 1965.

BROWN, MILTON P., *et al. Problems in marketing.* New York: McGraw-Hill, 1961.

BUREAU OF THE CENSUS. Miscellaneous data memorandum No. 3. Washington, D.C.: Bureau of the Census, 1958. (Dittoed.)

CHRISTIE, RICHARD, and MERTON, ROBERT K. Procedures for the sociological study of the values climate of medical schools. *J. medical Educ.,* 1958, **33**, 125–53.

COCHRAN, WILLIAM. *Sampling techniques.* New York: John Wiley & Sons, 1953.

COLBY, B., COLLIER, G. A., and POSTAL, S. K. Comparison of themes in folktales by the General Inquirer System. *J. Amer. Folklore,* 1963, **76**, 318–23.

COLOMBOTOS, JOHN. The effects of personal vs. telephone interviews on socially acceptable responses. Paper presented at the Annual Meeting of the American Association for Public Opinion Research, Groton, Connecticut, May 14, 1965.

CONTRA COSTA PROBATION DEPARTMENT. Time study. Martinez, California: Contra Costa Probation Department, 1959.

CRONBACH, L. J. *Essentials of psychological testing.* (2nd ed.) New York: Harper and Row, 1960.

DAVIS, JAMES H. *Increasing wholesale drug salesmen's effectiveness.* Columbus, Ohio: Bureau of Business Research, Ohio State University, 1948.

DEMING, W. EDWARDS. *Sample design in business research.* New York: John Wiley & Sons, 1960.

Department of Public Health Nursing, National League for Nursing. *A comparative study of costs in eleven public health nursing agencies.* New York: National League for Nursing, 1956.

Department of Social Welfare, State of California. *Independent adoption yardsticks.* Sacramento: Department of Social Welfare, 1956.

DOHRENWEND, B. S. Some effects of open and closed questions on respondent's answers. *Hum. Organization,* 1965, **24**, 175–84.

DOYLE, L. B. Expanding the editing function in language data processing. *Communications assoc. computing Machinery,* 1965, **8**, 238–43.

DUNPHY, D. Social change in self-analytic groups. Unpublished Ph.D. dissertation, Harvard University, 1964.

DUNPHY, D., STONE, P. J., and SMITH, M. S., The General Inquirer: Further developments in a computer system for content analysis of verbal data in the social sciences. *Behav. Sci.,* 1965, **10**, 468–80.

DURBIN, J., and STUART, A. Call-backs and clustering in sample surveys: An experimental study. *J. Royal statistical Soc. (A),* 1954, **117**, 387–428.

FARBER, D. J., GRISWOLD, R. E., and POLONSKY, I. P. SNOBOL, A string manipulation language. *J. assoc. computing Machinery,* 1964, **2**, 21–30.

FELLER, WILLIAM. *An introduction to probability theory and its applications: I.* New York: John Wiley & Sons, 1950.

GOODMAN, ROE, and CANNELL, CHARLES F. Sampling errors and components of interview costs in relation to sample design. Ann Arbor: Survey Research Center, University of Michigan, n. d. (Mimeographed.)

GREELEY, ANDREW M., and ROSSI, PETER H. *The education of Catholic Americans.* Chicago: Aldine, 1966.

HANSEN, MORRIS, HURWITZ, WILLIAM, and MADOW, WILLIAM. *Sample survey methods and theory, Volume I.* New York: John Wiley & Sons, 1953.

HANSON, ROBERT, and MARKS, ELI. Influence of the interviewer on the accuracy of survey results. *J. Amer. statistical Assoc.,* 1958, **53**, 635–55.

HAUCK, MATHEW, and STEINKAMP, STANLEY. *Survey reliability and interviewer competence.* Urbana, Ill.: University of Illinois, Bureau of Business and Economic Research, 1964.

HOCHSTIM, J. Comparison of three information gathering strategies in a population study of sociomedical variables. In *Proceedings of the Social Statistics Section, 122nd Annual Meeting, American Statistical Association.* Washington, D. C.: American Statistical Association, 1962. Pp. 154–59.

HOLSTI, O. R. An adaptation of the "General Inquirer" for the systematic analysis of political documents. *Behav. Sci.,* 1965, **9**, 382–88.

HYMAN, HERBERT H., *et al. Interviewing in social research.* Chicago: University of Chicago Press, 1954.

IKER, H. P., and HARWAY, N. T. A computer approach towards the analysis of content. *Behav. Sci.,* 1965, **10**, 173–82.

JEWISH CHILD CARE ASSOCIATION OF NEW YORK. Time study, May, 1952. New York: Jewish Child Care Association, 1952. (Mimeographed.)

JOHNSTONE, JOHN W. C., and RIVERA, RAMON J. *Volunteers for learning.* Chicago: Aldine, 1965.

JOSEPHSON, ERIC, and SUSSMAN, MARVIN. *A pilot study of visual impairment.* New York: American Foundation for the Blind, 1964.

KISH, LESLIE. *Survey sampling.* New York: John Wiley & Sons, 1965.

LOWE, FRANCIS, and MCCORMICK, THOMAS. Some survey sampling biases. *Pub. opin. Quart.,* 1955, **19**, 303–15.

MCDAVID, R. I., JR. The dialects of American English. In W. N. FRANCIS (Ed.), *The structure of American English.* New York: Ronald Press, 1958. Pp. 480–543.

MCPHERSON, W. Lobbying and communication processes: Content analysis by computer methods and supplement. Paper read at the American Political Science Association meetings, September, 1964. (Dittoed.)

MAYER, CHARLES. *Interviewing costs in survey research.* Ann Arbor: Bureau of Business Research, University of Michigan, 1964.

MOSER, C. A., and STUART, A. An experimental study of quota sampling. *J. Royal statistical Soc. (A),* 1953, **116**, 349–94.

NEHNEVAJSA, JIRI. The near system: A study in public acceptance. Washington, D. C.: Office of Civil Defense, Department of Defense, 1964.

OGILVIE, D. List of Icarian categories. Cambridge, Mass.: Laboratory of Social Relations, Harvard University, 1964. (Dittoed.)

PAIGE, J. M. Automated content analysis of "Letters from Jenny: A study in individual personality." Cambridge, Mass.: Department of Social Relations, Harvard University, 1964. (Dittoed.)

PAYNE, S. L. Are open-ended questions worth the effort? *J. marketing Res.,* 1965, **2**, 417–19.

PERRY, PAUL. Election survey procedures of the Gallup Poll. *Pub. opin. Quart.,* 1960, **24**, 531–42.

POLITZ, ALFRED, and SIMMONS, WILLARD. An attempt to get the 'not at homes' into the sample without call-backs. *J. Amer. statistical Assoc.* 1949, **44**, 9–31.

ROSSI, PETER H., and KATZ, ELIHU. *The profitable difference.* New York: Magazine Publishers Association, 1960.

SALESWEEK. Untitled article. December 12, 1960, pp. 12–13.

SCHEUCH, E., and STONE, P. J. The General Inquirer approach to an international retrieval system for survey archives. *Amer. behav. Scientist,* 1964, **7** (June), 23–28.

SHEATSLEY, PAUL. An analysis of interviewer characteristics and their relationship to performance: Parts I–III. *Intl. J. opinion and attitude Res.*, 1950, **4**, 473–98 and 1951, **5**, 79–94, 191–220.

SIMMONS, R. F. Answering English questions by computer: A survey. *Communications assoc. computing Machinery*, 1965, **8**, 53–65.

SMITH, M. S., *et al.* A content analysis of twenty presidential nomination acceptance speeches. Cambridge, Mass.: Department of Social Relations, Harvard University, 1965. (Dittoed.)

SOLOMON, H. (Ed.) *Studies in item analysis and prediction.* Stanford, California: Stanford University Press, 1961.

STEPHAN, FREDERICK, and MCCARTHY, PHILIP. *Sampling opinions.* New York: John Wiley & Sons, 1958.

STONE, P. J., BALES, R. F., NAMENWIRTH, J. Z., and OGILVIE, D. M. The General Inquirer: A computer system for analysis and retrieval based on the sentence as a unit of information. *Behav. Sci.*, 1962, **7**, 1–15.

STONE, P. J., and HUNT, E. B. A computer approach to content analysis. *Spring joint computer conf. Proc.*, 1963, pp. 241–56.

STONE, P. J., *et al. The General Inquirer: A computer approach to content analysis.* Cambridge, Mass.: M.I.T. Press, 1966.

UNITED STATES CENSUSES OF POPULATION AND HOUSING. 1960. *Enumeration time and cost study.* Washington, D.C.: U. S. Bureau of the Census, 1963.

WILLIAMS, ROBERT. Probability sampling in the field. *Pub. opin. Quart.*, 1950, **14**, 316–30.

Index

Activities enjoyed by interviewer, and interviewer value, 4, 101–4, 142–45, 151–52

Advance listing of special populations, 2, 39–45; costs of, 41, 43–45; problems with, 2, 42–45; use of optical scanner in, 185

Affectivity of respondent: effect on free response answers, 171–75; and sociability, 172–73, 175

Akin, K., 84, *6.5*n.

Analysis of survey results, 4, 191–92, 194; cost of, 24

Attitudes toward interviewing, and interviewer value, 4, 101–4, 106, 113, 131–37, 150–52

Availability of respondent, 8–16, 19–23, 26, 37; and community size, 11–16; and household size, 13, 37, *2.3*; and respondent characteristics, 8, 11–14

Bales, R. F., 156, 175

Bias: and availability of respondent, 10, 37; in computer dictionary construction, 176; in probability sampling with call-backs, 10, 13; in probability sampling with quotas, 7, 9–11, 13, 19–23, 31, 36–37; in quota sampling (uncontrolled), 6, 31; from socially acceptable answers, 54–57, 66

Birnbaum, Z. W., 27

Bradburn, N. M., 60, 110, 161, 172–75

Brown, M. P., 81, *6.4*n.

Call-backs: effect on travel time and costs, 78, 95–96; number required, 11–21, 59–62; for self-administered questionnaires, 48–50, 53; by telephone, 58; *see also* Probability sampling with call-backs

Cannell, C. F., 75, *6.3*n.

Caplovitz, D., 60, 110, 172–75

Career orientation of interviewer, and interviewer value, 4, 101, 103, 106, 113–14, 124–31, 150–51

Child-rearing attitudes of interviewer, and interviewer value, 103–4, 124–31

Christie, R., 147

Clerical time of interviewer, 3, 70–71, 73–74, 76–77

Clustering, 23; effect on travel time and costs, 59–60, 78, 93, 95–96

Cochran, W., 6n.

Coders, rating of interviewers by, 109–10

Coding: accuracy of manual *vs.* computer, 4, 162–65, 184; by computer, 4, 155–83 *passim;* cost of manual *vs.* computer, 4, 160, 164–65; errors in manual, 158–59, 163; of open-ended questions, 154–83 *passim;* use of optical scanners in, 184–89

Colby, B., 175

Colombotos, J., 65

Community size: and interview completion, 11–16, 19, *2.5–2.7;* and interviewer travel costs, 27–29; and interviewer value, 105, 146–47; *see also* Primary sampling unit

Computers, use of, in coding, 4, 155–83 *passim;* accuracy of, compared with manual coding, 4, 162–65, 184; advantages of, 4, 165–66; cost of, 160–61, 164–65; cost of, compared with manual coding, 4, 160, 164–65; dictionary for, 155–57, 160, 167–68; flexibility of, 4, 165–66; for information responses, 158–61; for latent responses, 166–75; problems in, 162–66; for thematic responses, 161–66

Cooperation rates, 2, 19; and interview length, 46; in personal interviews *vs.* other methods, 50–51, 63; in probability sampling with call-backs, 10, 37; in probability sampling with quotas, 10, 37; with self-administered questionnaires, 47–51, 53; with use of

NOTE: numerals in *italics* are table numbers.

ABOUT NORC

The National Opinion Research Center is a non-profit social research institute, founded in 1941 and affiliated with the University of Chicago since 1947.

The Center maintains a professionally-trained interviewing staff to conduct national surveys on a wide variety of topics, using representative cross-sections of the population, quota cross-sections, and samples of special populations.

Recent research includes studies of race relations, occupational prestige and social stratification, public political participation and attitudes, the components of happiness, educational needs, and career choice.

Staff members of the Center are skilled social scientists, many of whom also hold appointments in one of the academic departments of the University. NORC's Survey Research Service provides sampling, interviewing, and data processing facilities for other social scientists, and offers consultation on research design. In addition, the Center administers a formal training program for graduate students in the social sciences and related fields.

The research activities of the Center are financed through grants from and contracts with private foundations, government agencies, and colleges and universities. NORC is governed by a Board of Trustees chosen from among prominent social scientists, educators, and laymen interested in social research.

National Opinion Research Center
6030 South Ellis Avenue
Chicago, Illinois 60637